SURREALISM, FEMINISM, PSYCHOANALYSIS

To Saro Lusty-Cavallari
(whose own obsessions have proved a delightful distraction)
and in loving memory of my parents, Margot and Don

Surrealism, Feminism, Psychoanalysis

NATALYA LUSTY
University of Sydney, Australia

ASHGATE

Published by
Ashgate Publishing Limited
Gower House
Croft Road
Aldershot
Hampshire GU11 3HR
England

Ashgate Publishing Company
Suite 420
101 Cherry Street
Burlington, VT 05401-4405
USA

Ashgate website: http://www.ashgate.com

British Library Cataloguing in Publication Data
Lusty, Natalya
Surrealism, feminism, psychoanalysis 1. Surrealism 2. Women artists – History – 20th century 3. Feminism and art 4. Psychoanalysis
I. Title
709'.04063

Library of Congress Cataloging-in-Publication Data
Lusty, Natalya.
Surrealism, feminism, psychoanalysis / by Natalya Lusty.
p. cm.
Includes bibliographical references and index.
ISBN 978-0-7546-5336-3 (alk. paper)
1. Surrealism. 2. Women artists—History—20th century. 3. Feminism and art. 4. Psychoanalysis. I. Title.
N6494.S8L87 2007
700.82'0904—dc22

2007005515

ISBN 978-0-7546-5336-3

Printed and bound in Great Britain by MPG Books Ltd, Bodmin, Cornwall.

Contents

List of Illustrations

Acknowledgments

Grateful acknowledgment to the following friends, colleagues and readers for their generous support and encouragement of this project, at various stages during its development: Gilbert Caluya, Brandon Cavallari, Clare Corbould, Alice Gambrell, Anna Gibbs, Helen Groth, Kate Lilley, Bob and Pam Lusty, Julian Murphet, Julia Newbould, Elspeth Probyn, Linnell Secomb, Lyndsey Stonebridge, Ed Wright and Damon Young. Thanks to Marina Warner, Paul de Angelis and Carolyn Burke for speaking to me about Leonora Carrington and providing the sort of stories that make research so rewarding. Thanks to my editor, Ann Donahue for her patience and support.

I would like to thank the following institutions and organizations for facilitating research for this project: the Edward James Foundation, Sussex, the Jersey Heritage Museum, The MOMA Library and the Interlibrary Loan service at Fisher Library, University of Sydney.

I am extremely grateful to the Australian Academy of the Humanities for its financial support of this project in the form of a publication grant to assist in the cost of image reproduction. An early version of Chapter 2: "Masking the Crime of Femininity" appeared as "Eating the Maid: Leonora Carrington's 'The Debutante'" in *Challenging Modernism: New Readings in Literature and Culture*, ed. Stella Deen, Aldershot: Ashgate, 2002.

Chapter 1

Introduction: Disturbing Subjects: Surrealism, Feminism, Psychoanalysis

For Walter Benjamin Surrealism embodied the radical possibilities of modernism and in his famous 1929 essay, he locates the energies of Surrealist poetic practice within the rhetoric of civil rebellion at a point of historical crisis. In "Surrealism: The Last Snapshot of the European Intelligentsia" Benjamin invokes the motif of "the snapshot," that ubiquitous mode of recording everyday life, in order to define the movement's relationship to modernism. "[F]ed on the damp boredom of postwar Europe and the last trickle of French decadence" (1978: 177), Surrealism occupies a position, Benjamin argues, that is at once "anarchistic *fronde*" and "revolutionary discipline," a position that attempts to push "poetic life to the utmost limits of possibility" (178). But here "anarchistic *fronde*" becomes as much a description of Benjamin's own methodological approach and eclectic interests—as one who could never conform to the "revolutionary discipline" of the communist party, a movement he sympathized with but would never join—as it is of Surrealist aesthetic and political practice. Benjamin obliquely writes himself into this piece as the German observer who understands and is sympathetic to the intellectual crisis of modern Europe and the revolutionary spirit of Surrealism:

> The German observer is not standing at the head of the stream. That is his opportunity. He is in the valley. He can gauge the energies of the movement. As a German he is long acquainted with the crisis of the intelligentsia, or more precisely, with that of the humanistic concept of freedom .... (177)

Benjamin's insight into Surrealism is predicated upon his position as an outsider. As someone who shares the movement's spirit of rebellion but can critically examine its effects from a distance, Benjamin tracks its impetuous rush through the valley of history without being caught up in the intoxication of its idealism. In his Surrealist inspired work, *One Way Street*, Benjamin turns away from the mysterious in itself, what he saw as the overly ecstatic and transcendent nature of Surrealist poetic imagery, instead creating aphoristic, prose snapshots that reveal the illuminating and extraordinary paradoxes of the everyday. Reading this work, Cohen suggests that Benjamin "consistently turns an ironic discourse valorizing askesis and reason against Breton's capricious and elusive praise of unconscious inspiration" (1993: 178). In spite of his reservations about unconscious inspiration,

Benjamin's fascination with Surrealism was indeed predicated on its expansion of the field of experience into the domain of culture's marginalia; by pushing the aesthetic to extreme limits Surrealism dissolved the conceptual parameters between art and the everyday, between dream and waking life, mapping out a psychic materialism that opened up the revolutionary effects of desire. If *One Way Street* and the *Arcades Project* establish the legacy of Surrealism in Benjamin's work, these works nevertheless proceed through a productive ambivalence that establishes Benjamin's dialogic relationship with Surrealism.

It is in the paradox of the participant/observer (rhetorically elaborated by Benjamin as the paradox of anarchistic revolt and revolutionary discipline) that I want to locate the work of the subjects of this book; primarily that of Leonora Carrington and Claude Cahun but also that of Georges Bataille and then through the relationship of modernism and postmodernism that of Cindy Sherman and Hans Bellmer. Like the Benjamin of *One Way Street*, their work at particular moments is informed through the twin modes of active participation and detached observation, establishing a structural dynamic of complicity and resistance, homage and critique in relation to many of the central tenets of Bretonian Surrealism. Although this kind of relationship in many ways formed the modus operandi of a movement that continually redefined both its constitutive and substantive orthodoxy, their affiliation entails a critical distance that elaborates and expands many of the ideas and practices by which the movement conceived itself, and in ways that go beyond the often reductive materialist/idealist binary relationship between Bataille and Breton.

While it is a given that Surrealism proposed a broader conception of the political, aesthetic and psychical possibilities of culture, we might also ask with what lacunae has this expansion been made possible? What are the tropes, ambiguities, blind spots that haunt a Surrealist rhetoric and praxis? In locating the movement's historical and critical position at a point of crisis within a European intellectual tradition, Benjamin paved the way for a reading of Surrealism as the radical other of modernism. While such a configuration rested on Surrealism's sublation of art into contexts outside it, one that for Benjamin represented an illumination of "the crisis of the arts" that had yet to be as radically presented (184), it also entailed a subsequent tendency to reduce a conception of modernism to a high modernist literary defence of the aesthetic as the privileged domain of a highly-individualized critical voice. In the last ten years or so the terrain of modernist studies has of course been remapped alongside the various cultural and theoretical revolutions that have engendered a necessary reconfiguration of the artefacts that bear its sign. In the reshaping of this landscape new works and voices have emerged to challenge not only existing interpretations of modernist cultural production but to expand the very premise of a singular modernism with its oppositional framing of modernism and the avant-garde. Although it is now given that the boundaries of Surrealism and its relationship to modernism are less certain than we once thought them to be, the very contestation of those limits record the historical ambiguities and conflicts that mark any kind of artistic movement and its subsequent institutionalization within the academy. In framing my reading of these texts through their dialogical relationship to Surrealism, I am interested in the process by which certain avant-garde texts refuse, then and now, to be so easily accommodated within the normalizing narratives that inevitably come to inform a movement's place in history.

If Benjamin locates in Surrealism a critical turning point, he also reveals how Breton's *Nadja*, through its "moral exhibitionism," its "intoxication" achieves this by opening up the autobiographical self to the errant logic of what we might call a material and psychic *flânerie*; so that the traces of memory, both historical and individual, and the traces of the material presence of revolutionary and Bohemian Paris and its inhabitants, create what Benjamin calls "the true, creative synthesis between the art novel and the *roman-à-clef*" (180). But what is perhaps most astute about Benjamin's observation here, at least for my analysis, are the terms in which he frames Breton's fascination with Nadja herself. Defining the relationship between Breton and Nadja as akin to the relationship of the gentleman and his beloved in courtly love poetry, Benjamin observes, "The Lady, in esoteric love, matters least. So too for Breton. He is closer to the things that Nadja is close to than to her" (1978: 181).[1] In other words Benjamin points to the central paradox of *woman* within the movement; the tension between Nadja as inspired crazy muse and real life embodied subject, a tension that has come to haunt a feminist reading of Surrealism. While this tension stages both the fantasy and erasure of the female subject, it also opens up a debate—central to both Surrealism and feminist theory—between experience and theory, between artistic practice and interpretation.

Although the title of Breton's book, *Nadja* suggests that it is about the woman who goes by this name, we soon learn in the opening paragraph that the book is not about Nadja herself but about Breton, specifically Breton, the confessional writer haunted by the past:

> Who am I? If this once I were to rely on a proverb, then perhaps everything would amount to knowing whom I "haunt." I must admit that this last word is misleading, tending to establish between certain beings and myself relations that are stranger, more inescapable, more disturbing than I intended. Such a word means much more than it says, makes me, still alive, play a ghostly par, evidently referring to what I must have ceased to be in order to be *who* I am. (1928/1960: 11)

While the autobiographical subject in Breton's narrative is transparently opened up to the psychic and material manifestations of the everyday, as though living in a "glass house" night and day (18), the figurative constitution of the autobiographical subject as "ghostly" simultaneously renders it as amorphous and impermeable, one that refuses full knowledge or a unified self-contained subject. So we might ask, how does Nadja fit into Breton's narrative, what purpose does she serve? As Benjamin suggests Nadja is really the prop, akin to the lady in esoteric love or even the analysand in the "talking cure," which will assist Breton in uncovering the ghosts of his past. As a woman of the *déclassé* streets of Paris, one whose madness heroically ignites the surreal tenor of the narrative but whose eventual institutionalization brings about Breton's abandonment of his muse and a diatribe against psychiatry, Nadja serves as a prop to reunite Breton with the collective social past represented by Parisian revolutionary history and Breton's own individual past as a psychiatric intern during the war. In other words Nadja brings Breton closer to the key intellectual and social paradigms of his life up to this point—communism and psychiatry (and psychoanalysis). But if Breton's abandonment of Nadja uncannily re-enacts his earlier abandonment of a career in neuropsychiatric medicine, his quest for self-knowledge, as experimental and revolutionary as Benjamin claims, is nevertheless haunted by the spectre of Nadja's real-life incarceration.

If Breton poses the question "Who am I?" as central to the subject's crisis of representation, in the work of Leonora Carrington and Claude Cahun the process of self-revision is pivotal to the way in which they position the female subject in relationship to the wider goals of the Surrealist movement. In examining Carrington's early and late literary production (in the "The Debutante"and *The Hearing Trumpet*), we can gauge the transformation of her work, from her initial involvement with the Surrealist group in France during the 1930s to her later years in Mexico City, and her collaboration with Remedios Varo. Reading work from across this period demonstrates Carrington's changing relationship to the movement and the development of her own artistic and intellectual authority. These texts emerge out of the profoundly disturbing contexts of war, emotional and psychic crisis, and emigration, and reveal a series of revisions to the construction and representation of the self in narrative form that elucidate an important response to Breton's seminal exploration of subjectivity in relation to literary narrative. Although I concentrate on Carrington's writing, the fact that she is also a visual artist bears strikingly on the written work, in particular, the way in which visual forms and techniques are often transformed into writing effects. Of course this is significant within much Surrealist aesthetic practice where the interplay between visual and verbal language is central to its project of aesthetic innovation and its radical reconfiguration of the value of content over form.[2] In her writing, however, Carrington takes up a Bretonian interrogation of the self, increasingly expanding its terms of reference within and against the grain of a Surrealist construction and representation of the female subject. In reading "The Debutante" and *The Hearing Trumpet* as two different responses to the representation of the self, I have sought to provide a number of contextual and apposite readings that situate these works within the complex discursive and cultural fields from which they emerge. Invariably critical analyses of Carrington's work and other women Surrealists are disengaged from the larger debates within modernism; debates about genre, gender, class, race and politics, as well as questions of institutional and artistic affiliation, which are often taken for granted in readings of more canonical work. As such, in Chapter 2 I read "The Debutante's" thematic development of the cross-cultural exchange and commodification of women's bodies alongside Riviere's psychoanalytic examination of the newly professional intellectual woman's negotiation of the public sphere, outlined in her essay, "Womanliness as a Masquerade" (1929). The autobiographical context implicit in both these pieces unfolds what I call a complex dynamic of resistance and complicity, formed in relation to their respective negotiations of the Surrealist and psychoanalytic coterie structure. A feminist rediscovery of Carrington's writing and Riviere's essay in the 1980s and 1990s reflects the degree to which the themes taken up in their work have increasingly become important to contemporary feminist hermeneutics and theory.

In Chapter 3 I investigate the role of transgression and subversion in Carrington's late, Surrealist novel, *The Hearing Trumpet*, suggesting that it forms a precursor to contemporary feminist experimental writing. While this work suggests an allegiance to both feminism and Surrealism, its use of parody also undermines, or at least curbs, the ideological investments of these movements through a rereading of the Grail legend, one that draws on feminist and Surrealist derivations of the quest narrative theme. Reading the novel alongside Bataille's *Story of the Eye* and its own critical engagement with a Bretonian ficto-critical subject, I argue that both texts combine autobiography and a burlesque excess and fantasy to critique the quest narrative theme—the principal structuring device in *Nadja*. While Bataille turns to eroticism to examine the relationship between order and disorder that underlies all transgression, Carrington employs the categories of the hybrid and the grotesque to critique a Surrealist celebration of femininity as erotically transgressive. In de-eroticizing feminine transgression, Carrington replaces the figure of the *femme-enfant* with the maternal figure of the crone whose abject and culturally marginal status signifies a reworking of female spectacle as politically and aesthetically disruptive because of its failed transcendence. In Chapters 4 and 5 I shift the focus on Surrealist writing to the photographic self-portraits of Claude Cahun (Lucy Schwob) in the context of her different writing projects: journalism, translation, political tracts and experimental prose. Cahun's commitment to both Marxism and psychoanalysis in many ways makes her an exemplary Surrealist practitioner. And yet in using the photographic self-portrait to reveal what Susan Sontag has defined as the innately surreal capacity of photography to reveal the "fantastic disclosures" of the subject (1977: 53), Cahun signals the indeterminancy of gendered and sexual identity in a way that implicitly foregrounds the limitations of a Surrealist political and aesthetic investment in desire. In transposing Breton's question, "Who am I?" into "What do you want from me?" staged as a question internal and external to the subject, Cahun radically extends a Bretonian Surrealist investigation of the self, by foregrounding the psychic and social constraints that impede the revolutionary possibilities of desire. In self-consciously fashioning a lesbian subject, a subject in which gender and desire are seen as flexible as well as constrained, Cahun implicitly critiques Breton's often-homophobic idealization of heterosexuality.

In striking ways the work of Carrington, Cahun and Riviere pre-empt many of the critical concerns in contemporary feminist theory. If the central problem for feminism in its most recent past has centered around the possibility of a political feminist subject that does not preclude or assume to dissolve the differences between women, it may be that feminism must pull back from its sweeping political vision. If the cost of accountability means qualifying feminism's claims of unity and coming to terms with the instability of its subject, then it may also require a recognition of its own complicity in circumscribing what counts as feminist work; without indiscriminately diminishing its material and political gains. The central paradox for contemporary feminism is therefore not dissimilar to the paradox of positionality that informs the work of Carrington, Cahun and Riviere.[3] In moving from the modernist work of Carrington and Cahun to the postmodern work of Cindy Sherman, and then very briefly Judith Butler, I have attempted to map the continuity between both the past and the present, not simply in terms of how the present revisits the past, for example in terms of Sherman's engagement with Surrealism, but how the past pre-empts the present. In this sense Cahun's self-portraits stage an uncanny knowingness of the trajectory of the modern subject as it comes to inform queer and feminist readings of gendered and sexual identity. If Sedgwick argues that difference has become so fetishized within contemporary theory that theory itself no longer provides a cogent articulation of its effects, what, we might ask, do Cahun's images offer us in terms of a theory of the subject conceived within the rubric of a radical otherness before the advent of its material vaporization (1990: 23)? Given the uncanny currency of Cahun's work, how do we read the past from a moment of the over-determination of difference in the present? Although this risks a certain anachronistic projection, what Cahun's work nevertheless provides for a contemporary audience is an emerging dialog around the representation of sexual and political identity that we now take for granted.

In Chapter 6, the question of postmodernism's relationship with the avant-garde is explored through Cindy Sherman's engagement with the work of Hans Bellmer. While I argue that Sherman's "Sex Pictures" series unsettles a Surrealist violation of the female body, they also utilize the affective registers of "shock" in Bellmer's own work. As such I read Sherman's return to the past through what Matei Calinescu defines as the logic of renovation that defines postmodernism's aesthetic practice (1987: 275), but examining also how such a logic reveals a striking affinity with a Surrealist fascination with the outmoded. If the outmoded for Surrealism was one way in which to come to terms with the failed ambitions of the past by recycling the very objects that constituted its ruin, Sherman's engagement with Bellmer exhibits a similar process of recovery and critique. In recoding the affective resonances of "shock" that emanate from the seductively damaged bodies of Bellmer's dolls, Sherman exposes the compromised ambitions of Surrealism's own political and aesthetic ideology while also acknowledging the power of its image repertoire. While both Bellmer's and Sherman's work stages a certain resistance to traditional cultural narratives (Nazism and Surrealism respectively), as I argue, they both also risk internalizing, in part at least, the very ideologies they set out to critique.

Since the critical reception of Sherman's work has been framed through a binary reading that positions it as either the consumption of myth or as a clever deconstruction of myth, the final chapter of the book takes up this critical ambivalence in terms of the way in which the feminine subject itself has come to haunt the political project of feminism. In reading the reception of Sherman and Butler's work alongside each other, I am interested in the way in which theoretical and aesthetic modes of ambivalence, often developed through strategies of subversion and parody, are viewed suspiciously by certain modes of feminist critique precisely because they challenge the stability of the feminine subject. While Sherman's work stages what she calls "a love–hate" relationship with the construction of gender in contemporary culture, Butler's work interrogates the binary arrangement of gender, suggesting that the relationships *between* women are far more ambivalent than feminism has been willing to acknowledge; so that feminism itself has unwittingly produced its own modes of regulation. In her introduction to *Gender Trouble*, Judith Butler articulates the rhetorical turns of troublemaking in a way that exemplifies the strategies and ruses of power that both constrain the subject and also open up the possibility of defiance:

> Contemporary feminist debates over the meanings of gender lead time and again to a certain sense of trouble, as if the indeterminacy of gender might eventually culminate in the failure of feminism. Perhaps trouble need not carry such a negative valance. To make trouble was, within the reigning discourse of my childhood, something one should never do precisely because that would get one in trouble. The rebellion and its reprimand seemed to be caught up in the same terms, a phenomenon that gave rise to my first critical insight into the subtle ruse of power: The prevailing law threatened one with trouble, even put one in trouble, all to keep one out of trouble. Hence, I concluded that trouble is inevitable and the task, how best to make it, what best way to be in it. (1990, vii)

In reflecting on how Butler's theories of gender and Sherman's representation of the female body have troubled feminist theory, I want to suggest that while ambivalence itself is fraught with risk it does not preclude political agency but understands agency itself to be implicated in the very relations of power that it seeks to oppose. While such a model of power has been criticized for reducing material experience to symbolic or abstract theorizing, I contend that such a model actually reflects the contradictory and ambivalent conditions of individual women's lives.

If the history of academic feminism reveals a certain territorialization, the constitution of proper and improper feminists acts, what is perhaps most prescient about the work of Carrington and Cahun, as well as Sherman in a different historical moment, is their interrogation and critical reflection on what was proper and not proper to Surrealist ideology and practice, mining these tensions for their own aesthetic and political effect. Their work repeatedly troubles ways of reading Surrealism that ultimately expands our sense of the possibilities of the movement beyond its familiar tropes and expectations of women. As such, this book takes up sites of conflict as necessary to the process of developing and thinking critically about strategies of interdisciplinarity and intertextuality, revealing how the tensions of what Alice Gambrell calls "insider–outsider" affiliation came to shape the work itself (1997:13). In Carrington's writing, the figure of the hybrid is her most persistent strategy for mapping out an epistemology of the self that refuses the static and regulatory cultural forms of femininity. Employed as a feminist *and* a Surrealist strategy, the hybrid produces an anxiety of difference that refuses to resolve the tensions that it inaugurates. In Cahun's self-portraits the fashioning of a lesbian identity disturbs the familial-erotic dynamic of heterosexuality, implicitly critiquing a Surrealist heterosexualization of desire. In Sherman's recent work the sense of aesthetic disintegration is staged through the reduction of the female and male body to comically atomized sexual organs, substituting a "real" body with comically perverse mannequins or sex dolls. Indeed the indeterminancy of Sherman's bodies signals a sense of anarchic celebration, a moving on from all that has gone before, while still containing its mythic traces.

Intellectual Obsessions and Feminist Reading Strategies

In her Introduction to the second edition of *Between Men*, Eve Sedgwick, in her indomitable fashion, writes: "Obsessions are the most durable form of intellectual capital."[4] Taking my cue from Sedgwick I want to reflect on my own fascination with Surrealism within the context of what I, and others have noted as feminism's cautious fascination with Surrealism.[5] My own obsession can be traced to a visit, one rainy afternoon, to a women's bookshop in Amsterdam, a time when such places still held their novelty value for anyone wanting their fill of feminist texts; a time before the woman's bookshop itself became an historically outmoded site. It was here that I first came across the work of Leonora Carrington and other women Surrealists in Chadwick's impressive survey, *Women Artists and the Surrealist Movement*. Unable to buy the book, I spent an entire afternoon reading it from start to finish under the congenial gaze of the bookshop owner. After I had finished I felt compelled to buy *something*, as a gesture of gratitude. As if to accommodate the financial reality of its customers, at the back of the shop, behind the glossy art books, dense works of theory and pristine anthologies, were row upon row of second hand books for sale. After a quick search of the shelves I came across a very battered 1970s paperback copy of Phyllys Chesler's *Women and Madness*. Like the found object, which forms a new life out of the very obsolescence of its old one, Chesler's book, in the ensuing years, came to invoke the uncanniness of that afternoon, since it served as a reminder of Surrealism's own obsession with women and madness if not also the troubled relations between Surrealism and feminism.

To gauge feminism's fascination with Surrealism is therefore a complicated affair. In her essay, "The Alchemy of the Word" written in 1978, Angela Carter describes Surrealism as a movement concerned ultimately with the celebration of wonder, a wonder intricately woven from the everyday as if wonder itself could be a self-sustaining mode of perception: "Surrealism's undercurrent of joy, of delight, springs from its faith in humankind's ability to recreate itself; the conviction that struggle *can* bring something better" (1978: 67). Carter's excitement over Surrealism, nearly fifty years after its initial impact, registers a profound sense of the possibilities of art as a way of life, one that incorporated desire, philosophy and politics in equal measure whilst maintaining a way of "living on the edges of the senses" (69). But Carter also registers her ambivalence toward Surrealism in terms of a guilty pleasure she must renounce: "The surrealists were not good with women. That is why, although I thought they were wonderful, I had to give them up in the end" (73). The tension between fascination and aversion that informs Carter's response to the Surrealists is a tension that Surrealism itself exposed as the driving force of human desire. But if Surrealism was not good *with* women, is there a way in which we might say that Surrealism was in many ways good *for* women. And how might this rhetorical distinction shape a feminist critical approach to understanding the paradoxical position of women in the movement? In her introduction to *Women Artists and the Surrealist Movement*, Whitney Chadwick delineated what has become the defining tension in all subsequent critical work on the women Surrealists:

> "The problem of woman," André Breton wrote in 1929, "is the most marvellous and disturbing problem in all the world." No artistic movement since Romanticism has elevated the image of woman to as significant a role in the creative life of man as Surrealism did; no group or movement has ever defined such a revolutionary role for her. And no other movement has had such a large number of active participants, their presence recorded in the poetry and art of male Surrealists, and in the catalogues of the international Surrealist exhibitions of 1935 (Copenhagen and Prague), 1936 (London and New York), 1938 (Paris), 1940 (Mexico City), and 1947 (Paris). Yet the actual role, or roles played by women artists in the Surrealist movement has been more difficult to evaluate, for their own histories have often remained buried under those of male Surrealists who have gained wider public recognition. (1985: 7)[6]

The paradox defined here by Chadwick is the simultaneous absence and presence of "woman" within Surrealism. That is, her historical absence from overviews and accounts of the movement despite her heightened visibility as a subject of desire, indeed as the very emblem of Surrealist revolutionary practice.[7] Since the publication of Chadwick's early survey, this absence has been considerably modified, with an ever-increasing number of important interventions, restoring the availability of the work of women Surrealists as well as critical appraisals of it.[8] However, the central paradox of women's metaphorical presence and historical absence still seems to haunt many of these recent critical reflections and will no doubt continue to inform critical work. While women functioned as muses, scribes and emblems of and for its revolutionary cause in the early part of the movement, the large numbers of women writers, artists, intellectuals and political activists who became associated with the movement during the 1930s and 1940s[9], and who have only more recently become subjects of intellectual inquiry and evaluation, have inevitably shifted the contours of the movement and its relationship to the wider cultural and historical zone of modernism.

If, as Walter Benjamin suggests, Surrealism functioned as the radical other of modernism, women were often the figurative and literal embodiment of that alterity. But given the concentration of women flocking to the movement in its later years as well as those who had been there from the beginning, their presence has also imbued the movement with a certain tension and self-reflexivity. While Benjamin's analysis of *Nadja* draws attention to the conservative tenor of Breton's emancipatory vocabulary, reminding us of the problematic tension between Nadja as the aestheticized subject of Breton's narrative and her own experience of mental illness, poverty, and eventual institutionalization, his comments nevertheless remind us of the value accorded to the experience of modernism's others—women, children, the mad, the exotic primitive—as a way in which to guarantee the movement's continuation and authenticity.[10] Similarly, feminist readings of Surrealism have endeavored to illustrate how the transgressive function of Surrealism as the radical other of modernism has rested on its appropriation of the disturbed female psyche and the violated female body as a metaphor for its revolutionary aesthetic and political practice. In light of this, the work of Cahun and Carrington reflects the tension between experience and representation, or what today is seen as the very crux of a contemporary feminist political and social ethic—the tension between theory and practice. Their work raises questions that although once considered more marginal to modernism are now at the center of contemporary theoretical debate and discussion.

While the problem of definition plagues a critical evaluation of the disciplinary codes of Surrealism, feminist readings of Surrealism are rarely unanimous. The aim of this book is to situate the work of Carrington, Riviere and Cahun in the cultural and political contexts of these movements and disciplines; that is, to read them as pointed responses to modernist aesthetic and ideological practice. This is in contrast to a critical tendency to represent women Surrealists as apolitical, attracted to the formal properties of a Surrealist aesthetic rather than engaged with the political and cultural contexts of the movement. Too often the women Surrealists are represented as politically naïve or disinterested in the political and aesthetic debates of the movement, in contrast to their work, which is interpreted as exhibiting a spontaneously inspired affinity with Surrealist ideas and themes. An example of this response is Chadwick's own early reading of the work of Lee Miller:

> Like many of the women artists who came to surrealism in increasing numbers during the 1930's, she [Lee Miller] had no interest in theory or politics, and no commitment to Surrealism's collective goals … Her connections with the group were entirely personal rather than formal and she is closer to the newly liberated woman of the 1920's than to Breton's etherealised vision of the Surrealist woman (1985: 39–42).

What I find problematic here is Chadwick's implicit refusal to grant a political or theoretical voice to Miller's work despite the fact that works such as *Revenge on Culture* (1940) (see cover illustration) reverberate overt political and cultural themes about the construction of the "ruinous" female body within Surrealist aesthetics. If anything, Miller's photographs have constructed an important visual and historical narrative of those involved with the Surrealist group over a twenty year period, one which reflects a quite different narrative to the one left by Man Ray. Miller often incorporated into her work a particular kind of Surrealist irony as a way to reflect the interrelation of the personal and the political, and frequently along gendered lines. Her portrait of the famous Surrealist couple, Max Ernst and Dorothea Tanning, in the Arizona desert, distorts the size of each figure so that an enormous Ernst looms large over a diminutive Tanning serving as a wry comment on the public stature of these two artists. One would have thought that this constitutes a very explicit statement of the gender politics of the movement. While Man Ray is noted for his highly stylized portraits of famous modernist figures, Lee Miller, by contrast, invariably captures the collective and collaborative spirit of those in and around the Surrealist group, choosing the group portrait or the Surrealist couple, over the often highly-fetishized individual portrait favored by Man Ray.[11] Whether or not Miller's association with the movement was formal or personal, she was certainly an active presence in the various coterie structures formed in and around the Surrealist movement. Similarly, her war photographs importantly shift the focus of the Surrealist gaze from the often-violated erotic female body to the fragile and ruined masculine body of war, and the monumental destruction of "culture" that war brought.[12] Indeed Miller's powerfully evocative photograph, *Revenge on Culture* addresses the cultural violence endemic to the representation of femininity at the same time that it reveals a loss of innocence brought about by war. In representing the figure of the ruined woman as a monument now destroyed, Miller wryly suggests that Culture, represented as woman, has been broken and ruined alongside the aesthetic ideology that constructs her as such.[13] Taken at a point of crisis for the Surrealist movement, as many of its members were either interned in war camps or attempting to emigrate or involved in resistance activities, we could hardly find a more prophetic or political statement about the construction and destruction of aesthetic culture.

In an early essay on Carrington's fiction, Peter G. Christensen argues that her work is "inherently ahistorical and that it lacks a sense of the role that women have played in society" (1991: 149). Christensen thus concludes, "Carrington does not depict the relationships of women and men as the products of complex social and economic forces" (149). What Christensen's essay seems to imply is that Carrington does not depict the realities of men's and women's lives in a mimetic or realist genre, which, given her allegiance to Surrealism, seems quite absurd. Furthermore, this argument is used to question the "feminist" nature of her work, especially the early fiction. In fact, as my reading of her early and late fiction suggests, Carrington's work provides a profound analysis of the hierarchical arrangements of social institutions and discourses, including Surrealist ones. Although women Surrealists such as Miller and Carrington certainly played little part in the Marxist debates that formed one aspect of the movement's ideological base, neither did many of the men.[14] The critical tendency to read the work of women Surrealists as politically naïve or as intuitively zoned into a Surrealist sensibility replicates the way in which the Surrealists themselves invariably positioned women artists and writers as inspired and inspiring marginal figures. But to think that women artists and writers did not respond to these ideological configurations of female subjectivity is itself politically naïve. Moreover, to read the politics of the movement along gendered lines is to overlook key figures such as Claude Cahun. Strongly committed to the Surrealist project of combining Freud and Marx, and as a member of the Association of Revolutionary Artists and Writers, along with Breton, Cahun played a significant role in the political side of the movement, for which Breton held her in high esteem.[15] But Cahun's work was also inflected by other intellectual and social concerns that reflected her own radical interdisciplinarity.

In her introduction to *Surrealism and Women*, Gwen Raaberg notes that despite the large numbers of women attracted to the Surrealist movement, the marginal roles assigned to women in society were often replicated within the movement: "Woman functioned … as an idealised Other, … as an object for the projection of unresolved anxieties, and continued to be identified in traditional terms of body, irrationality, and nature" (1991: 8). As we have seen in *Nadja*, the female muse provides the visionary insight; the psychic identifications that give meaning to the chance encounters of the novel, but her failure to sustain the conditions of convulsive beauty and Breton's ensuing frustration with his muse, also suggest the precariousness of the conceptual enterprise underwriting the novel. The figure of Nadja, the woman and the muse, thus reveals a tension between representation and experience that complicates the heroic trajectory of the autobiographical narrative, reminding us of Frederic Jameson's contention that "the *idea* of Surrealism is a more liberating experience than the actual texts" (1971: 101). In Carolyn Dean's work on Claude Cahun, she argues, "the surrealists' anti-bourgeois sentiments—at least in the realm of gender and sexuality—sustained the dichotomies between heterosexuality and homosexuality, pure and impure" (1996: 78). While Dean is careful not to completely expunge the undeniably radical elements of the movement, her argument illustrates how the oppositional categories of Surrealism—the pure and the impure—often produced their own prescribed and entrenched hierarchies. Shaped by and largely challenging a pervasive Catholic morality, Surrealism sought to mine female sexuality for its libidinous, transgressive qualities. However, as has become clear Breton's theoretical concerns were themselves shaped by particular moral and sexual prejudices of his own (Polizzotti, 1997: 524). Dean has thus usefully illustrated the conservative idealism embedded within Breton's Surrealist revolutionary rhetoric:

> [Breton's] problem with bourgeois morality was that it was not moral or pure enough, and he countered it with an idealised, liberated, natural heterosexuality purged of the tainted, repressed, and hence compromised bourgeois ideal of love that *produced* adultery, treachery and presumably, homosexuality. (1996: 78)

Chadwick's identification of the simultaneous absence and presence of women within Surrealism as well as Dean's critique of the paradoxical function of categories such as the pure and impure reveals what Calinescu defines as the paradox of avant-garde politics itself, its "elitist-antielitist approach": the formation of an elite committed to an anti-elitist aesthetic and political program (1987: 104). In wedding radical politics to the pursuit of new forms of creative expression, the movement attempted to open up aesthetic inquiry and practice to marginal experience, to include the effects of chance, irrationality and the unconscious to reignite the mystery buried by the rational, external world. If this was often achieved, as I have suggested, through the celebration and mimicry of the marginalized voices of those who occupied positions outside the elite cultural and economic center, such a strategy was invariably cannibalistic in that it subsumed, often unproblematically, the voice and identity of the other as part of its own supposedly radical position. But like any politics that claims to speak through the marginal, disenfranchized voice, Surrealism also gave that voice a material reality and a political presence even as it attempted to prescribe the terms of its articulation.

Psychoanalysis and Surrealism

In establishing art and life as part of the same radical drive, Surrealism unfolds the importance of psychoanalysis to its very conception. In providing a key to the unconscious, to an area of the psyche that could only be accessed in ways other than through rational or conscious states, Surrealism found in psychoanalysis a model on which to develop a theory of creativity bound up in the mystery of unconscious desires and associations, a move which sealed the trope of the enigmatic woman as its most potent erotic symbol. Although automatism was important in the early years of Surrealism, this was gradually replaced by the category of the marvelous, often represented through the enigma of feminine sexuality. The mystery of feminine sexuality invariably disclosed the contradictory emotional responses of fascination and disgust; while feminine sexuality inspired the male artist to unleash his own desires in order to transcend a rational, masculinized subjectivity, its excessive and disturbing qualities also threatened to contaminate his innovative, critical endeavors. In *Nadja*, we see this ambivalence in play as Breton moves from his initial excitement over the poetic possibilities of an erotic encounter with Nadja to eventual disgust that such encounters form the familiar experience of Nadja's life on the streets of Paris. If Surrealism embodied many of its innovative concepts in actual female figures, psychoanalysis similarly elaborated many of its most important concepts in the context of its work with women patients. Both have subsequently proved to be important for feminist analyses of the representation of feminine subjectivity and desire. While it may be argued that Surrealism could not have been conceived without the advent of psychoanalysis[16], the relationship between the two was as difficult as has been the relationship between feminism and psychoanalysis or indeed Surrealism and feminism. Breton's formulation of woman as "the most marvelous and disturbing question in all the world" echoes Freud's own puzzled inquiry, *Was will das Weib*? ("What does woman want?").[17] Moreover, Freud's muted response to Breton's flattering and enthusiastic letters and his failure to understand Breton's aesthetic interest in psychoanalysis ("I am afraid it is unclear to me what surrealism is and *what it wants*" [my italics] (cited in Jones, 1974: 468)), strangely rehearses his obsession with the riddle of femininity, *Was will das Weib*? Here the doubling of Freud's question, "what does Surrealism/Woman want" uncannily collapses the troubled relationship between subjectivity, desire and femininity in Freudian psychoanalysis onto Surrealism's own troubling appropriation of the female other. The simultaneous erasure and fantasy of woman as other within Surrealism and Freudian psychoanalysis is indicative of a long and troubled representation of femininity within Western aesthetic and philosophical systems. The radical impetus behind movements such as Surrealism and psychoanalysis, however, was also instrumental in enabling women artists and intellectuals to contribute in ways that often marked them as "different" and "valuable" even if the terms of difference and value were themselves allegorized and contested in the work that they produced. As such the discursive and aesthetic parameters of both Surrealism and psychoanalysis were irrevocably altered by the participation of women, even if these effects were only fully apparent decades later—as becomes strikingly evident in the case of Cahun and Riviere.[18]

In describing psychoanalytic theory as "a story of where the wild things are" (1993: 18) Adam Phillips underscores the literariness of psychoanalysis, inferring that the wildness of psychic life, those areas of experience prohibited by the rational or formal limits of language, needs a mode of articulation that matches its fantastic complexity. Of course this opens up one of the central contradictions of psychoanalysis; its claims to scientific authority in spite of the wildness of its evocative and interpretative claims. But if psychoanalysis is a story of where the wild things are, it is a story saturated at every turn with conflict, one which discloses the duplicity of psychic life itself; as Jameson suggests, for Freud there are always two stories at work in the topology of the psyche; one conscious and the other suppressed (1971: 98). The failure of Breton and Freud to communicate in spite of the seemingly common ground that they shared points to what both men found most irresistible as well as what they feared in the antithesis between science and literature. While Breton was indebted to the observations of psychoanalysis, he was nevertheless circumspect about its therapeutic goal. In giving up a career in neuropsychiatric medicine to become a writer and the leader of an avant-garde movement committed to aesthetic and political transformation, Breton was more interested in tapping the energies of the unconscious for a new mode of living, one which gave free rein to the ambiguities and mysteries that govern our waking lives. In this sense he was deeply sceptical about the scientific claims of psychoanalysis even as he adopted scientific terms himself to describe the various activities and projects of his movement. Likewise Freud's own analytic writing discloses an avid fascination with the literary that at times seems to almost compete with his attempts to define psychoanalysis in the scientific terms that would give his discipline the status of a respected field of knowledge. Throughout much of his work Freud elevated the status of the creative writer precisely because he or she was someone who could listen to the possible developments of the unconscious and lend them artistic expression instead of suppressing them. In suggesting that we can only come to know of the existence of the unconscious through its various effects—works of art, childhood play, dreams, jokes and slips of the tongue, neurotic symptoms—Freud stressed above all the figurative quality of the unconscious; as such using the creative arts to furnish evidence of its existence made perfect sense even if he felt compelled to show how psychoanalytic interpretation authenticated the very insights that literature only implicitly conveyed. In his 1907 essay "Delusions and Dreams in Jensen's *Gradiva*," Freud writes against existing scientific theories that propose dreaming to be a mere physiological process, aligning himself with the insights of creative writers who, he suggests, have come closer to revealing the hidden depths of how the mind works than any field of knowledge:

> Creative writers are valuable allies and their evidence is to be prized highly, for they are apt to know a whole host of things between heaven and earth of which our philosophy has not yet us dream. In their knowledge of the mind they are far in advance of us everyday people, for they draw upon sources which we have not yet opened up for science. (PFL, vol. 14: 34)

In replaying Hamlet's line to Horatio ("There are more things in heaven and earth than are dreamed of in your philosophy"), Freud cleverly invokes Shakespeare's own scepticism toward empirical science as the ground on which to justify his own turn to literature as an explanation for the uncanny effects of the unconscious. But while Freud gives credit to the writer for disclosing the existence of unconscious mechanisms governing the fantasies that constitute his creative output, he laments the ambiguity that still shrouds even the writer's own understanding of his work, suggesting that analytic interpretation alone holds the key to understanding the latent thoughts or desires revealed through its manifest content. But as Mary Jacobus has shown, Freud's fascination with Jensen's story reveals a striking parallel between the story's hero and Freud himself: "Jensen's hero is at once a 'scientist' and a 'fantasist'" (1982: 120). As both scientist and fantasist, Freud attempts to interpret what had previously been seen as unintelligible but in a way that proposed the mind as still ultimately unknowable or at least duplicitous to it's self. In working through the twin modes of unintelligibility and interpretation, in confounding the distinction between fantasy and reality, Freud implicitly rethought the very terms of science itself, knowing full well the precariousness of his endeavors: "The author of *The Interpretation of Dreams* has ventured, in the face of the reproaches of strict science, to become a partisan of antiquity and superstition" (PFL, vol. 14: 33). While we might want to distance the scientific claims made on behalf of psychoanalysis in its more positivist vein, Freud seems to have implicitly understood that the stories that science tells are not so different from the fabulist creations of writers and artists in so far as both are informative and interpretive.

But even if we acknowledge that Freud's insistence on scientific credibility registers his desire for legitimation in a world that largely values empirical evidence or "strict science," the tension between its scientific and hermeneutic status has continued to haunt psychoanalysis' usefulness for literature and art as well as feminism. In the context of feminism's own rejection of psychoanalysis in favor of materialist understanding of social relations, Jacqueline Rose points to the marginalization of psychoanalysis by a dominant culture that seeks still to value the self-evident empirical realty of our lives over and above the messy, sometimes contradictory effects of our desires—and the implications for feminism in terms of its own historical marginalization. Rose argues that the usefulness of psychoanalysis for feminism often hinges on whether one sees Freud as being "descriptive" or "prescriptive" about women. And yet, she asserts, this is to really miss the point since what Freud's theory of the unconscious most usefully offers feminism is a theory that discloses the "failure" of identity as the norm:

> The unconscious constantly reveals the 'failure' of identity. Because there is no continuity of psychic life, so there is no stability of sexual identity, no position for women (or for men) which is ever simply achieved ... psychoanalysis becomes one of the few places in our culture where it is recognised as more than a fact of individual pathology that most women do not painlessly slip into their roles as women, if indeed they do at all. (1986: 91)

In establishing the discontinuity of psychic life through his theory of the unconscious, Freud challenged the self-evidence of all truths about identity, whether they are seen as natural or socially inscribed. As such Freud's self no longer constitutes a singular "I" but is dispersed across multiple and competing identities and identifications. It is therefore no coincidence that Carrington, Riviere and Cahun, and also Sherman, all utilize the trope of the mask—with all its Freudian possibilities and difficulties—to problematize the experience of identity and self-representation in a way that critically reflects on the nexus between subject and object, agency and desire. The notion of "the double," central in much of this work, reflects a general aura of ambiguity and duplicity characterizing not only the representation of the self but also those strategies of complicity and resistance that define any intellectual or artistic affiliation. What this book hopes to do is map some of the tensions as well as the commonalities that run through the movements and institutions of Surrealism, feminism and psychoanalysis, by indicating the ways that each of these fields of social or artistic inquiry emerged to shape similar questions around art, politics and subjectivity; sometimes the connections between these domains are transparently articulated, sometimes they are latent.

Notes

1 See Natalya Lusty, "Surrealism's Banging Door," for a detailed reading of Breton's relationship to Nadja and her haunting of his text.

2 The most striking examples of this are Max Ernst's collage-novels and Magritte's word paintings.

3 In reading modernist women's work as a critical genealogy of contemporary debates about the competing values of "experience" and "theory," Alice Gambrell has uncovered academic feminism's own troubled and troubling paradoxes: the way in which feminism itself has "enabled and excluded certain kinds of discussions"(1997: 6).

4 See http://www.duke.edu/~sedgwic/WRITING/BETWEEN.htm: Internet.

5 See Conley's introduction to *The Automatic Woman: The Representation of Woman in Surrealism.*

6 Chadwick goes on to recount how her initial attempts to uncover material on women Surrealists resulted in the assumption that "while the lives of male Surrealists may be considered 'history', attempts to piece together the lives of the women involved constituted a search for mere 'gossip'"(7).

7 In *L'Armour Fou: Photography and Surrealism*, Rosalind Krauss positions Surrealist photography as the "feminine" Other of straight photography, and defines "woman" and "photograph" as figures of each other's condition: ambivalent, blurred, indistinct and lacking in "authority."

8 Included here would be Marina Warner's edited series of Leonora Carrington's fiction for Virago in the late 1980s and early 1990s as well as critical work initially done by Susan Rubin Suleiman, Mary Ann Caws, Reneé Riese Hubert, and more recently by Katherine Conley, Annette Shandler Levitt and Alice Gambrell. Also Penelope Rosemont's anthology of work by Surrealist women writers has made a significant contribution to the field by making available in English previously untranslated or unavailable work by women Surrealists.

9 Leonora Carrington, Giselle Prassinos, Jaqueline Lamba, Dora Marr, Frida Kahlo, Léonor Finni, Lee Miller, Meret Oppenheim, Valentine Penrose, Remedios Varo, Nancy Cunnard and Claude Cahun were all active as artists, writers and intellectuals within the Surrealist group in the 1930s and early 1940s. See Whitney Chadwick, *Women Artists and the Surrealist Movement* and Penelope Rosemont, *Surrealist Women: An International Anthology* for more detailed biographical information.

10 Alice Gambrell argues that during the late 1930s and early 1940s, Breton "spent a great deal of time as entrepreneur and patron to a scattered group of younger artists … [and] began … quite consciously to seek out and promote work by writers and visual artists, who, for him, embodied and made literal those carefully constructed fictions of difference and alterity" (42).

11 Examples of Miller's photographs of groups and couples include: Picasso and Dora Maar (1936), Adie, Lee Miller and Nusch Eluard at Antibes (1937), Leonora Carrington, Lee Miller, Ady and Nusch Eluard at Lambs Creek, England (1937), Nusch and Paul Eluard in their apartment in Paris (1944), Ernst and Tanning in the Arizona Desert (1946), E.L.T. Messens, Max Ernst, Leonora Carrington and Paul Eluard in Paris (1937) and a number of portraits of Carrington and Ernst in 1939 in St Martin d'Ardèche.

12 These photographs were exhibited at the Ivan Dougherty Gallery in Sydney in 1999. Looking at the collection as a whole one is struck by the political forcefulness of the images. In this series Miller contrasts the clean, almost poetic destruction of buildings and monuments with the human corpse's prolonged and visceral process of decay. Miller seems to dwell on the wounded body of the soldier as a new kind of aesthetic icon, turning from the ruinous and erotic body of Surrealist aesthetics to the fragile masculine body of war. In contrast the photograph of herself in Hitler's bath creates a more subtle dissonance in relation to the shock effect of much Surrealist photography.

13 For an account of Miller's role as a photojournalist during the war and a close reading of her photograph of Hitler's Bathtub, see Carolyn Burke's excellent article, "Lee Miller in Hitler's Bathtub."

14 Neither Ernst nor Dali, key figures in the movement at various times, showed any interest in the Marxist debates that reached a critical point during the 1930s.

15 In his autobiography, Breton recommends Cahun's political pamphlet, *Les Paris sont ouverts* as "a truly evocative image" of Surrealism's involvement with the French communist party during the early 1930s (1993: 133).

16 See Kevin Brophy, *Creativity: Psychoanalysis, Surrealism and Creative Writing*.

17 "The great question that has never been answered and which I have not been able to answer, despite my thirty years of research into the feminine soul, is 'What does a woman want?'" (Sigmund Freud, cited in Ernest Jones, *The Life and Work of Sigmund Freud*).

18 As Stephen Heath notes, neither Freud nor Jones ever responded to Riviere's paper and it only began to receive critical attention in the context of representation and sexual difference in connection with film theory. Of course, Butler also returns to Riviere in order to articulate her theory of gender performativity and parody.

Chapter 2

Masking the Crime of Femininity

Nanny do let's pretend that I'm a hungry hyena and you're a bone!

– Lewis Carroll, *Through the Looking Glass*

Introduction

Throughout the 1930s Surrealism became ever more preoccupied with the experiences of marginal groups: of women, children, non-western cultures and the insane. Investing their experiences and acts with a political resonance that reflected back onto the revolutionary tenor of the movement,[1] marginality came to signify Surrealism's opposition to normative bourgeois culture. In the *Second Manifesto of Surrealism* Breton writes, "every means must be worth trying, in order to lay waste to the ideas of *family, country, religion*" (1930/1972: 128).[2] While Breton's chance encounter with Nadja had precipitated an earlier attempt to combine Marx and Freud, in the uncertain political climate of the 1930s, he became intent on reconfiguring the political and epistemological ground of the movement through the lens of "experience" itself. It is therefore not surprising that it is during this period that the "Researches expérimentales," a series of investigations into various modes of irrational knowledge, were published in *Le Surréalisme au service de la revolution*. Increasingly transfixed by the transformative potential of repressed and libidinal forces as sites of resistance to hegemonic cultural formations, as well as the nature of psychic contagion as a sign of a collective imaginary, the Surrealist's work of this period reflects a sustained rethinking of the personal and social dimensions of desire and its potential to be harnessed in non-institutionalized forms of political and social action. If experience itself became the privileged mode of knowledge for the Surrealists during this period, it was an experience disseminated through the lived realities of those who occupied the peripheries of metropolitan cultural life: as such it was an experience that everywhere bore the blazon of alterity and crisis as the authentically possible ground of a revolutionary aesthetic and political practice.

It was during this decade, a period in which Breton occupied an increasingly entrepreneurial role, that Leonora Carrington made her debut into the Surrealist movement. Only twenty years of age and striking because of her dark Irish beauty and eccentric humor, Breton was to become one of her most ardent admirers and supporters. In praising her "boundless human authenticity" and transgressive independence, Breton was unequivocal in his promotion of her as an "authentic"

Surrealist heroine.[3] His inclusion of Carrington in the important and canonical *Anthology of Black Humour* reveals his admiration for her trademark "black humor" and unconventional performative manner. British born and raised, Carrington was introduced to Max Ernst at his London exhibition in 1937. Already a great admirer of his work—her mother had given her Herbert Read's book on Surrealism the year before—Ernst in turn became enamored with the young, rebellious British artist. Following a trip to Cornwall with members and associates of the Surrealist group, including Max Ernst, Man Ray, Nusch and Paul Eluard, Lee Miller and Roland Penrose, Carrington fled to Paris to be with Ernst. Intent on escaping the conservative and watchful eye of her upper-class family, Carrington seemed to have found in the Surrealist movement a sympathetic bohemian environment for her own rebellious nature and spirited imagination.[4] However, as tensions within the Surrealist group intensified and the animosity between Ernst's wife, Marie-Berthe, and Carrington became intolerable, Ernst and Carrington moved to St Martin-d'Ardèche in the South of France.[5] Here they began working and living together and playing host to a string of visitors in the final years before the war; collaborating on publications, paintings and sculptures and exhibiting in the two important Surrealist shows of the decade, in Paris in 1938 and in Amsterdam in 1939.[6]

During this period—around 1937 to 1938—Carrington wrote what would become her most anthologized work, the masterful and macabre story, "The Debutante." In this narrative the image of the debutante as both child and woman, caught in the transitory space of adolescence, references the Surrealist category of the *femme-enfant* and records the cross-class commodification and cultural exchange of women's bodies. The theme of unruly adolescence evoked by the debutante's violent resistance to her "coming out" also recalls two notorious criminal cases involving young women in Paris in the early 1930s; those of the Papin Sisters and Violette Nozière.[7] Like Nadja, these women became emblems for Surrealism's anti-bourgeois aesthetic and social revolt; their crimes read as evidence of a deep psychic backlash against an increasingly corrupt social and political post-war France. In paying homage to the *spectacle* of violence and terror unleashed by these crimes, the Surrealists sought to capture the complicated relationship of the unconscious to social and political reality; to see in these crimes a form of psychic contagion that might account for their own paranoid fears of fascism as well as their ongoing resistance to a naïve communist realist aesthetic. But the Surrealists' glorification of these crimes also illustrates the problematic nature of the figure of the "ruined" woman as a metaphor for, and embodiment of, Surrealist revolutionary ideology. In its critique of the commodified spectacle of the debutante, Carrington's narrative presents a scene of adolescent violence and rebellion that evokes a Surrealist celebration and eroticization of female violence.

Originally written in French and published as part of the collection *La Dame Ovale* in Paris in 1939, "The Debutante" examines the question of feminine and sexual identity within the socio-cultural and political world of the 1930s; including the changing role of the debutante during this period. Throughout the course of this short narrative, the body of the debutante, traditionally the commodified emblem of heterosexual and heterosocial ritual, becomes tropologically marked by the disruptive logic of hybridity, effected through the representation of a violent masking. In exploring the themes of masking and passing, Carrington's text registers the violence enacted in the cultural shaping of the feminine body as well as the codes of violence inherent to Surrealist aesthetic practice. Presented as an adolescent scene of rebellion, Carrington's debutante experience in this story, as in other autobiographical commentaries about this period of her life, conjures the racial, sexual and class narratives of violence in the 1930s. However, Carrington's repeated autobiographical discussion of her experience as a debutante in 1936 elliptically signals her other momentous "introduction" shortly after this event—her formal debut into the Surrealist group in 1937 as the young lover of Max Ernst. This introduction is formalized in Carrington's early Surrealist short stories, "The House of Fear" and "The Debutante." In these publications Max Ernst and André Breton provide introductions to the work which inscribe Carrington within an erotically charged entrepreneurial relationship. These texts imbue a culture of patronage and introduction intrinsic to the operation of Surrealist coterie politics and artistic production which resemble in part the rituals of debutante culture with its own system of patronage, hierarchy and authenticity. In choosing to write her first published stories in French, Carrington signals her rejection of her upper-class English family, at the same time augmenting her affiliation with the Surrealist movement. Moreover, Carrington's narrative exploration of the commodified body of the debutante addresses a wider cultural and aesthetic exchange of women, including the exchange of women's literal and figurative bodies within the Surrealist movement. While the narrative employs a Surrealist aesthetic economy of violence, rebellion and hybridity to offer a satirical account of the world of Edwardian manners, it also critiques this economy by foregrounding gender and class in a way that disrupts the "revolutionary" rhetoric of canonical Surrealist aesthetic and political ideology.[8] While the violence performed in the narrative reinforces a canonical Surrealist taxonomy of violence, through its themes of masking and passing, it also unfolds the dynamics of power inherent in a Surrealist celebration of female violence.

Masking the Intellectual Woman

I begin examining the themes of masking and feminine identity in "The Debutante" by turning to Joan Riviere's 1929 psychoanalytic essay, "Womanliness as a Masquerade" and the personal and public context in which it emerged, in order to disclose some of the complexities and contradictions for modernist women writers and intellectuals. As I will show, Riviere's delineation of femininity as masquerade in terms of a theory of aggression and conflict resolution, one that is inflected by the boundaries of race and class, shares certain salient features with Carrington's attempts to represent an epistemology of the self, more complex than a conventional Surrealist dichotomization of woman as pure and impure, idealized and debased. Riviere's article is important here precisely for the way in which it describes the politics of praxis for modernist women intellectuals and writers as well as for its tracing of the violence of gendered masking strategies. While I have no evidence of Carrington's familiarity with this piece, I hope that a brief analysis of the essay will demonstrate its relevance in terms of the wider cultural debates concerning women's newly acquired intellectual and artistic roles. More specifically, her essay raises a series of questions around masking and performance rituals, which are important for my reading of Carrington's aesthetic representation of violence and transgression.[9]

First published in the *International Journal of Psychoanalysis* in 1929, Riviere's article contributed to the important work on sexual difference already carried out by Freud and Ernest Jones. Jones' essay on female sexuality had appeared in the same journal in 1927 and it is this essay that Riviere addresses in her introductory remarks. It is not surprising that Riviere makes mention of Jones' essay in light of the fact that this issue was itself a commemoration of Jones' fiftieth birthday, an occasion for which Freud wrote an open letter in praise of Jones' tireless dedication to the cause.[10] As such Riviere prefaces her essay with a tribute to Jones' extensive work in the field before providing a more detailed reading of his "roughly … schematic classification" (1929: 303) of female sexuality. Indeed the innovative nature of Riviere's essay lies in its awareness of the changing social and cultural status of women and the implications of this in terms of the psychic patterns of gendered performance; that is, an analysis of feminine identity within the context of the newly participating intellectual and professional woman. At the center of Riviere's article is an account of an intellectual woman who moves between a "masculine" intellectual professional performance, which includes public speaking and writing and a "hyper-feminine" display of flirtatious and coquettish behavior, adopted upon completion of her public performance. Under analysis it is revealed that Riviere's subject has "quite conscious feelings of rivalry and superiority" toward many of her male colleagues and that her coquettish behavior toward them "was an unconscious attempt to ward off the anxiety which would ensue on account of the reprisals she anticipated … after her intellectual performance" (305). The subject's masquerade of the "guiltless and innocent" unknowing woman, represented by her display of hyper-femininity, is a strategy that diminishes the success of her intellectual performance. According to both analysand and analyst, this behavior is inappropriate, reflecting the ambivalent cultural position of the intellectual woman in this period: she is damned for performing as a man and damned for performing as a woman to hide her performance as a man.

Riviere concludes, however, "womanliness … could be assumed and worn as a mask, both to hide the possession of masculinity and to avert the reprisals expected if she were found to possess it" (306). Up to this point Riviere's paper is straightforward, but in a move that posits the radical nature of her anti-essentialist position, she declares that there is no difference between "womanliness," which, by nature of her "lack" is only a dissimulation of masculinity, and the masquerade, a dissimulation of dissimulated masculinity.[11] Thus, the reassurance that the masquerade is just that quickly spills over into the disturbing awareness that there is only ever the mask, a disturbance that constitutes the alienation (and rebellion) of *Woman's* being. Further investigating the analysand's performance of the gender masquerade, Riviere uncovers a series of daydreams and fantasies, which are marked by both race and class. The fantasies, originating from the analysand's childhood in the American South, revolve around the fear of attack from a Negro man. In an effort to thwart or delay the imagined attack the analysand offers herself sexually to him; in a variation of this scenario the subject reports that she assumes the menial role of washing clothes so as to disguise both her power and privilege in the face of any immanent threat.

It becomes clear, then, that Riviere's analytical development of the "masquerade" has its origin in racialised fantasies of violence and sexualized fantasies of race; scenarios that display the subject's cross-class and cross-race identifications, as well as the transgressive sexual desires, which may serve to detract from the powerlessness the white woman experiences in relation to the law of the father. In Riviere's narrative the threat of what lies behind the mask is the "darkness" and "danger" that the subject herself imagines: a sexual and racial taboo which has been culturally transferred and which threatens to unleash the retributive paternal fear of miscegenation. And yet clearly the masking strategy is a performance that stages a rebellion as well as an attempt at mastery and control. Ann Pellegrini argues:

> Putting herself in the place of a lower-class woman, black or white, or a black man, the white woman can look back at and down on her other(ed) self. Because Riviere nowhere explicitly addresses the social conditions or historical context in which the woman's psychical defences against anxiety are negotiated, she leaves out of consideration an explicit engagement with questions of power, resistance, and complicity. (138)

It is precisely these (left-out) questions of power, resistance and complicity, which I want to explore in my reading of "The Debutante." Firstly however, I want to indicate what it is about Riviere's essay that proves useful as a frame for Carrington's own early relationship to Surrealism.

While Riviere's essay avoids direct reference to the social and historical context underlying her analysand's experience, her essay is explicitly framed by an awareness of a cultural and historical shift in the gendered identifications of the intellectual woman:

> Not long ago intellectual pursuits for women were associated almost exclusively with an overtly masculine type of woman, who in pronounced cases made no secret of her wish or claim to be a man. This has now changed. Of all the women engaged in professional work to-day, it would be hard to say whether the greater number are more feminine than masculine in their mode of life and character (303–4).

In focusing on a very specific type of woman—the intellectual woman newly competing within the male-defined institution or discipline—Riviere's piece is poignantly self-reflective. The "intermediate" type of woman who displays all the codes of "appropriate" femininity, other than her intellectual performance, is in fact a "type" that Riviere would have frequently encountered in the coterie world of psychoanalysis. Women such as Loë Kann, Lou Andreas-Salomé and Riviere herself were all variously described as erotically attractive, fiercely intelligent and independent. And yet in his letter of introduction to Freud, Jones describes Riviere as "a case of typical hysteria" who has "a strong masculine identification" and "a strong complex about being a well born lady" (*The Complete Correspondence*, 1993: 339). Nevertheless, in this same letter Jones confesses that his analysis of Riviere had been "the worst failure I had ever had," though he concedes, without irony, that she is "unusually intelligent" (339). He also notes that she is extremely useful to the cause (of psychoanalysis) primarily because of her fluency in German and English; Riviere would eventually become an important mediator between Freud and the English-speaking world as one of his most gifted and respected translators. Riviere had been in analysis with Jones for nearly four years before being recommended to Freud for analysis. After Freud's initial sessions with Riviere, his letters to Jones become particularly stern, admonishing him for his failure to carefully read his patient: "Mrs Riviere does not appear to me as black as you had painted her … In my experience you have not to scratch too deeply the skin of a so called masculine woman to bring her femininity to light … No doubt she is very clever and clear-headed" (351). While the letters between Freud and Jones reveal the formidable nature of Riviere's intellect and Freud's astute awareness of her capacity to contribute to the cause, they also poignantly unfold the contested terrain of feminine performance in the context of professional life that is the very subject of Riviere's paper.

The tension in Riviere's piece between the subject under analysis and her own position within the coterie world of psychoanalysis reveals the more general problem of the relationship between modernist women intellectuals and the disciplinary fields in which they worked. In light of this relationship Stephen Heath asks:

> What did it mean to be an intellectual and a woman, an intellectual woman? The question for Riviere's patient in the paper can hardly but have been a question for her too (as it was widely in the writing of the period, the question of identity as a woman …). (1986: 46–7)

The question of identity as a woman became increasingly important in the years between the wars, and is exemplified by Freud's notorious question: "What does a woman want?"; a statement that would become increasingly important to feminist analyses of subjectivity and desire. Echoing Freud's consternation, Breton declared during this period that women constituted the most "marvelous and disturbing problem in all the world." Breton had rejected the model of the professional New Woman as too entrenched within a modernist bourgeois literary establishment. Instead, Surrealism relied on the rhetorical paradox of the idealized and transgressive woman as the emblem of its poetical practice, revealing both the Romantic and Symbolist influences on literary Surrealism. Breton's reputation for the public support and promotion of women within the movement, particularly throughout the 1930s, stood in stark contrast to his more traditional and conservative expectations of the women he became personally involved with.[12] Likewise Freud could express pessimism about the benefits for women brought about by the feminist movement in spite of his more general support and encouragement of, and indeed profound respect for, women in professional life.[13]

Reading Riviere's analysis of her subject as a mask for her own relationship to psychoanalysis suggests the encoded ways in which women modernists might illustrate the complexity of their disciplinary affiliation. The question of Riviere's position within this piece and within a male dominated psychoanalytic coterie is masked by her analysis of the "other" woman, the intellectual woman who is both the subject and object of her analysis. As an object of analytical exchange between Jones and Freud, as well as a significant contributor to the field of psychoanalysis, Riviere's essay may be read as a pointed response to the position of women within the profession. In framing her piece with Jones' own earlier essay on femininity, Riviere provides an important correction to his straightforward reading of the intellectual woman as inherently masculine. In light of Riviere's correction it is extraordinary that neither Jones nor Freud ever responded to Riviere's important paper on femininity and the masquerade. The silence of her male colleagues upon the publication of this essay may have inhibited any further work in this area, since Riviere never again returned to the important questions raised in her essay. Riviere's life and work thus reveals the often-conflicting political motivations behind modernist women's intellectual production at the same time that her psychoanalytic analysis of the violence of gendered masking strategies attempts to trace its etiology. If Riviere's article describes the symptoms of this experience, Carrington's "The Debutante" explores the political, cultural and aesthetic structures informing it.

Carrington's Surreal Debut

The surreal narrative of "The Debutante" commences with an early morning visit to the zoo by the protagonist of the story, the debutante. A place she visits frequently, preferring, as she informs us, the company of the animals at the zoo to friendship with girls her own age, the debutante manages to persuade her friend the hyena to attend her coming out ball in her place. Smuggling the animal back to her room, the debutante assists in preparing an elaborate disguise for the hyena, becoming a willing accomplice in the murder of her maid, Mary. Neatly chewing around the edges of the maid's face, the hyena constructs her mask from human skin before consuming the rest of her body, save for one or two bones she stuffs in a fleur-de-lis bag that she takes to the party, in case she gets hungry. Thus costumed in all the accoutrements of debutante wear—ball gown, high heels and gloves—the hyena sets out for the ball wearing the face of the reluctant debutante's maid. Meanwhile, the reluctant debutante, "tired by the day's emotions" sits down to read *Gulliver's Travels*. The ruse is unsuccessful, however, because the hyena's overwhelming smell, alluded to throughout the story, attracts the attention of the other guests. The tale ends abruptly when the debutante's mother enters her daughter's bedroom, "pale with rage," and exclaims:

> We'd just sat down at table ... when that thing sitting in your place got up and shouted, "So I smell a bit strong, what? Well I don't eat cakes!" Whereupon it tore off its face and ate it. And with one great bound disappeared through the window. (48)

Shifting in tone between artlessness and canniness, the narrator of the tale recalls Lewis Carroll's Alice narrator, whose own desire for transformation is registered by her favorite parlour game "Let's Pretend ...," and which incites her remark: "Nurse! Do let's pretend that I'm a hungry hyena and you're a bone" (18). The "black humor" in Carrington's narrative is thus established through the literal rendering of Alice's cannibal fantasy and through the dissonant effect of simple declarative sentences narrating a tale of grotesque and absurd violence. When the hyena first mentions her plan of tearing off the maid's face, the reluctant debutante replies with curious but faultless logic: "It's not practical, ... She'll probably die if she hasn't got a face. Somebody will certainly find the corpse, and we'll be put in prison" (47). The narrator's response is reminiscent of Alice's own practical but absurd powers of reasoning in both *Through the Looking Glass* and *Alice's Adventures in Wonderland*. Here Carrington's narrative recalls the tension between Alice as innocent unknowing girl and Alice as intrepid explorer; a tension that is also illustrative of the contradictory performance of caricatured femininity and intellectual competence for the intellectual woman in Riviere's essay. Alice's double persona (as artless and canny) is developed in Carrington's text through the double figure of the reluctant debutante, who withdraws from social action, *and* the hybrid hyena-maid, whose attendance at the ball constitutes a disruptive presence.

Drawn to the rebellious quality of Carroll's writing, with its satire on Victorian mores and literature as well as its use of the fantastic, many of the Surrealists payed homage to Carroll by referencing or illustrating his work. Breton included him in both *The Anthology of Black Humour* and *The Dictionary of Surrealism,* while Ernst and Dali completed illustrations of the Alice series. Dali's illustrations for *Alice in Wonderland* draw on the figure of the *femme-enfant*, highlighting the overt eroticism of Alice's child-woman status. These illustrations repeat in emblematic form a blank ink silhouette of Alice's "womanly" body about to jump through a skipping rope. The prominence of warm hues throughout the illustrations—hot pink, orange, red and yellow seeping into each other, often from black outline or concentrations of black ink—emphasize the libidinal and oneiric quality of Alice's adventures. Max Ernst's life-long fascination with Carroll intensified during his time with Carrington in the South of France. His paintings *Alice in 1939* and *Alice in 1941* belong to a series of decalcomania portraits of Carrington, which extensively explore the theme of "the lost beloved" as the ruin of the world (Wilson, 1991: 368). Like Dali, Ernst appeals to the incestuous and erotic nature of the *femme-enfant* as an exemplary model for his recreation of Alice and in doing so reminds us of his closing illustration for Carrington's debut publication, *The House of Fear*. In this image, a horse's head, proud and aloof, is contrasted with the adolescent body of a girl (an Alice figure), in modest Edwardian dress, thrown upside down on a rock, her hand clutching her head in a pose that records the consternation of her abandonment and ruin. Sarah Wilson ironically comments on how this image prophetically encapsulates the effect on Carrington of Ernst's imprisonment as an enemy alien, producing in the process powerful "elisions between pictorial inversion, sexual abandonment and the abandonment of reason" (368).

Like Dali and Ernst, Carrington explores the ambiguous status of the child-woman figure. But rather than present her as an icon of erotic transformation, Carrington dwells on the logical contradiction of her status as both child and woman. The space of transition, or, the contradiction of being two things at once, is repeatedly explored in Carrington's fiction through the hybrid figures of the child-woman (the debutante) and the feral woman. These figures problematize the dichotomous relationships of adulthood and childhood, as well as of nature and culture, the civilized and the uncivilized, in much the same way that Carroll's work destabilizes the ubiquitous binary position of logic and nonsense. As Camille Paglia points out:

> In Carroll, manners and social laws are disconnected from humane or "civilising" values. They have a mathematical beauty but no moral meaning: they are *absurd*. But this absurdity is predicated not on a democratic notion of their relativism but on their arbitrary, divine incomprehensibility. In the Alice books, manners are meaningless but still retain their hierarchical force. (553)

Like Carroll, Carrington comically exposes the arbitrariness of masking rituals within social hierarchies. Carrington's satire on the English upper-class debutante ritual resembles Carroll's own lampooning of Victorian manners and rituals, nowhere better illustrated than in his satirical rendering of the "madness" of the tea party ceremony. In Carrington's story the cultural and class-bound nature of the debutante ritual, its very "Englishness," becomes the focus for a satirical reflection on the absurd and violent codes vested in rituals of the proper and the authentic. The act of passing at the heart of the substitution ploy in the story reveals how the public display of manners works to reinforce the arbitrary codes of power invested in categories of class and gender.

While Carrington's story unfolds the importance of her Anglo literary heritage, her reworking of "experience" in the narrative takes on a particularly subtle and astute edge. The reluctant debutante of the story closely mirrors Carrington's own resistance to her experience as a debutante in 1935.[14] Mary, the maid in the narrative, matches Carrington's own working-class Irish nanny, Mary Kavanaugh. Similarly, the debutante's reluctance in the narrative reflects Carrington's repeated failure to adopt the conventional mask of appropriate upper class feminine behavior and her increasing rebelliousness within the family home. In an interview with her literary agent, Paul de Angelis, Carrington reflects on her experience of her own debutante season:

> ... I was presented at court ... That was the last court of George V. I was on the marriage market ... I went through the season in London, the Royal garden party, ... Then you go to Ascot, the races, and you're in the Royal enclosure. And if you please, in those days, if you were a woman, you were not allowed to bet. You weren't even allowed to the paddock where they show the horses. So I took a book. I mean, what would you do? It was Huxley's *Eyeless in Gaza,* which I read all the way through. (1991: 34)

Like the fictional heroine in "The Debutante," this autobiographical account places Carrington's resistance to the codes of heterosocial behavior within the conventional trope of the woman reader as a figure whose seduction by the romance plot is seen to circumvent her moral and social responsibilities. In shifting the scene of rebellion from the contemporary and popular *Eyeless in Gaza,* a sentimental romance that warns of the fate of an uppity intellectual woman, to Swift's canonical but iconoclastic *Gulliver's Travels*, Carrington strategically connects her narrative with a tradition of English satire and its practice of humorous social critique, rather than the more "feminine" tradition of frustrated romance, represented by Huxley's text.[15] However, the trope of the woman reader, historically theorized as both complicit and resistant, underscores the way the narrative action of the story is structured around themes of complicity and resistance or rather rebellious social withdrawal (the reluctant debutante) and disruptive social participation (the masked hyena).[16] The ambivalence of this strategy obliquely signals the paradoxical position of the woman artist within the Surrealist movement as well as the affective ambivalence registered by the intellectual performance of Riviere's subject, whereby adopting the mask of femininity constitutes a strategy that is at once conformist and transgressive.

Breton's selection of "The Debutante" for *The Anthology of Black Humour* further establishes Carrington's connection to an overtly masculinist literary tradition; in part because she was one of only two women represented in the *Anthology*, but also because she appears to adopt a form of humor that Breton defines as "the mortal enemy of sentimentality" (1939/1997: xix), a humor predicated on a dark, often aggressive sensibility. Although the anthology was published in 1939, on the eve of the German invasion of Paris, it did not appear until 1945, having been deemed subversive by the Vichy regime's censorship board.

The irony of the *Anthology's* belated arrival rests on Breton's very conception of "black humor" as a "process that allows us to remove the overly distressing aspects of reality" but only when "exercised at the expense of others" (Breton cited in Polizzotti: 416). Indeed Breton's compilation of the most subversively macabre writers in the European tradition, including de Sade, Fourier, Nietzsche, Carroll, Swift, Lautréamont, Appollinnaire and other contemporary writers closely associated with the spirit of Surrealism, had taken a number of years to complete and occurred during a particularly momentous period for both Breton and the Surrealist movement more generally. In the years that Breton had been assembling his anthology, he had definitively split from the French Communist Party over its support of Stalin, formed the short-lived anti-fascist group, Contra-Attaque with Bataille, and drafted with Trotsky one of the group's most significant manifestos on politics and art, "For an Independent Revolutionary Art" (1938). The latter manifesto, in particular, served to crystallize Breton's fervent desire to defend the intellectual conditions under which creative activity takes shape from the totalitarian manipulations of both the right and the left. For Breton, the revolutionary potential of art lies precisely in the anarchic and subjective conditions of its creation; for it to be constrained by either political propaganda or market forces is to threaten its critical and radical autonomy. From the perspective of the manifesto's central thesis, the absolute freedom of cultural expression, Breton's *Anthology of Black Humour* becomes a celebration of literature's subversive potential.

The anarchic rebelliousness of Breton's idea of humor is further elaborated in the short introductions to the individual authors represented in the volume. In these introductory essays Carrington and Swift are linked via a literary performance of masking. While Swift, "the true initiator" of black humor, is described as donning an impassive glacial mask, despite being a man who was constantly outraged (Breton: 3), Carrington is described as wearing "the mask that can save her from the hostility of conformism" (335). Breton's description of Carrington's literary style as a form of masquerade shrewdly registers the hyena's own violent masking in her story as well as Carrington's reputation for unconventional and often socially disruptive behavior. Breton, in fact, recounts two such episodes in his introduction, as if to remind us of Carrington's ability to tantalize an audience in both literary and performative modes. The first one involves Carrington's attendance at an important dinner in a restaurant during which she began lathering her feet with the mustard provided on the table. When questioned about her odd behavior, Carrington merely replied that her feet were sore (Breton: 335). The second story Breton tells involves his presence at a dinner at which Carrington served her guests dishes from a sixteenth century English cookbook, improvising certain ingredients that were unavailable to her. To this episode Breton comments rather wryly: "I will admit that a hare stuffed with oysters, to which she obliged me to do honour for the benefit of all those who had preferred to content themselves with its aroma, induced me to space out those feasts a bit" (335). Carrington's proclivity for eccentric social performances greatly enhanced her reputation within the group since it reinforced the importance of the marvellous within the experience of the everyday. It is not surprising therefore that Breton defines Carrington's artistic authority using the trope of the "beautiful divine witch," who initiates and performs spectacular rituals for the consumption of the male Surrealist imagination, facilitating the poetic function of woman as transgressive other:

> Michelet, who so beautifully did justice to the *Witch*, highlights among her gifts two that are invaluable, because granted only to women: "the illuminism of lucid madness" and "the sublime power of *solitary conception*."... Who today could answer the description better than Leonora Carrington? (Breton, 1941/1977: 335)

While Breton stresses the marvelous nature of Carrington's inspired performances, reminding us of his description of Jacqueline Lamba as "scandalously beautiful" at the beginning of *Mad Love*, he nevertheless acknowledges the startling force of her creative endeavors by granting her "the sublime power of solitary conception." But in many ways "The Debutante" reminds us that Carrington had already adopted the role of the rebellious and defiant *femme-enfant* long before she met the Surrealists. Similarly her relationship to the Surrealists was always mediated by her status as an outsider. As an upper class British woman, Carrrington's status was all the more exotic and exoticized. But while her rebellious sensibility may have been shaped by her personal rejection of her family, with its gender bias and aristocratic pretensions, she nevertheless adopted a Surrealist anti-bourgeois rhetoric. Having been brought up as a Catholic, Carrington also shared their blasphemous humor and their rejection of Catholicism's institutional triumvirate of family, state and church. Indeed the satirical depiction of the reluctant debutante's uptight mother registers a Surrealist rejection of the overly ambitious bourgeois mother figure. But given the fact that Carrington was only twenty years of age when she wrote "The Debutante," her social and political ideas were still very much inchoate. Like so many of the women that came to Surrealism in the 1930s, she was a generation (25 years) younger than her male peers such as Breton and Ernst and valued precisely because she represented a new lease of life for the movement.[17] Breton's description of Carrington as "superb in her refusals, with a boundless human authenticity"(Polizzotti, 1997: 448) illustrates the role ascribed to many of the young women that came to be associated with the movement throughout this decade. In representing a kind of "authentic" Surrealist spirit, Breton, and critics that have followed, read Carrington's work as spontaneously imbibing a Surrealist sensibility. But despite Breton's recuperation of Carrington's artistic performance within the traditional Surrealist trope of the beautiful, crazy muse, he acknowledges the resistant and ironic capacity of her masking strategy (both within and outside the text) when he concludes: "Over these and many other exploits ... reigns a smooth mocking gaze" (335).

This is significant when we consider that in his introduction to the *Anthology* Breton presents humor itself as a masking strategy. Quoting Freud, Breton reminds us of the liberating quality of humor as a literary mode:

> It is now time to acquaint ourselves with some of the characteristics of humour. Like wit and the comic, humour has in it a *liberating* element. But it has also *something fine and elevating*, which is lacking in the other two ways of deriving pleasure from intellectual activity. Obviously what is fine about it is the triumph of narcissism, the ego's victorious assertion of its own invulnerability. It refuses to be hurt by the arrows of reality or be compelled to suffer. It insists that it is impervious to wounds dealt by the outside world, in fact, that these are merely occasions for affording it pleasure. (Freud, cited in Breton, 1997: xviii)

For Freud, and for Breton too, humor is in essence a kind of masquerading whereby that which would normally constitute trauma and vulnerability becomes a source of pleasure and hence power: "the ego's victorious assertion of its own vulnerability." The use of black humor by both Swift and Carrington suggests the way in which satire *twists* its subject into something other, masking and therefore transforming "the real." This closely coincides with Breton's description of Carrington's literary style as a kind of masquerading performance (where she can "don and remove the mask that can save [her] from the hostility of conformism"). Like Freud's psychoanalytic interpretation of humor, Carrington's narrative reveals both critical and complicit strategies of displacement.

In his Preface to Carrington's debut publication, "The House of Fear," subtitled "Loplop Presents the Bride of the Wind," Ernst also introduces Carrington to a Surrealist reading public, but more explicitly stages the dynamics of power reminiscent of the chaperoned debutante's presentation to the world of upper class society. Casting both himself and Carrington in their mythological roles, Ernst adopts a tone that is whimsical, though churlish:

> Who is the Bride of the Wind? Can she read? Can she write French without mistakes? What wood does she burn to keep warm? She warms herself with her intense life, her mystery, her poetry. She has read nothing, but drunk everything. She can't read. And yet the nightingale saw her, sitting on the stone of spring, reading. (Preface, "The House of Fear," 1938/1988: 26)

While Breton acknowledges the "sublime power" of Carrington's "solitary conception" in his introduction to "The Debutante," Ernst presents her here as a *conducteur merveilleusement magnétique*, a term used to describe the function of the *femme enfant* for the male Surrealist imagination.[18] Drawing attention to Carrington's adoption of French in these stories, Ernst instructs her readers that the quality of the stories rests on their "inspired" and "intoxicated" sensibility rather than their literary skills. Here the Bride of the Wind, who cannot read or write French without mistakes, produces her fiction through a kind of immaculate conception, with Loplop, the Bird Superior, as her chaperone and guide. The preface thus establishes a hierarchical and eroticized relationship between Carrington and Ernst, framing their literary and personal association through a series of binary categories: experience/inexperience, artist/muse, professional/amateur, and teacher/pupil.

Carrington's adoption of French, a language in which she was far from fluent despite having been taught at home by a French governess, indicates a certain pragmatic move in terms of her association with the Surrealists. As Marina Warner argues, however, her adoption of a language she had only begun to master adds a certain profundity and uniqueness to the tone of her stories:

> Carrington tells a tale in a unique tone of voice, that deadpan innocence of the masters of the macabre. The simplicity of her syntax, and the cool sequential structure of her narratives… owes something to her adoption of French … . But unfamiliarity [with French] does not cramp her style; rather it sharpens the flavour of ingenious knowingness which enchanted the Surrealists. (Introduction to *The Seventh Horse and Other Tales*, n.p.)

Warner's astute observations of Carrington's literary style contrast with Ernst's more ambivalent praise in his preface. While Ernst dwells on Carrington's spelling mistakes and shrouds her work in a collection of unintelligible and abstract statements, Warner celebrates the understated genius of Carrington's turn of phrase.

"The Debutante's" publication history reveals its importance not only within the context of Breton's trans-historical construction of the Surrealist category of "black humor" but also within a contemporary feminist revival of modernist women's writing.[19] "The Debutante's" inclusion in a number of feminist anthologies (by Angela Carter, Marina Warner and others)[20] throughout the 1980s and 1990s highlights what Alice Gambrell has outlined as an ongoing interest for contemporary feminist work in the process of "back-talk." Gambrell reads Carrington's work within the context of a cultural history of academic feminism, finding in the work of a number of interwar women writers and artists—such as Carrington, H.D., Frida Kahlo and Zora Neale Hurston—an engagement with the issues of alterity and difference in a way that pre-empts contemporary feminist critical practice. Examining the complicated relationship between past and present and the problem of disciplinary affiliation more generally, Gambrell explores

> what it meant, during the 1930s and 1940s, for women to work within the boundaries of schools, movements, or disciplines in which, under more usual circumstances, they would have occupied the position of "Other": the object of investigation, the eroticised source of inspiration, the respondent in—though rarely the initiator of—an interlocutionary exchange. (1997: 1)

Calling this kind of engagement "insider-outsider activity," after de Lauretis's work in the problematizing of identity and practise, theory and experience, Gambrell argues that it forms part of the complex history of modernist women's intellectual modes of interrogation and can hardly be, as it often is, conceived as a newly emergent postmodern concern. In light of Gambrell's argument it appears that one of the reasons for the "rediscovery" of women such as Carrington, Kahlo, Hurston and H.D. (and here we might add Joan Riviere) in the 1980s and early 1990s is that at about this time feminists began to reconceptualize their own work—literary and cultural—as a complex dynamic of complicity and resistance. Increasingly during this period, issues of race, class and sexuality became intrinsic to a rethinking of the relationship between theory and praxis, in part because they highlighted the material experience of positionality. As with the interwar work that Gambrell examines, "experience" became an important heuristic for feminist politics.

Both Riviere and Carrington, working within and against canonical disciplines, use the trope of the mask as a strategy for negotiating and illustrating the strategies of power that emerge from the dynamic of complicity and resistance. In "The Debutante" this is effected through a doubling and absenting of the self. Through the narrative events of social withdrawal and disruptive participation, "The Debutante" sets in play a rhetorical turn of ambivalence, which references the wider cultural position of *Woman* as allegory, as the object and condition of representation (as crazy muse, *femme-enfant*, and so on) and the historically specific female subject negotiating the conditions of her inscribed image. In her story, skin becomes the fetishised site for the enabling strategies of masking and passing, evoking the surface materiality of all forms of feminized display as well as the threshold between an inside marked "natural" and an outside marked "cultural." The strategies of masking and passing (here and also significantly in the work of Claude Cahun and Frida Kahlo) become culturally gendered and racialized responses to the disabling position of women and the lower social classes. Through the hyena's performance of passing, the narrative conflates the animal and human body, as well as the social roles of working-class maid and upper-class debutante. Thus the hybrid figure unfolds a series of combinations—hyena-maid, maid-debutante and animal-human—that work against a unified or stable interpretation of this figure. Here hybridity represents the very anxiety of classification, what Homi K. Bhabha calls "that ambivalent turn of the discriminated subject into the terrifying exorbitant object of paranoid classification—a disturbing questioning of the images and presences of authority" (1994: 113). Thus the conflation of the animal and human body in the narrative registers a modernist collapse of the reasoned knowing subject while also exploring new kinds of subject positions and ways to represent a more dynamic and complex epistemology of the self.[21] While Carrington's work acknowledges the importance of destabilizing canonical Surrealist constructions of female "otherness" by embedding her surreal narrative in her own lived experience, she nevertheless adopts a masculinist tradition of ironic critique to displace a Surrealist tendency to reify the experience of the other.

As an "object of paranoid classification" the hybrid hyena-debutante in this text (and the many other hybrid identities in Carrington's paintings and stories from this period) evokes the subject's marginalization, alienation and position as grotesque outsider. Echoing Gulliver's sense of alienation and displacement in Swift's novel, the protagonist in the "The Debutante" begins her narration with a confession of misanthropic withdrawal:

> When I was a debutante, I often went to the zoo. I went so often that I knew the animals better than girls of my own age. Indeed it was in order to get away from people that I found myself at the zoo everyday. The animal I got to know best was a young hyena. She knew me too. She was very intelligent. I taught her French and she taught me her language. In this way we passed many pleasant hours. (44)

The debutante's rejection of social interaction at the beginning of the narrative prefigures her ultimate refusal to participate in the formal rite of passage from childhood play to the marriage market. This echoes Gulliver's own escape from the responsibilities and demands of a wife and children as well as Alice's resistance to the formal lessons of instruction provided by her elder sister. The intellectual exchange between the hyena and the debutante further reminds us of Alice's communicative attempts with the black kitten in *Through the Looking Glass* and Gulliver's encounters with unfamiliar beings throughout his travels. In all three texts anti-social behavior leads to an extraordinary journey or event, one that interrogates the given nature of institutional practices and the arbitrary effects of power relations. Carrington's relationship to both Swift and Carroll is thus carefully orchestrated not only within Breton's *Anthology* but also in her own narrative.

The hybrid body of the masked hyena also disrupts the logic of serial reproduction, exemplified by the figure of the conventional debutante, who, as an object of exchange between men, becomes a serialized body on display. The spectacle of the debutante's body, paraded in an expensive and elaborate gown, contrasts to the image of the *faceless* wage labor servant who haunts the narrative's action. The removal of the maid's face macabrely registers the impersonal treatment of the working class domestic at the same time that it underscores their indispensable role in masking the often unseemly behavior of the upper classes. Furthermore, the narrative mobilizes the trope of hybridity to satirically depict the debutante's increasingly devalued and comic status among the upper and middle classes. The debutante's traditionally symbolic status as "pure" and "noble," color-coded through the fetishization of her "whiteness" and her "blue blood,"[22] had begun to erode by the early decades of the twentieth century. Increasingly debutante culture took on the terms and references of commodity culture, signaled in the literature of the period with the term "the marriage market." In her history and analysis of debutante culture, Margaret Pringle has shown how money and not blood became the currency of exchange as this traditionally aristocratic ritual was opened up to more entrepreneurial families. At the same moment that the blood of the aristocracy became "diluted," the debutante ritual was increasingly compared to the "primitive" mating rituals of non-western countries. In her examination of this story and its strategic use of the debutante, Alice Gambrell argues that

> … with increasing popular awareness of developments within the discipline of anthropology, a series of smugly self-mocking "debutante jokes"—which compared debutante rituals to puberty rites among non-Western peoples—started to emerge from the upper classes. Edith Wharton's *The Age of Innocence* (1920), for example, is filled with jokes of this kind. While these jokes successfully mocked the pretensions of those who presumed that their activities stood for the height of "civilization," they also required a generic (and utterly problematic) hypothesis of a "primitive" cultural "other" to serve as the ultimate butt of the joke. Thus, while Carrington's short story bears some resemblance to this kind of humour, her tone is quite different: she undermines its smugness by foregrounding violence in an extremely disruptive way. (1998: 208)

If the hyena-maid represents the partially successful infiltration of the middle-class other into an aristocratic debutante coterie, as well as its violent expulsion, then the violence in Carrington's story also strongly evokes the violence of paternal anxiety over miscegenation.

Surreal Violence

In foregrounding violence in the debutante's masking performance, Carrington's narrative dramatizes the violent cultural shaping of the female body, suggesting that notions of the "primitive" and the "civilized" are themselves caught up in a racial and gendered class narrative of privilege and power. While the narrative dramatizes the cross-class commodification of women's bodies it also self-consciously exposes the violent human cost of maintaining upper class ritual at the expense of lower social classes. The hyena's attendance at the ball, its very domestication, provokes a blood-lust that metaphorises the latent violence invested in an aristocratic maintenance of bloodlines. The figure of the violated maid and the latent "blood-lust" of the masked hyena, who kills in order to attend the ball, powerfully evokes the Surrealist fascination with female criminality, in particular the two notorious criminal cases involving young women in Paris in 1933—those of Violette Nozière and Christine and Léa Papin.[23] Violette Nozière was eighteen years old when she was accused of poisoning her parents, supposedly because they had refused to allow her to attend a party. The Papin Sisters, previously dutiful household maids, had violently murdered their employer and her daughter.[24] The themes of violence, femininity, and class evoked in Carrington's narrative are central to the controversy that erupted over these criminal cases in popular and intellectual circles, both at the time of the events and for years to come.[25] When both cases came to court, the sensationalist Parisian press presented these women as "monsters" and "cannibals," unleashing a wave of "anti-woman hysteria" (Rosemont, 1998: 42) throughout France, despite evidence that the Papin sisters had been subjected to an oppressive code of silence by their employer and Nozière's initial claim that she had been repeatedly raped by her father, a prosperous and respected middle-class father and husband.

In her autobiography Simone de Beauvoir records that the trials of all three women coincided over a three month period toward the end of 1933, and precipitated a legal correspondent to call for the harshest penalties to be given to "all cases of youthful delinquency" (1992: 109). However, the misogyny and hysteria surrounding these cases was evident not only in the popular press but in writers such as Janet Flanner, the Paris correspondent for *The New Yorker*. In her article on Nozière, Flanner writes:

> Violette killed her father like a cannibal, because she wanted to eat and drink up the savings that were his French life and blood ... Violette was, one fears not the last of the faked-silver-foxed, hard-toothed, modern young monsters of mediocre looks and without any sense of the business of life ... . (1936/1972: 158–9)

The language and tone of Flanner's piece reflects a modernist cultural anxiety over the corrupting influence of consumer culture on young women, as well as an anxiety over women's increasing independence and assertiveness. Violette's greatest crime, according to Flanner, is her wasteful consumption of the nationalist and paternal symbols of French bourgeois culture, her father's hard earned savings, which for Flanner is the unquestioned—here at least—"business of life." Flanner's representation of Violette as a "faked-silver foxed, hard-toothed, modern young monster" recalls the trope of the modern woman as a voracious consumer, eating away at the traditional moral values of bourgeois culture. In leaving out of consideration any mention of the violent incestuous relationship that Violette claimed had occurred with her father, Flanner's polemical piece reflects how the Nozière case dramatically divided French society. According to Roudinesco

> In the press and in public opinion, there were two adversary camps. One, which was the patriotic and conservative majority, was convinced of Baptiste's [the father] probity, and saw him as the victim of a perverse creature. The other, the minority, recommended a certain prudence. In the fall of 1933, all of France was obsessed with the Nozière affair. (1990: 18)

The Surrealists sided with the minority, championing Noziére as a heroine whose crime could be read as a backlash against an increasingly corrupt social order, in particular the hypocrisy of the bourgeois family, an institution that harboured incest and perversion.[26] A special pamphlet, *Violette Nozières* came out in December 1933, with poems and drawings illustrating the case, by many prominent Surrealists, including Breton, Péret, and Crével. Magritte also provided an illustration—*L'impromptu de Versailles* (1933)—which depicted a disturbing visual narrative of the events. In this image the incestuous relationship between Violette and her father is made graphic with a young Violette sitting on the lap of her father, his hand disappearing under her dress. Looking on this scene of incestuous desire is a man with a white beard and a bowler hat, who bears a striking likeness to Freud. The facial expressions of rapture on both father and daughter seem to gloss any sense of trauma experienced by Nozière.

In 1933, the same year as the Nozière and Papin scandals, Jacques Lacan published "Motives of Paranoid Crime," a psychoanalytic case study of the Papin Sisters, in the Surrealist journal, *Minotaure*. During this period, Lacan had begun to associate with the Surrealists, becoming particularly interested in Dali's essay on the "paranoid-critical" method.[27] In the midst of his doctoral thesis on paranoia, Lacan was drawn to the sensational nature of the crime and its lack of any obvious motive, and took the opportunity to test his own theories. Providing graphic detail of the sisters' crime, Lacan's essay bears the stamp of a Surrealist fascination with violence and transgression:

> Each seized an adversary, tore her eyes from their sockets (a deed unheard of, it was said, in the annals of crime), and brained her. Next, with the aid of what could be found within reach, hammer, tin pitcher, kitchen knife, they assaulted the bodies of their victims, bashing their faces, baring their genitals, and deeply slashing the thighs and buttocks of one in order to soil with blood the members of the other. They then washed the instruments of these atrocious rites, cleansed themselves, and retired to the same bed. "That's a clean job of it!" ... Such is the phrase they exchanged, which seemed to restore to them a sober tone, empty of all emotion, after the bloody orgy. (1933/1988: 7)

Lacan's description is indebted to a Surrealist obsession with enucleation as a symbol for the crisis of modernist visuality and the epistemological and ontological uncertainties of the self; it also frames the sisters' crime in terms of a surrealist disjunction of propriety and scandal through the contrasting detail of sordid violence and conscientious cleanliness. Although his reading of the motives for the crime differ from that of the Surrealists, as it did from contemporary orthodox psychiatry and general public opinion, he nevertheless shares with them an interest in the graphic spectacle of female criminality. Rather than claim that the sisters were reprehensible monsters guilty of a heinous crime or victims of bourgeois hypocrisy out for class revenge, Lacan argues that they were suffering from paranoia and thus "questioned the fundamental responsibility of the Papin sisters for the murders" (Lane, 1993: 34). Noting that the sisters exhibit an emotional attachment akin to the bonds of identical twins, Lacan draws on Freud's explanation of paranoia in the Schreber case, as an unsuccessful defence against repressed homosexual desire, one that unfolds a manifest connection between external judgement and internal persecution. For Lacan, the sisters exhibit perfect symptoms of paranoid psychosis born of repressed homosexual desire; that is, their disavowed desire for each other gives rise to a persecution complex which in turn produces a confusion of boundaries between male and female, self and other. This is born out by Christine's confession in prison that "I really think that in another life I must have been my sister's husband" (1933/1988: 9). Lacan contends that in murdering their employers the sisters were performing an act of self-persecution, seeing in them a specular double of themselves. Evidence of this is suggested by Christine's attempt, when separated from her sister, to rip out her own eyes and subject herself to acts of violence and erotic display that bear a resemblance to her original crime. On closer scrutiny of the maid's lives, however, it is revealed that comments about domestic duties were relayed through a series of notes left on trays. When asked whether her employers were kind, Christine responded that she did not know since in the six years of their service they had never spoken directly to her. Lacan thus speculates that the "accusatory" silence that existed between the sisters and their employers fueled their persecution complex:

> If one observes that the masters seem strangely to have lacked human sympathy, we can only reply that the haughty indifference of the domestics was but a response to this attitude; "one doesn't speak to the other." Yet this silence could not be empty, even if it was obscure in the eyes of the actors. (7)

In closely reading the social and psychical details of the case, Lacan reveals that paranoia is not "a straightforward response—or even a deliberate answer—to cultural pressure and alienation because psychosis seems to illustrate an asymmetrical relation between the social and the psychical" (Lane, 1993: 35). Although Lacan mentions the details of the sisters' background, including their strange relationship with their employers, ultimately he provides a rhetorical reading of the event that locates the meaning of the crime in the symbolic silence of the relations between the two groups; a silence which is thus transferred into widespread public and intellectual confusion over a motive for the crime.

In her account of the Papin affair de Beauvoir exemplifies this confusion. Although initially she claims full understanding of the event in terms of class revenge, much like the Surrealists, in the end de Beauvoir too becomes fascinated by its seemingly inexplicable nature. At the time of the Papin affair, she and Sartre were confined to Rouen. With few friends or family to distract them, de Beauvoir reports that they became obsessed by the news of the day, in particular the Papin affair:

> We were attracted by any sort of extreme, just as we were by psychoses or neuroses … Abnormality we found positively attractive. One of our inconsistencies was our refusal to accept the idea of the subconscious. Yet Gide, the Surrealists, and, despite our resistance, Freud himself had all convinced us that in every person their lurks what André Breton called *un infracassable noyau de nuit*, an indestructible kernel of darkness, something that cannot break up social conventions or the common currency of human speech, but does, now and then, burst out in a peculiarly scandalous fashion. (1992: 107)

Although de Beauvoir's account registers the social and political significance of the crime in terms of class relations and the conservative nature of the judiciary, it also reveals a degree of confusion over its motive or cause. While she sets out regarding the Papin sisters as victims of bourgeois brutality and hypocrisy (108), she concludes by rethinking her original position in the face of a widely accepted diagnosis of the sisters' paranoia: "We were therefore wrong in regarding their excesses as being due to the hand of rough justice" (109). What is interesting about de Beauvoir's account is that, despite her commitment to a political and feminist reading of the crime, she has also imbibed a Surrealist reading of female criminality as "marvelous," as "an indestructible kernel of darkness." Similarly, she is struck, like them, by the publication in the mainstream press, of a set of photographs of the sisters taken before and after the crimes:

> How well-behaved Christine and Léa looked in the old photograph that some papers printed, with their ringlets and white collars! How had they been transformed into the haggard Furies that pictures taken after their arrest displayed for public obloquy? (108)

While de Beauvoir's reticence in initially interpreting the Papin crime indicates her general style of philosophical reflection, in the end she reads their experience through the seductive trajectory of the ruined woman, made palpable through a series of visible somatic signs. It was this discordant quality produced by the "Before" and "After" photographs (see Plate 1) that had inspired the Surrealists to reproduce these images in their journal, *Le surréalisme au service de la révolution* (No. 5, May 15, 1933). The visual *frisson* of these images exemplified the Surrealist aesthetic principle of "convulsive beauty," registering the problematic dichotomization of feminine sexuality as ethereal and transcendent and as violently excessive and corporeal.

The various readings of these crimes—by Flanner, Lacan, de Beauvoir and the Surrealists—unravels the complex nexus between femininity, class, trauma, rebellion and psychosis as they came to operate in these events. In particular, the Surrealists' interest in female criminality and their use of these women as emblems of an aesthetic and social revolutionary cause seems to gloss over the very real sense of trauma and loss of meaning experienced by these women. For the Surrealists the rebellious female criminal, like the madwoman, exemplifies what Roudinesco calls a new vision of femininity: "Baudelarian, nocturnal, dangerous and fragile" (20), a spectral figure, who, though dangerously tantalizing is nevertheless made powerless by her working class status and her experience of a trauma she can never articulate or understand. Here the trope of the "ruined" woman surfaces in the Surrealist fantasy of feminine criminality and psychosis as a revolutionary aesthetic and social category, one which reduces her to a silent, enigmatic spectacle.

While "The Debutante" stages the themes of rebellion and violence through the reluctant debutante's scene of unruly adolescence, it complicates a Surrealist celebration of female rebellion by foregrounding the importance of race and class in the construction and performance of female paranoia. The hyena's working class cockney diction: "So I smell a bit strong, what?," together with its refusal of the class-bound ritual of eating cake, registers the animal's status in a way that collapses the working class body of the maid (the domestic) onto the undomesticated body of the hyena, foregrounding the female body's abject and liminal cultural status. The hyena's smell and its hairiness ("her hands ... were too hairy to look like mine") emerge as a trope for the grotesque leaking body, a body that has escaped the processes of socialization and the successful mask of idealized and commodified femininity. It is the strong and noticeable smell of the hyena that brings about its own unmasking at the party. The mother's repeated plea that her daughter wash before the party (because the smell of the hidden hyena has permeated the daughter's bedroom), together with her traumatic outburst over the hyena's presence, suggests the repressed horror of the unclean woman and the implicit violence of propriety.

Hybrid Figures

In choosing the figure of the hyena for her story about social rebellion, Carrington registers the animal's mythological and zoological status as a sexually hybrid creature. A recurring animal in Carrington's Surrealist bestiary, the hyena is symbolic of sexual transgression and hybridity. Once thought to be hermaphroditic, because the male and female genitals are almost identical—the female having both testicles and an enlarged clitoris—the hyena has endured a reputation for profanity and sexual deviancy, including homosexuality. The hyena has also been maligned within Christianity and folklore. In medieval mythology it was believed that sorcerers hunted with packs of hyenas and that witches road upon their backs.[28] Also renowned as a harbinger of death, the hyena is often associated with the devil's dark wisdom, primarily because of its human-like mocking laughter; a characteristic that satirically reinforces Carrington's trademark "black humor."

In referencing the ambiguity of the hyena's sexual and cultural status, the hybrid body of the hyena-maid disrupts the static and closed body of bourgeois individualism as well as the sealed and spectral body of commodity culture. Mary Russo argues that the grotesque body functions as a libidinal multiplicity through its refusal of the singular and its embracement of the multiple and the possible: "the grotesque body is the open, protruding, extended, secreting body, the body of becoming, process and change" (62–3). Russo's analysis also unfolds a modernist and postmodernist articulation of the hybrid. Within contemporary theoretical parlance, hybridity has taken on a postcolonial understanding of race and sexuality formed at the site of a nineteenth- and twentieth-century discourse on eugenics, signaled in Carrington's narrative by debutante culture's fetishization of blood and genealogy within the historically analogous rise of fascism in Europe.[29] Tracing the cultural anxiety of miscegenation within a postcolonial narrative of modernist cultural history, Bhabha writes:

> Hybridity intervenes in the exercise of authority not merely to indicate the impossibility of its identity but to represent the unpredictability of its presence ... The display of hybridity—its peculiar 'replication'—terrorises authority with the ruse of recognition, *its mimicry, its mockery* (114–15). (Emphasis mine)

In light of Bhabha's extensive theorization of the hybrid, I would argue that Carrington's use of the hybrid form in this story is in part a response to the impossibility of the female subject's identity within the "authoritarian" codes and practices, not only of the bourgeois and upper-class family, but of Surrealist aesthetic ideology and practice. In canonical Surrealist cultural production, the grotesque female body is often deployed as a topos of mutability and instability, one which registers a misogynistic violence that is inherent to its anti-bourgeois political and aesthetic order. While Carrington may have concurred with the political and aesthetic import of much Surrealist imagery, her work critically engages with the repeated dichotomization of female embodiment as both pure and abject. Like Riviere's subject, who moves between caricatured femininity and intellectual authority as a reflection of the compromised role of the newly emerging professional woman, Carrington's use of masking strategies and hybrid configurations, together with the modes of irony and satire, betray the problematic nature of artistic authority for the Surrealist woman artist or writer: they also suggest a desire to disrupt and mock any such hierarchy of authority.

Conclusion

The multiple ambiguities and possibilities of the hybrid enact both the "nowhere" of female identity, signaled by the reluctant debutante's social withdrawal into the utopic textual world of *Gulliver's Travels* as well as its mimicry and mockery of paternal and professional codes of authority, signaled by the masked hyena's sadistic and disruptive presence at the ball. Carrington's aesthetic and textual practice thus interrogates the "authority" of Surrealist cultural production and professional and personal patronage. In its unmasking of the violence inherent in the commodified exchange of the female body, Carrington's story critiques the narratives of authenticity and purity produced by canonical Surrealism and the class bound institution of debutante culture. As a text which marks Carrington's debut into the Surrealist movement, "The Debutante" maps out a resistance to the codes of prescribed femininity in the culture of the debutante ritual within the context of her participation in the Surrealist coterie. In staging the themes of violence and feminine propriety within her narrative, Carrington weds her narrative to the spectre of violence unleashed by a Surrealist celebration of female criminality and violence. The Surrealist's homage to Nozière and the Papin sisters suggests the way in which women's "authentic" experiences were mined for political and aesthetic effect. In Lacan's reading of the Papin sisters' crime and Magritte's smug depiction of incest in his portrait of Nozière, as in

Breton's and Ernst's introductions to Carrington's narrative, the full meaning of women's experiences and writing is interpreted and mediated by the male Surrealist. Moreover, the publication of the "Before and After" photos of the Papin Sisters in *Le Surréalisme au service de la révolution* evokes the Surrealist representation of woman as both pure and abject, a trope that reinforces the dialectical foundation of its aesthetic practice.

Carrington would later exploit (ironically) the "Before and After" effect for her own political and aesthetic ends. In 1942 she published an account of her psychotic breakdown during the war, in the Surrealist journal, *VVV*. Her autobiographical narrative, *Down Below*, was accompanied with a photograph of the author "before" the events she describes, dressed as a debutante in the company of her mother. The image presents, like the "Before" photograph of the Papin sisters, an image of feminine purity and conformity. Appearing at the conclusion of the essay, however, the image sets up what Alice Gambrell describes as an "interpretive dissonance," contrasting "the essay's many verbal images of degradation and vulnerability with a photographic representation of deliberately constructed purity and protectedness" (1998: 83–4). This dissonance is further replicated in the essay through Carrington's use of her characteristic black humor to describe her exchange between a series of powerful male figures. Like "The Debutante," *Down Below* records Carrington's resistance to the pervasive cultural exchange and manipulation of women's bodies and experiences during this period.

Notes

1 Roudinesco notes that during this new phase, Breton increasingly became preoccupied with "new technique[s] for arriving at a knowledge of reality" (1990: 31).

2 While much of this manifesto reads as a public outing of various former members, it comes as no surprise that in the decade to come Breton would seek to open the movement up to new members. Some of those celebrated by the Surrealists during the 1930s included the fourteen-year-old writer, Gisèle Prassinos, the Czech painter Toyen, Meret Oppenheim, Leonora Carrington, Frida Kahlo and the Chinese-Cuban painter Wilfredo Lam. Alice Gambrell argues that during the late thirties and early forties, Breton "spent a great deal of time as entrepreneur and patron to a scattered group of younger artists ... [and] began ... quite consciously to seek out and promote work by writers and visual artists, who, for him, embodied and made literal those carefully constructed fictions of difference and alterity" (1997: 42).

3 Polizzotti notes Breton's fondness for Carrington: "Breton, for his part, was very taken with the stunning Englishwoman, whom he later described as 'superb in her refusals, with a boundless human authenticity'" (448).

4 Chadwick argues that Carrington's portrait of her friend Joan Powell (painted before her encounter with Surrealism), holding a copy of Jean Cocteau's *Les Enfants Terribles,* presents an image of woman as "worldly, independent and tough." Chadwick suggests that Cocteau's novel, published in 1930, became a symbol of alienated and rebellious

youth and seems to signify for Carrington "an emblem of revolt both literary and bohemian" (67–8).

5 Polizzotti provides a striking portrait of Carrington during this period when he writes: "Fleeing both Carrington's conventional upper-class family and the crazily jealous Marie-Berthe, the couple went to live in Ernst's country house in the Saint-Martin-d'Ardèche, among the Côte-du-Rhône vineyards. Lively and uninhibited, equally talented as a writer and painter, the darkly beautiful Carrington brought to Surrealism a keen sense of black humor all her own" (448).

6 For details of Carrington's life during this period see Whitney Chadwick(1985). For publication dates see introduction by Marina Warner in *The House of Fear: Notes From Down Below*.

7 It is more than likely that Carrington was familiar with both these cases. Although both crimes occurred in 1933, they instantly attracted notoriety, being widely discussed in the press and throughout France for years to come. As late as 1937 the Nozière affair resurfaced when Violette, after a religious conversion and reconciliation with her mother, retracted all accusations leveled against her father. Also Carrington may have discussed the case with Ernst since he had been part of the group of Surrealists who had contributed to the special pamphlet dedicated to Nozière. See Roudinesco, 19–21.

8 I use the term "canonical" here to refer to early Surrealist political and aesthetic constructions, particularly those formulated by Breton throughout the 1920s. While Carrington's work certainly became more canonical during the late 1930s and early 1940s, I think historically, it has suffered from lack of inclusion in retrospective guides to Surrealism. That is, until feminist scholars such as Whitney Chadwick and Susan Rubin Suleiman began their important work on the women Surrealists.

9 There is no evidence that Carrington, or any of the Surrealists ever read Riviere's essay. Its inclusion here is appositional since both texts, written almost a decade apart, explore the importance of masking strategies to modernist women's identity. Indeed the significance of Riviere's essay was not fully recognized until feminist theory began to explore issues of female spectatorship and gender performance. See Mary Ann Doane, "Film and the Masquerade: Theorizing the Female Spectator" (1991) and Judith Butler's *Gender Trouble* (1990).

10 For details of Riviere's life see Lisa Appignanesi and John Forrester, *Freud's Women* and Athol Hughes, "Joan Riviere: Her Life and Work" in *The Inner World and Joan Riviere: Collected Papers, 1920–1958*, ed. Athol Hughes, London and New York: Karnac, 1991, pp. 1–43.

11 Judith Butler adopts a similar strategy to Riviere when she writes: "gender is a kind of imitation for which there is no original." For Butler's own referencing of Riviere in her account of the masquerade and the theory of gender performativity see *Gender Trouble: Feminism and the Subversion of Identity*, Chapters 2 and 6.

12 See Polizzotti, 1997: 431.

13 Lisa Appignanesi and John Forrester argue that: "Freud's views on women were as erratic as anyone else's. He could fire off the dissmissive quip: 'A woman who feels restless consults a physician or goes shopping', but he was equally able to observe during the Nazi occupation of Vienna that 'The women are the most capable' and that 'In general women hold up better than men.' During the Vienna Psycho-Analytical Society discussions of 1906 on the 'Natural Position of Women,' he is quoted as having said: 'A woman cannot earn a living and raise children at the same time. Women as

a group profit nothing by the modern feminist movement; at best a few individuals profit'" (3).

14 In interviews with Marina Warner and Paul de Angelis, Carrington has repeatedly spoken about her experience as a debutante. See Interview with Paul de Angelis, *El Paseante 17*

15 "Huxley, as Jessica Mitford notes in her autobiography *Hons and Rebels,* enjoyed a brief vogue among artistically inclined British debutantes during the 1930s." See Gambrell, 1997: 78.

16 In the following exchange from *Love in a Cold Climate*, written between the wars, Nancy Mitford provides an example of the increasing resistance to, and parody of, debutante culture by prospective debutantes themselves: "Polly says: 'This coming out seems a great bore—do you enjoy it, Fanny?' to which Fanny replies 'I had never thought … Girls had to come out, I knew. It is a stage in their existence'" (239).

17 Carrington was three years older than Ernst's son, Jimmy Ernst, and Breton was in his early forties when Carrington first met him.

18 See Warner's introduction to *The House of Fear*, 15.

19 In his "Introduction," Polizzotti notes that the *Anthology of Black Humour* started out as an attempt to create "a showcase of the Surrealist conception of humor and a way for its impecunious author to earn a quick advance …" (v).

20 Two anthologies, in particular, *Wayward Girls and Wicked Women: An Anthology of Stories*, ed. Angela Carter and *That Kind of Woman: Stories From the Left Bank and Beyond*, eds. Bronte Adams and Trudi Tate, reflect the growing visibility of Carrington's work as well as the way in which "The Debutante" has become an exemplary story about the crisis of gendered identity both between the wars and more recently within a contemporary feminist framework.

21 It is important to note that the hybrid of the animal and the human body cannot be sustained, as the events of the narrative make clear. The hyena-maid hybrid does not successfully pass as a debutante at the party.

22 The cultural historian Angela Lambert suggests that the expression "blue blood" derives from "the sangre azul claimed by certain families of Castile, as being uncontaminated by Moorish, Jewish or other admixture; probably founded on the blueness of the veins of people of fair complexion (OED). Thus racism and anti-Semitism are also inherent in the idea of blue-bloodedness" (15).

23 The Surrealists also celebrated Aimée, who was the subject of Lacan's doctoral thesis; a woman also suffering paranoia who had attempted murder.

24 For details of both crimes see Elisabeth Roudinesco (1990), Janet Flanner (1973), Martin Jay (1994), Penelope Rosemont (1998) and Christopher Lane (1993).

25 As Rosemont notes the Surrealist's interest in these two criminal cases was later echoed by others: Genet's play *The Maids* was based on the Papin sisters and Claude Chabrol made a film in the 1970s on Nozière, titled *Violette*. More recently Nancy Meckler's film *Sister My Sister* (1994) attempts to read the Papin affair from the perspective of the sister's incestuous lesbian relationship and the class relationship between the maids and their employers.

26 Polizzotti suggests: "Breton in particular felt a visceral commitment to the case … For him supporting Violette Nozières meant spitting in the face of the parents he still resented" (393).

27 Lacan would eventually confirm many of Dali's insights on paranoia and interpretation in his doctoral thesis, *De la psychose paranoïaque dans ses rapports avec la personnalité* (Polizzotti, 384).

28 From "The Bestiary": http://pages.prodigy.com/Christory/hyena.htm.

29 In her interview with Paul de Angelis, Carrington suggests that once she met the Surrealists in London she became aware for the first time of "who Hitler really was" and that later when she moved to Paris to be with the group, Hitler became the most common topic of conversation (*El Paseante* 17, n.p.).

Chapter 3

Surrealist Transgression and Feminist Subversion

Introduction

In her essay, "Dialogue and Double Allegiance: Some Contemporary Women Artists and the Historical Avant-Garde" (1998), Susan Rubin Suleiman reflects on her use of the term "double allegiance" to describe a certain critical and creative dynamic in the work of contemporary avant-garde feminist writers. Suleiman initially applied the term to those postmodernist writers (Kathy Acker and Angela Carter) who were inspired by the avant-garde work of male predecessors such as Bataille and Aragon but who were also interested in feminist critiques of the power relations inherent in the discourses of predominantly male avant-garde movements such as Surrealism. In this recent essay, Suleiman revises this concept to include not only artistic practice but also critical practice:

> Dialogism does not simply *occur*; it is also, to a large extent, *staged* by the critic who juxtaposes works and makes them speak to each other, perhaps even inventing the very words one work might address to the other. (1998:133)

In reading Leonora Carrington's late Surrealist novel, *The Hearing Trumpet* alongside Bataille's early pornographic novel, *Story of the Eye*, I am interested in the ways in which these texts are shaped by a profound critical exegesis of Surrealism; one mired in the illumination of the blind spots of Surrealist political and aesthetic practice. Extending Suleiman's argument, I would suggest that my own analysis produces a critical staging that positions both the text and the reader within a framework of discursive and political negotiation, one that moves equivocally between the imagined dialogues between texts as well as their historical differences and their accumulated value within the canon. I would also argue that "double allegiance" is the defining characteristic of Carrington and Bataille's texts in so far as they attempt to push beyond the limits of the aesthetic and political boundaries that came to define Bretonian Surrealism throughout the 1920s and 1930s; one as Surrealism's "enemy from within" and the other with a "smooth, mocking gaze,"[1] characterizations which exemplify the parodic strategies and inverted significations that mark these texts as insider/outsider works. Historically, these texts are situated at either end of the movement and therefore reflect a unique relationship to the contingencies of their time and place. Each text however had been in its initial moment of circulation marginal to the movement only to have its status later revived within and against the terms of a Surrealist enterprise that had begun to be stripped of its radical impetus by the time these works were re-evaluated. Indeed their subsequent reassessment forms part of a leftist and feminist critical reaction to Surrealism's increasing reification within the literary canon. But while it is easy to see a certain reworking of Bretonian Surrealism in these texts, and a close reading does indeed legitimate such a critical move, they are in striking ways also indebted to the critical momentum that inaugurated the aesthetic and political concerns of the first Surrealist manifesto.

Written in 1927 but published anonymously in the same year as Breton's *Nadja*, in 1928, *Story of the Eye* was in many ways an underground text since its explicit pornographic content made it impossible to be published under Bataille's own name.[2] Although some of Bataille's contemporaries, including Breton, were aware of the novel's author, the use of the pseudonym, Lord Auch (an abbreviation of *aux chiottes* which, when combined with Lord translates as "god relieving himself") guaranteed authorial anonymity and the text's connection to the literal name of the father while underscoring the novel's obsession with a rearrangement of the high and the low. The prohibition of paternal legacy registered by Bataille's choice of authorial mask also evokes what Michel Surya refers to as Bataille's mongrel status within French avant-garde circles during this period, as a respected scholar and archivist and as the author of obscene literature (2002: 116). It was this profound paradox that Breton had in mind when he referred to Bataille as the "excremental philosopher," at once praising Bataille's capacity for intellectual rigor if only to question its application to a base materialism that for Breton threatened to undermine the very foundations of its own logic. Bataille's own resistance to Breton's dogmatic policing of Surrealism—with the counter-accusation that Breton wields his power like a "priest" and a "cop"[3]—signified his anti-authoritarianism even in the context of the then radical aims of Surrealism. Breton's recuperation of the transgressive into the logic of the marvelous signaled, for Bataille, a homogenous move toward idealism that bespoke the necessary failure of the revolutionary ideal of rupture. Only through the unmediated affirmation of waste, expenditure and destruction "to the point of shame" could one find "the uninterpretable truth of existence" (124): against the marvelous Bataille would institute an absolute affirmation of the monstrous, one stripped of any consoling idealism.[4]

Bataille's capacity to exceed the very limits of Surrealism made him an exemplary figure for the generation of French post-structuralist writers who emerged as the leading intellectual power brokers following the explosive events of May 1968. The group that gathered around *Tel Quel* (Foucault, Derrida, Kristeva, Barthes and Sollers) in the late 1960s and early 1970s were, like their Surrealist predecessors, attempting to connect political and social change with a symbolic attack on literary and philosophical tradition. Bataille's marginal and ultra-left status in a movement that by this time had already begun to be reclaimed by the center, made him an exemplary figure to underwrite the radical aims of the new French avant-garde. In spanning two different generations (two different avant-gardes) Bataille's work has come to represent *the* counter-discourse of both modernist and postmodernist epochs. But in reclaiming Bataille for a philosophical revolution that inaugurates theory as the new avant-garde, the rich historical context out of which Bataille's voice emerged, one grounded in an active intellectual engagement with Surrealism in all of its disparate aesthetic and political actualities, is invariably reduced to a mythical rendering of the utter opposition between Breton and Bataille. Writing in 1946, after the energies of antagonism had settled into a more reflective account of those early years, Bataille concluded: "I would now like to affirm [Surrealism] from within as the demand to which I have submitted and as the dissatisfaction I exemplify" (1994: 49). While my own reading of the novel points to the tensions between the Surrealism of Bataille and Breton, it does so without losing the framework of proximity that governs all dialogic engagement.

Written in Mexico City at some point in the early 1950s[5] Carrington's *The Hearing Trumpet* was circulated and read privately for many years before the manuscript was lost, only to be rediscovered and published as *Le Cornet acoustique* in France in 1974, and later in English in 1977. Initial reactions to the English translation of the novel were sympathetic and interested if not spectacular.[6] It was not until the late 1980s and early 1990s that Carrington's writing began to attract critical attention when the feminist publishing house, Virago, reprinted much of Carrington's short fiction as well as the non-fiction work, *Down Below* and her only novel, *The Hearing Trumpet*. By this point there had been growing interest in the women Surrealists as a result of Whitney Chadwick's comprehensive survey, *Women Artists and the Surrealist Movement* (1985) as well as critical attention by writers such as Marina Warner and Susan Rubin Suleiman. It is in the context of a feminist revisionist approach to the history of modernism that Carrington's novel was resurrected as a lost classic of Surrealism. But, as a late work of the movement, one which satirically inverts many of its formal and thematic concerns, it was also hailed as an important precursor to feminist revisionist fiction, a category of literature that increasingly came to represent a kind of feminist avant-garde in so far as it combined an experimentation with narrative form alongside a dialogical political engagement with modernist avant-garde uber-texts. In this sense, *The Hearing Trumpet* also carries a double historical inscription, as a lost Surrealist classic *and* as a founding text of feminist experimental writing.

The autobiographical and historical contexts out of which Carrington and Bataille's texts were initially created and circulated are central to my analysis of their critical place within Surrealism. In reading Carrington's novel alongside Bataille's, I want to examine how these two works combine parody, autobiography and fantasy to explore Surrealism's aesthetic violation of the human body as central to the movement's anti-institutional and anti-bourgeois politics and aesthetics. However, I also want to argue that these texts offer an implicit critique of a Bretonian transcendent vision, defined in *The Second Manifesto* as the ideal point at which all contradictions cease (1972: 123–4).

Here, Breton's desire for unity produces an idealism that encompasses everything from the idea itself to his exaltation of heterosexual romantic love. In contrast to a Bretonian idealism, Carrington and Bataille's texts sustain rather than resolve contradiction; in these works a burlesque excess is figuratively deployed in a way that produces a representational politics of monstrosity. While Bataille turns to eroticism to examine the relationship between order and disorder that underlies all transgression, Carrington employs the categories of the hybrid and the grotesque to critique a Surrealist celebration of femininity as erotically transgressive. In de-eroticizing feminine transgression, Carrington replaces the figure of the *femme-enfant* with the maternal figure of the crone whose abject and culturally marginal status signifies a reworking of female spectacle as politically and aesthetically disruptive because of its failed transcendence. While the modes of autobiography and self-analysis are central narrative devices in Carrington and Bataille's texts, these modes are deployed in a way that complicates the privileged status of the experiential in Surrealist literary narrative. In Breton's *Nadja* the heroic construction of the self proceeds through an encounter with the everyday world of the street ("the only region of valid experience") and the haunting effects produced by the narrative reconstruction of the autobiographical subject. As Benjamin reminds us, it is Nadja's *déclassé* status that provides Breton with an "authentic" connection to the experiential and revolutionary world of the street. In Bataille and Carrington's texts, the field of experience offers no such intelligibility or coherence of the self; rather experience itself is constantly thwarted by an unrestrained excess that inserts perversion and desublimation against Breton's containment and recuperation of desire in the heroic quest. Both texts incorporate autobiographical reflection in order to critique the stability of the authorial voice; that is each text inscribes a process of rupture—between objects and words, between fantasy and experience and between narrative styles and genres—which reflects a privileging of the spatial form of the labyrinth over a transcendent unity. While Carrington satirically inverts a Surrealist celebration of the *femme-enfant*, installing in its place a series of monstrous and transgressive heroines, Bataille's erotically violent quest narrative parodies a Bretonian idealization of the marvelous and its concomitant exaltation of the heterosexual romantic encounter.[7] In Bataille and Carrington's texts the operation of desire and fantasy unfolds through a series of lexical, mythological and narrative substitutions and transformations which, as in a great deal of Surrealist work, challenge the cultural and discursive codes which underpin bourgeois aesthetic and political ideology. In both these texts the modes of fiction and autobiography come together in a way that suggests transgression itself signifies a certain crisis of subjectivity and the representation of the self, one that operates within and against the terms of a Bretonian aesthetic and political practice.

Surrealism and The Haruspical Eye[8]

The very title and substantive content of Bataille's first novel registers a Surrealist interest in the enucleated eye as a symbol of its anti-rationalist polemic and as a motif for a post-war crisis of masculine subjectivity and "ways of seeing." While the recurring image of the detached or violated eye forms part of a general modernist aesthetics of violence toward, and scrutiny of, the body,[9] within a Surrealist aesthetic this iconic image locates a more specific cultural obsession whereby the process of displacement produces the much-desired discordant effect exemplified by Lautréamont's famous coupling of an umbrella and a sewing machine on a dissecting table. The sexual connotation of this coupling registers not simply the unconscious dimension of the creative act, but underlines the symbiotic relationship between form and content, so that Surrealist experimental techniques such as frottage, decalcomania, and collage reveal strategies of dissection, displacement and doubling that produce a shifting of the boundaries of both aesthetic form and meaning. However, in the axis between avant-garde culture and a newly emerging science of psychoanalysis, the location of the artist/writer as deviant other, outside of both cultural and aesthetic norms, is invariably inseparable from the strategies and effects they employ. The logic of the Surrealist object, like that of Surrealist identity, in its persistent employment of the alter-ego,[10] implicitly involves strategies of displacement and doubling, requiring us to look at what it has been as well as what it might become—a strategy that registers the object and the subject's signification within a discourse of memory and desire.

While the recurring image of the detached or violated eye registers the psychoanalytic, indeed Oedipal foundations of Surrealist aesthetics, enucleation invariably involves a fetishistic violence directed toward the female body, one that unfolds a profound displacement of masculine trauma.[11] Outside of Bataille's text, two of the most important examples of ocular violation for my analysis are Man Ray's "Object to be Destroyed" (see Plate 2) and the slit eye in *Un chien andalou*, both of which demonstrate a fairly straightforward connection between ocular violation and masculine anxiety. The first version of Man Ray's "Object to be Destroyed" was created in 1923 but as its title predicts, was later destroyed. The object was recreated in 1933, this time in response to Man Ray's anger at Lee Miller's resignation as his photographic assistant in order to set up her own photographic studio in New York. Cutting out a photograph of Miller's eye, the photographer's most vulnerable organ, Man Ray attached it to the arm of a metronome with an invitation to the spectator to "destroy the object". Here we witness acutely the sense of the surreal as a culture of systematic displacement, a culture invested in the processes of desire rather than truth. Since the function of the metronome is "to keep time," we can imagine that this is precisely the role Man Ray desires for his former assistant; fixed to the arm of the metronome, Lee Miller remains the time keeper, the traditional role assigned to the photographer's assistant in the dark room. A year earlier Man Ray had published a sketch of the object with the accompanying text: "Cut out the eye from a photograph of one who has been loved but is seen no more. Attach the eye to the pendulum of the metronome and regulate the weight to suit the tempo desired. Keep doing to the limit of endurance. With a hammer well-aimed, try to destroy the whole at a single blow" (quoted in Caws, 2004: 114). The phallic aggressivity expressed by the frenetic movement of the metronome needle, holding in place the castrated eye of Man Ray's ex-lover and soon-to-be rival, suggests his profound anxiety over Miller's desire for professional independence, and indeed her abandonment of her former roles as lover, model, muse and photographer's assistant.

The slit eye in Dali and Buñuel's *Un chien andalou* is perhaps Surrealism's most violent and memorable moment of ocular violation; indeed the film's central analogy of a cloud eclipsing the moon and of a razor slicing an eyeball has become cinema's defining expression of surreality, one which fully realized the inherently oneiric qualities of avant-garde cinema. Made in 1929, the film shares many of the formal and thematic concerns of *Story of the Eye*. The infamous shot of a razor slicing through the center of the eye takes place toward the end of the prologue, which opens with the caption, "Once upon a time;" the fairytale connotation of this opening shot is violently shattered by the image of a woman having her eye slit by a man who is possibly her lover, producing a discordant coupling of different levels of reality. Here the slit eye metaphorizes both romantic and narrative blindness as our attempts to read coherently are continually frustrated by the film's disjointed anti-linear structure which follows the logic of collage in its use of montage, double exposure and dissolve. These filmic devices capture the dislocated logic of the unconscious so that the slit eye, through its violent "opening up," becomes a symbol of inner vision. On the employment of this device Inez Hedges writes:

> A recurrent surrealist theme is that it is necessary to blind oneself to "objective" reality in order to gain inner vision. Surrealism inverts the terms of blindness and sight, proposing various methods for acceding to true vision. (117)

The violence so persistently enacted through this particular iconographic form points to a Surrealist rhetoric of the marvelous, a freeing of the unconscious through the violent disconnection of everyday ways of seeing and perceiving.[12] Hedges' observations explain in part the prolific occurrence of the violated eye within Surrealist aesthetics but perhaps fail to fully account for the connection between enucleation, libidinal desire and masculine anxiety. As in Man Ray's "Object to be Destroyed," the slit eye in *Un chien andalou* signals an acute agressivity by the male desiring subject against the body of the desired object, so that the violation of the eye, *the* organ of desire and identity, produces an annihilation that registers the seductive terror of the love object.

In his essay "Eye," published in *Documents* in 1930, Bataille signals his enthusiasm for the film's affective discharge of desire and fear, one that demonstrates the overarching significance of the slit eye scene in providing the film's devastating critique of the seductive attraction of the cinematic apparatus. Bataille begins this essay by noting: "It seems impossible, in fact, to judge the eye using any word other than *seductive*, since nothing is more attractive in the bodies of animals and men. But extreme seductiveness is probably at the boundary of horror" (*Visions of Excess*: 1985: 17) and goes on to conclude:

> In this respect, the eye could be related to the cutting edge, whose appearance provokes both bitter and contradictory reactions; this is what the makers of the *Andalusian Dog* must have hideously and obscurely experienced when, among the first images of the film, they determined the bloody loves of these two beings. That a razor would cut open the dazzling eye of a young and charming woman—this is precisely what a young man would have admired to the point of madness ... a young man who by chance holding in his hand a coffee spoon, suddenly wanted to take an eye in that spoon. (17)

It is hardly surprising that Bataille was one of the film's most ardent supporters since it explores similar terrain to his own account of ocular violation, one that seemingly transforms the verbal play of objects in Bataille's own text into an iconography of displacement through the aggressive use of montage. In highlighting the film's transfiguration of one object into another—from the lover's longing gaze at the lunar surface to the slitting of the beloved's "dazzling" eye and its imagined spilling into the smooth hollow of a coffee spoon—Bataille registers his fascination with the fetishistic transformation of the libidinal object at the same time pointing to its production of affective ambivalence. The coupling of seduction and horror which inaugurates the description of the lugubrious eye becomes for Bataille a more general manifestation of the confusing but powerful effect produced by the film:

> This film can be distinguished from banal avant-garde productions, with which one might be tempted to confuse it, in that the screenplay predominates. Several very explicit facts appear in successive order, without logical connection it is true, but penetrating so far into horror that the spectators are caught up as directly as they are in an adventure film. Caught up and even precisely caught by the throat, and without artifice; do these spectators know, in fact, where they—the authors of this film, or people like them—will stop? (19)

For Bataille, the slitting of the eye is a metaphor for the filmic images' capacity to rupture normative modes of visual pleasure, one that performs a critical assault on the ethical detachment of the spectator; indeed the film's mobilization of a seductive horror underlines the erotic and sadistic dimension of the cinematic apparatus itself with its ingenious use of montage providing a "cutting edge" that momentarily blinds in order to liberate the image from mimetic codes and logical connections. Whether we see the film as an analogue for the unconscious or as an evocation of the dream mechanism, Bataille's essay reveals the power of avant-garde film to capture the "extreme seductiveness" of cinema only to take the spectator to the very "boundary of horror." Moreover, the central thesis of

Bataille's essay reinforces the affective ambivalence that underlies the connection between death and eroticism in *Story of the Eye*.

Stories of the "I"

In his structuralist reading of *Story of the Eye*, Roland Barthes argues that Bataille's narrative is driven not so much by the characters and their sado-masochistic erotic play but by the object of the eye itself and the linguistic play and fantasy that it generates. The text is thus centrally concerned with the transformation and displacement of narrative and lexical form inaugurated first by the chain of objects connected with the eye (eggs, testicles, and the sun) and secondly by the chain of liquids connected to those objects (tears, egg yolks, sperm) as well as other liquids such as milk, blood and urine which are also linked throughout the novel back to the globular objects in the first metaphoric chain. Barthes concludes therefore that Bataille's text produces a conflation of the erotic and the linguistic in a way that refuses to privilege one over the other: "*Story of the Eye* is not a deep work. Everything in it is on the surface; there is no hierarchy. The metaphor is laid out in its entirety; it is circular and explicit, with no secret reference behind it" (1982: 123). While Barthes' reading usefully encapsulates the circular and anti-teleological structure of the narrative, it nevertheless institutes its own interpretative hierarchy by privileging form over content in a way that divests the novel of both the experiential and representational force of eroticism and violence. In Barthes' textualist reading of the novel, erotic and linguistic transgression becomes one and the same; indeed in his attempt to render transparent the linguistic meaning of the novel, Barthes disavows its experiential quality, in particular the experience of the erotic encounter and the meaning that it occupies throughout Bataille's critical and creative work.

I would argue that Bataille's novel can be read as a nascent form of his theory of eroticism and its privileged relationship to "inner experience," one that manifests the affective ambivalence underlying all erotic experience—pleasure and anguish. As Suleiman argues "The characteristic feeling accompanying transgression is one of intense pleasure (at the exceeding of boundaries) *and* of intense anguish (at the full realization of the force of those boundaries)" (1995: 317). In *Story of the Eye* the extreme limits of erotic experience disclose the very rupture of knowledge as a coherent system as well as the boundaries that determine the self in relation to the other; erotic transgression, indeed all transgression operates as a supplement to systemic knowledge, disclosing an excessive and non-productive expenditure at the heart of being: death, eroticism, loss, mutability, waste and putrefaction are for Bataille not simply the other of life, but an expression of its absolute manifestation but one that nevertheless exists outside of rational and systemic thought. Eroticism, like sacrifice, opens up the body to a vulnerability and violence that unleashes a raw and profound experience of life, one which makes manifest the interminable presence of death as a shadow that haunts life, implicitly challenging what he defines as the banal inertia of bourgeois values of orderliness, utility and propriety. Just as semantic transgression involves both the simultaneous loss and creation of meaning, the transgressive erotic encounter involves both the recognition and violation of the other as well as the maintenance and loss of the self. Later in *Eroticism* Bataille reveals the paradox of erotic experience insofar as it "upsets an ordered system on which our efficiency and reputation depend" while indicating how "the individual splits up and his unity is shattered from the first instant of the sexual crisis" (1957/1994: 105). In this sense eroticism represents an intensification of experience that loosens the individual from ordered consciousness, one which involves the "plethoric life of the body" coming up against "the mind's resistance" (105). The "inner experience" that results from erotic transgression encapsulates both the body's desire for pleasure and the mind's anguish and resistance to it. As Suzanne Guerlac argues, Bataille's interest in the binary relationship of interdiction and transgression emphasizes "the irrational (emotional) nature of interdiction itself and, in this sense, the irrational foundation of reason …" (1990: 96).

We might ask, then, in what sense is *Story of the Eye* an attempt to come to terms with the affective ambivalence (seduction and horror, pleasure and anguish, desire and fear) that underlies eroticism and its connection with death. The structure of the erotic quest in Part I of the novel is developed through a series of obscene erotic spectacles that propel the narrative fantasy toward its climatic scene of extreme brutality and transgression. In all of these scenes the narrative imparts its own repetitive logic of eroticism in which only death can illuminate the meaning of the erotic event for the central protagonists, the narrator and Simone. The first of these obscene spectacles occurs early in the novel:

> I remember that one day, when we were in a car tooling along at top speed, we crashed into a cyclist, an apparently very young and very pretty girl. Her head was almost totally ripped off by the wheels … The horror and despair at so much bloody flesh, nauseating in part, and in part very beautiful, was fairly equivalent to our usual impression on seeing one another. Simone was tall and lovely … But on a sensual level, she so bluntly craved any upheaval that the faintest call from the senses gave her a look directly suggestive of all things linked to a deep sexuality, such as blood, suffocation, sudden terror, crime; things indefinitely destroying human bliss and honesty. (11)

Here the tension between seduction and horror (beauty and nausea) defines the relationship between the narrator and Simone; indeed the nauseating but beautiful sight of the decapitated young girl suggests that their relationship and the fantasy that it generates occupies a world without normal ethical restraints or responsibilities. It is rather the existential frame of their sexual activity that drives the narration, one that reveals taboo and transgression as itself the genesis of anguish and desire. As their erotic reverie continues the narrator declares: "We had abandoned the real world, the one made up solely of dressed people … Our personal hallucination now developed as boundlessly as perhaps the total nightmare of human society ..." (29). In contrast to the world of "dressed people" the world that the couple inhabit is the pure existential moment of erotic desire, a world of symbolic nakedness, in which death consummates the full meaning of desire since it alone mirrors the complete dissolution and discontinuity of the self that the erotic encounter entails. In the introduction to *Eroticism* Bataille outlines how nakedness is the very symbol of this dissolution, one that connects the naked body in the erotic encounter with the naked body of the corpse. He writes: "The whole business of eroticism is to destroy the self-contained character of the participators as they are in their normal lives. Stripping naked is a decisive action. Nakedness offers a contrast to self-possession ..." (1994: 17).

The novel's exploration of sex and death continues with the suicide of Marcelle, whose mental anguish and shame seems to drive the libidinal intensity and pleasure of the two lovers, Simone and the narrator:

> I will merely report that Marcelle hanged herself after a dreadful incident ... I cut the rope, but she was quite dead. We laid her out on the carpet. Simone saw I was getting a hard-on and she started tossing me off. I too stretched out on the carpet. It was impossible to do otherwise; Simone was still a virgin and I fucked her for the first time, next to the corpse. (43)

It is extremely significant in terms of Bataille's theory of eroticism that the sexual consummation of the two protagonists occurs in the presence of a death, next to the "irritatingly open eyes" of Marcelle's corpse. Here the anxiety of loss that attends to the erotic experience is made parodically literal in the figure of Marcelle. The cyclical pattern of the orgy established at the scene of death will culminate in the last horrific act of the novel, the rape and murder of the priest, bringing together the central characters of the novel's erotic triangle (Marcelle, Simone and the narrator) as well as its central object, the eye:

> Now I stood up and, while Simone lay on her side, I drew her thighs apart, and found myself facing something I imagine I had been waiting for in the same way that a guillotine waits for a neck to slice. I even felt as if my eyes were bulging from my head, erectile with horror; in *Simone's* hairy vagina I saw the wan blue eye of *Marcelle*, gazing at me through tears of urine. Streaks of come in the streaming hair helped give that dreamy vision a disastrous sadness. (67)

Having desecrated the most powerful symbols of the church, the host and the chalice, Simone performs the final act of transgression by inserting into her "slobbery flesh" the enucleated eye of the priest. But in seeing the eye of Marcelle, the narrator confirms that this final act is but a repetition of all previous erotic transgressions. In other words, each "obscene spectacle" is a return to, and an elaboration of, the original erotic experience of attraction and repulsion that links death to eroticism. The use of repetition is, as Sontag notes, the economical form of the pornographic imagination: "There are no gratuitous or non-functioning feelings; no musings, whether speculative or imagistic, which are irrelevant to the business at hand … everything must bear upon the erotic situation" (111–12). In the "total universe" proposed by the pornographic imagination, individual subjectivity is transposed into the endless possibilities for exchange. The transfiguration of one object into another throughout the narrative is repeated in the doubling of the two protagonists, the narrator and Simone, who share the same fantasies and have an understanding of the other in a way that suggests that they are intrapsychic, or the one psyche manifesting variations of its subconscious. Within the moment of the erotic encounter this also represents a fusion of self and other that necessitates a radical loss of self, one that emerges in the text as the paradox of a shared "personal hallucination." However, the uncanny return of Marcelle's eye in the final spectacle of erotic excess suggests that in order for erotic transgression to unfold and in order for the moment of radical self-loss to be fully realized, the presence of the anguished or shaming gaze of the other must be present. In other words it is Marcelle who becomes the symbol of death itself, a death that makes possible Simone and the narrator's erotic consummation. Within the structural schema of transgression and interdiction Simone's anguished gaze represents the threshold or limit that marks the crossing over from the ordered realm of prohibition into the disordered realm of transgression.

While both Barthes and Sontag's essays reveal the circular and enclosed world of the novel's narrative fantasy, when read through the autobiographical and critically interpretative scaffolding of Part II, parodically entitled, "Coincidences," the enclosed world of eroticism is opened up in a way that refuses, I would argue, a purely textualist reading. Adopting a reflexive analytic tone, Bataille, the emerging writer under analysis with Adrien Borel, produces a psychoanalytically inflected "interpretation" of the events in Part I. More significantly, Bataille locates the origins of his narrative in the traumatic family context of his early adolescence:

> I was about fourteen when my affection for my [blind] father turned into a deep and unconscious hatred … One night, we were awakened, my mother and I, by vehement words that the syphilitic was literally howling in his room: he had suddenly gone mad. I went for the doctor … The doctor had withdrawn to the next room with my mother and I had remained with the blind lunatic, when he shrieked: "Doctor, let me know when your [sic] done fucking my wife!" For me, that utterance, which in a split second annihilated the demoralizing effects of a strict upbringing, left me with something like a steady obligation, unconscious and unwilled: the necessity of finding an equivalent to that sentence in any situation I happened to be in; and this largely explains *Story of the Eye.* (72–3)

Closely reading the revelations in Part II, Suleiman locates the significance of Bataille's transgression in the body of the mother: "The knowledge that a 'strict upbringing' has always tried to repress, in a male child, is that his mother's body is *also* that of a woman" (1995: 327). She argues that the knowledge of the duplicity of the asexual maternal and the sexual feminine is the very contradiction of the coexistence of transgression and prohibition—the fascination and the terror, the fear and the desire—provoked by the mother's sexuality. Here, the son's horror powerfully evokes the Oedipal drama—"a confrontation with an all-powerful father and a traumatized son, a confrontation staged across the body of the mother" (1985: 85). In self-consciously drawing attention to the Oedipal origins of his story, Bataille explicitly unmasks the transgressive dimension of the erotic. This is significant when we consider that it was through his analysis with Borel that Bataille began writing *Story of the Eye*. According to Elisabeth Roudinesco, the work of transference had unleashed Bataille's literary creativity and the novel was discussed at every session and often revised after their meetings (1997: 122). But Roudinesco also points to Bataille's (and other Surrealist's) separation of the literary and theoretical dimension of psychoanalysis and its use as a treatment for neuroses: "To sympathise with the Freudian revolution was for [him] an intellectual act, whereas to go to an analyst merely meant one wanted to have one's malady dealt with as directly as possible" (121). And yet Bataille himself draws attention to the therapeutic value of analysis for his writing, and by implication his intellectual development, when he claims: "the first book I wrote ... I was able to write it only when psychoanalysed, yes, as I came out of it. And I believe I am able to say that it is only by being liberated in this way that I was able to write" (Surya: 99). While any reading of the novel needs to be mindful of not simply reducing the text to a series of neurotic symptoms, nevertheless, the autobiographical scaffolding which frames the novel cannot be separated from its emergence through analysis; in many ways this text constitutes an exploration of the unconscious that goes beyond Breton's experiments with automatic writing precisely because it traces the link between fantasy, the unconscious and creative writing.

In this sense Bataille's analytic interpretation in Part II provides an explicit disclosure of the genesis of fantasy and its relationship to creative writing akin to the model developed in Freud's essay, "Creative Writers and Daydreaming" (1908); an essay that Bataille's analyst, Borel would have certainly been familiar with, given his extensive analytical work with creative writers, many of them Surrealists.[13] In his essay, Freud defines the operation of fantasy as a temporal compression in which "past, present and future are strung together on the thread of one desire that unites all three" (2003: 29): that is, a current provocation triggers some past impression or memory of a certain moment in which the wish could have been fulfilled, which in turn presents a future whereby the successful realization of the wish might be satisfied. For Freud, fantasy, whether in the form of a daydream or the creative work of a writer exhibits the same temporal process, which in either case has become a substitute for the structural conditions of childhood play. What does differentiate these two categories, however, is the move toward either concealment or disclosure that attends to the content of these fantasies. For Freud, what distinguishes an *ars poetica* from ordinary fantasies, are the aesthetic conditions that make possible our imaginative enjoyment of the content of a writer's fantasies; for this to occur those fantasies have to be sufficiently disguised in order for the writer to overcome the feelings of shame ordinarily attached to intimate self-disclosure. Although Freud's argument is developed around the example of popular fiction, what we can take from the essay in general is the central importance of repression to fantasy life and by implication, creative production; through formal aesthetic criteria the artist overcomes the feelings of repulsion attached to the ego's fantasies and transforms otherwise individual neurotic symptoms into culturally sanctioned and pleasure-yielding works of art. Here pleasure is defined in relation to both the audience's experience of the work as a legitimate and mediated form of normally repressed fantasies, as well as the author's successful conversion of private neurotic symptom into a creative ambition that overcomes what would otherwise remain a source of shame.

There are several important implications of Freud's essay for my interpretation of the novel. Reading the two sections together, "Coincidences" becomes an explicit psychoanalytic interpretation—one that borders on parody—of the fictional nature of the story in Part I; that is, it lays before us in concrete detail the psychic scaffolding of the creative process as it comes into being in the text. As Barthes suggests, this is no ordinary novel since it moves "within a kind of essence of make-believe" (120). In other words, the "coincidences" between the memories of Part II and the fantasies in Part I trace the transposition of erotic obsession into linguistic play, revealing how the author's fantasies and obsessions are shaped into formal aesthetic codes. These obsessions, originating in the traumatic Oedipal relations of Bataille's childhood, but which were re-emerging through his analysis with Borel, disclose the central importance of psychoanalytic case history to the novel's structure. Embedding erotic fantasy within linguistic strategies and combinatory effects, Bataille reduces language to an obscene economy that mirrors the displaced and dispersed subject of psychoanalysis. As in the narrative of the Freudian case history, interpretation proceeds through a series of fetishized meanings extracted or displaced from the whole account. But in unmasking the very process by which the creative writer converts neurotic symptom into a work of art, Bataille also reinstates the feelings of shame and repulsion that are, according to Freud, successfully masked by the aesthetic apparatus. In other words, it presents a very "naked" account of the creative process, one that almost mimics Freud's outline of the temporal development of fantasy for the creative artist but also discloses the limitations of Freud's theory in terms of how writers may utilize the structural effects of play to master painful realities. If Bataille's novel suggests that it is the memory of childhood fantasy and those obsessions that are formed as a result that constitutes the very enigma of the creative process, this is reinforced by Breton in the first Surrealist manifesto: "The mind which plunges into Surrealism relives with glowing excitement the best part of childhood. … From childhood memories, and from a few others, there emanates a sentiment of being unintegrated, and then later of *having gone astray*, which I hold to be the most fertile that exists" (1924/1972: 40). Like the child in play who moves seamlessly between fantasy and reality, Bataille switches between different masks and voices, from the creative to the analytic writer.

In conclusion I want to argue that *Story of the Eye* is a profound engagement with two of the most important intellectual movements of Bataille's day—

Surrealism and psychoanalysis. The proximity of this narrative to these intellectual paradigms has tended to be overlooked since a poststructuralist reading of Bataille's work often equates "transgression with polysemia and the infinite play of *significance*, characterized as the literary equivalent of perversity" (Geurlac, 1997: 23). Bataille's engagement, however, is part homage and part parody in the sense that what Bataille found most useful in either was that which defined his own scepticism, his own desire to explore beyond what either had to offer. In this sense, transgression very much defined Bataille's whole approach to writing, bearing in mind that transgression itself is only ever defined in relation to the limit it transcends. Similarly, parody always involves a textual doubling that requires us to look at what the subject of parody has been and what it becomes. And as Freud was keen to remind us, parody (like caricature and travesty) is invariably directed towards those people or things that command respect and seriousness. The excessive nature of the erotic quest in Part I reveals itself as a parody of the quest narrative as a source of heroic self-discovery. The novel turns upside down the romanticized adventures of the wandering Surrealist's enchanted quest for self-knowledge, one that proceeds through the marvelous encounters of the everyday urban sublime. This becomes particularly apparent in the conclusion to the narrative in Part I, recalling, as it does, the endless proliferation of wrongdoing in Elizabethan rogue literature, a genre premised on the distortion of the heroic quest by bringing to light those vices that normally remain hidden:

> Two hours later, Sir Edmund and I were sporting false black beards … In this way, we kept disappearing all through Andalusia, a country of yellow earth and yellow sky, to my eyes an immense chamber-pot flooded with sunlight, where each day, as a new character, I raped a likewise transformed Simone. Especially towards noon, on the ground and in the blazing sun, under the reddish eyes of Sir Edmund.
>
> On the fourth day, at Gibraltar, the Englishman purchased a yacht, and we set sail towards new adventures with a crew of Negroes. (67)

Typical of the generic conventions of rogue literature, Bataille's novel ends with the promise of ever-new adventures in ever-new exotic lands, explicitly replacing a Surrealist urban sublime with the spatial no-where land of literary fantasy. This is a fitting, if not satiric, ending for a story that has as its goal the uncovering of the erotic and violent vices and fantasies of its central protagonists. Bataille's parodic gloss on the quest theme reaches its final climatic moment through the use of the anti-heroic blinding sun imagery, which explicitly contrasts with Breton's later celebration of the sun in his long poem, *Fata Morgana*, written in Marseilles during the war. Breton's poem is a classic example of an idealism "in which love undergoes hermetic transmutation and ends as a sun, signifier of hope" (Sarwin, 1997: 124), and which could not be further from Bataille's own figuration of the sun as blinding and castrating; an immense bowl of yellow urine threatening to anoint those below. The excessive violence and eroticism of his narrative thus writes itself against a Bretonian transcendent vision, one that idealizes the heroic quest of the wandering Surrealist and his chance encounters with the enigmatic woman.

And yet what are we to make of the sexual politics of Bataille's transgressions? In his reading of the text, Barthes suggests that what is most fascinating about the operation of the pornographic in this narrative is that it appears to be non-phallic; or rather he suggests it is ocular or testicular in a way that destabilizes the phallic as key signifier (125). Throughout the narrative we are presented with an image of the vagina as a terrifyingly voracious organ, one that consumes an array of ovoid objects: an egg, an eye and a bull's testicle. The act of coitus, normally associated with penetration and conjunction, is replaced with an explicit sexuality of commodity and consumption. In many ways the text performs an intricate and repeated tracing of the fetishistic process: fetishism as the play of substitutions and sublimations. The object of the eye, with all its metonymic freedom, is open to a vast exchange of meanings and associations, which link it to the non-phallic male genital, the testicle. The image of the vagina dentata, also a key signifier throughout the text, seems to preclude here an understanding of the female genitals as simply lack, signifying them instead as that which can castrate or consume but which are themselves uncastratable. In the final pages of the story the enucleated eye—everywhere in Bataille's oeuvre a symbol of a declining masculinist transcendent tradition—is returned to the body's two lowest orifices, the anus and the vagina. The eye, a potent symbol of Enlightenment ideology and rationality, becomes debased and feminized, through its association with the "low"; in other words, the vagina dentata, as a synecdoche for the monstrous feminine, becomes the texts most powerful symbol of transgression. While Bataille's narrative is in no sense a feminist polemic against the aggressively phallic nature of Surrealist aesthetics or a Western epistemological tradition, its general destabilization of the phallic's transcendent place within Surrealist aesthetics, does disrupt the revolutionary and experimental tenor of Breton's idealization of heterosexual romantic love. As Carolyn Dean has revealed in her cogent analysis of the relationship between pornography and the social body after World War One, a Surrealist interest in eroticism and its more explicit pornographic representations reveals "pornography's increasingly forceful association with the metaphorical shattering of the dignified, constrained, and yet wilful self that underpins democratic citizenship" (2001: 227). Since it is the male body that underwrites the social order, ingrained in fantasies about the destruction of the social body is an implicit threat to male bodily integrity. This explains in part Breton's anxiety about the role of sexuality (both its practice and its representation) in the movement, nowhere more pronounced than in his dogmatic policing of the parameters of enquiry in the "Reserches sur la sexualité." While these investigations demonstrate an unprecedented candour in their discussion of love, sexual practice and desire, Breton's contributions nevertheless reveal a "moral" containment of the erotic that for Bataille, at least, indicates repressed anxiety rather than uninhibited social research.

As such, I would argue, that what is being transgressed above all in Bataille's novel are the very limits of Surrealism's own exploration of sexuality and the unconscious. As Surya repeatedly points out, Bataille's problem with Surrealism was that it did not go far enough—in its reading of Sade, Freud, Marx or Nietzsche—but rather hung on to a "utopian blindness" and a "superior authority" that in the end replicated the bourgeois values it was attempting to overthrow. Against Breton's Icarian idealism, Bataille conceived of a Surrealism "taken to the limits and 'made monstrous'" (407). However, in Surrealism's Oedipal drama, the confrontation between the all-powerful father (Breton) and the traumatized son (Bataille) reveals a proximity that registers the trope of the feminine as paradoxically monstrous and ideal—*the* defining disjunction of Surrealist aesthetic practice.

Feminist Transgression

> The Surrealists were not good with women.
> That is why, although I thought they were wonderful,
> I had to give them up in the end.
>
> – "The Alchemy of the Word," Angela Carter

The themes of violence and transgression, propriety and social ritual resonate throughout Carrington's visual and textual work. In *The Hearing Trumpet* they are taken up in a satirically comic mode and explored at the intersection between myth, fantasy and autobiographical anecdote. Written in Mexico City sometime between the late 1940s and early 1950s, the novel weaves autobiographical and historical vignettes into an ironic retelling of the Grail legend. At the center of the novel are a series of transgressive female characters that attempt to subvert various cultural institutions and practices. The novel disrupts a Surrealist idealization of femininity through its parodic representation of female transgression: the novel's central character, Marian Leatherby ("let her be") explicitly challenges a Surrealist idealization of the *femme-enfan*t, and celebrates—through the magical hearing trumpet—the symbolic nature of the ear and a female storytelling tradition. In defiance of a Surrealist fetishization of the *femme-enfant*, Carrington's intrepid heroine sports a rather gallant beard and at the age of ninety-two leads a group of senile old women in revolt against their corrupt institution.[14] Framing Marian's own narrative of rebellion and the quest for self-knowledge is the story of the winking Abbess, Dona Rosalinda, whose portrait hangs in the dining room of the old ladies home. Dona Rosalinda's perverse escapades are chronicled in a book written by the Confessor of the Abbey, and which eventually falls into Marian's hands. As their stories begin to merge the novel moves toward its apocalyptic ending in which a new ice age restores the Grail to Hecate and a non-Christian female (and feminist) underground tradition, forcing the surviving inhabitants to a cavern "down below" the earth.[15] Through the characters of Marian and her alter-ego, Dona Rosalinda, the two most celebrated female figures within Surrealism, the *femme-enfant* and the madwoman, are transposed into the figure of the transgressive crone: it is the paradoxical wisdom of senility as opposed to madness, hybridity and excess as opposed to the dissected and disarticulated female body, that Carrington's novel celebrates.[16] The cross-dressing Abbess, a majestic and monstrous figure of excess, who winks at all below her in "a most disconcerting mixture of mockery and malevolence," allegorically signals Carrington's own transgressive textual practice. Through the motif of her wink, the novel sets in place its ironic tone, one in which laughter and excess foreground the disruptive materiality of the body and its subversive position within a feminist aesthetics.

In her chapter on feminist intertextuality in *Subversive Intent*, Suleiman traces the connection between parody and the practice of intertextuality via Bakhtin's work on carnival (1990: 142–3).[17] Following Bakhtin, Suleiman reveals how parody sets up a distance between language and reality so that its attraction for feminist writers lies in the fact that it performs a rereading and a recontextualization of received texts and ideas. While it is necessary to caution against an over-zealous attempt to see carnival as an a priori transgressive gesture, as Suleiman does, its very emphasis on change and renewal, even as "a *licensed* affair," suggests how carnivalized discourse might work to disrupt the codified effects of conventional aesthetic practice (143). In Carrington's novel, the competing ideological claims of Surrealism and feminism are negotiated through a parodic voice that recalibrates their effects in startling ways. *The Hearing Trumpet* is a difficult text precisely because its satirical posture obviates the idealism invariably attached to any social and political movement but nevertheless finds in these discourses powerful, if precarious, critical models. In casting a critical gaze over various social and cultural institutions: the church, the bourgeois family, institutions for the elderly and the insane as well as Surrealism, Carrington's characteristic black humor takes a particularly playful turn without ever losing the disturbing undercurrent that marks her idiosyncratic sense of the droll and the macabre. Placed by her family in an institution for senile old ladies, Marian—the outlaw and accomplice in Malory's Grail saga—sets out on a quest which leads her to Dona Rosalinda's own somewhat surreal search for the holy grail, and with it arcane knowledge. While on one level Carrington mocks the obsessive search for ideal knowledge, the novel is nevertheless concerned with the relationship between knowledge and myth so that parody and self-parody work together to unfold the tension between the past and the future; how things are and how one wants them to be.

Souvenirs

> Feminist nostalgia ... looks back not only to what
> feminism desires, but to what it desires different, and differently,
> both now and in the future.
>
> —Mary Jacobus *First Things*

For a novel that incorporates feminist fantasy and Surrealist effects, *The Hearing Trumpet* is strangely, if ironically, nostalgic. While the novel celebrates a new phase in Carrington's life, it also unleashes an unruly collection of souvenirs from the past, from Surrealism, the Bible, classical and Celtic mythology and the fairy tale tradition. If the enucleated eye is a privileged trope in Surrealist aesthetic practice, Carrington's text inverts this signification by formulating the hearing trumpet or ear as its fetishized object *par excellence*. As the novel's most surreally prophetic object, the hearing trumpet sets up a playful tension between the scopophilic and the aural, between looking and listening, the peeping tom and the eavesdropper, as well as highlighting the aural nature of a storytelling tradition.[18] This eponymous object continually draws attention to the way in which the narrative unfolds through the deviant actions of spying, confessing and eavesdropping—a strategy which hinders any clear understanding of the events and characters of the novel. The opening words of the novel mark the trumpet's central importance within the text:

> When Carmella gave me the present of a hearing trumpet she may have forseen some of the consequences. Carmella is not what I would call malicious, she just happens to have a curious sense of humour. The trumpet was certainly a fine specimen of its kind, without really being modern. It was, however, exceptionally pretty, being encrusted with silver and mother o' pearl motifs and grandly curved like a buffalo's horn. The aesthetic presence of this object was not its only quality, the hearing trumpet magnified sound to such a degree that ordinary conversation became quite audible even to my ears. (3)

With the aid of this beautifully decorated instrument, the hard-of-hearing Marian is able to eavesdrop on her family and thus learn of their sinister plot to send her away to an institution. This begins a narrative device in which the hearing trumpet serves to uncover a number of plots and counter-plots throughout the text, revealing its central role in idiosyncratically driving the narrative logic of the text; or rather its displacement of any form of narrative logic. As an outmoded object, found by Carmella at the market, the hearing trumpet recalls the many unusual objects found by Breton and other Surrealists at the Paris flea market thereby allegorizing a Surrealist interest in the psychological underpinning of the everyday object; through displacement, chance, play and transgression the found object exceeds the limits of its utilitarian function, crystallizing the latent and manifest nature of the creative process itself. In subverting the normative expectations of narrative logic and coherence, Carrington's hearing trumpet registers the novel's preoccupation with the intersection between fantasy and "the real". Indeed the novel is filled with competing narratives that seem to move between the mundane and petty domestic world of the institution and the inmates' imaginative escape through their creation of fantastical visions and stories. These disparate narrative threads, literally woven into the text, produce a collage of myth, fairy tale, legend and personal memoir, which seem to acoustically reverberate through the magical hearing trumpet. As an instrument that enables heightened perception, the hearing trumpet becomes the aural equivalent of the enucleated eye's association with inner vision. Carrington's inverted signification points to a self-conscious investment in the anarchic and embodied nature of storytelling, stressing how other modes of perception, apart from the eye, reveal the body as a complex cogniscent mechanism. But as Susan Stewart argues "the literary's nostalgia for oral forms is a nostalgia for the presence of the body and the face-to-face, a dream of unmediated communication that, of course, could never be approximated even in the oral—a dream of an eternalised present, a future-past" (1991: 90).

For Carrington, however, the iconographic significance of the hearing trumpet predates Marian's acoustic reveries in the novel. In Max Ernst's painting, *Napoleon in the Wilderness* (1941), a strange whimsical trumpet appears in the hand of a female figure that seems to have sprung from the sinister rock and coral formations of a world in ruin. This painting formed part of a suite of decalcomania works, in which Carrington's semi-naked figure haunts a series of eerie landscapes, richly textured and abundant with mythological hybrid forms. Between periods of internment during the war, Ernst had managed to continue painting, producing haunting images of his abandoned lover in works that evoke his own sense of loss and grief in macabre scenes that promise both decay and renewal. In *Napoleon in the Wilderness* Carrington's fragile form is draped in a majestic cloak, holding an ornate trumpet, similar to the novel's description of Marian's hearing trumpet as "grandly curved like a buffalo's horn." Between 1935 and 1945, Ernst had also executed a number of drawings of detached ears and eyes. In particular, his drawing, *The Lent Ear* (1935) reminds us that a hearing trumpet is above all a substitute or "lent" ear. In the years leading up to the war, Ernst and Carrington had been living and working together in St Martin-d'Ardèche in the South of France. When Ernst was interned as an enemy alien, Carrington became increasingly distraught and fled to Spain where she was committed to an asylum. Shortly after, Ernst managed to secure release papers and returned to the farmhouse; with Carrington absent and the war intensifying, Ernst retrieved work by both himself and Carrington and left for Marseilles, joining Breton and other Surrealists waiting to emigrate to the United States. A photograph from 1941 shows a collection of paintings by Ernst and Carrington hung in the garden of the Villa Bel Air, a large country home that provided a temporary refuge for those Surrealists waiting to flee France. Among this collection is Ernst's *The Lent Ear* as well as Carrington's *Portrait of Max Ernst* (1939). In Carrington's portrait, a shaman-like Ernst, draped in a magenta feathered cloak, stands in the midst of an arctic landscape, holding in his hand a magical lantern containing a miniature white horse in mid gallop. The coiled energy of the horse trapped in the lantern is evocative of Carrington's alter-ego, the mythological Celtic horse, the Bride of the Wind, and contrasts strikingly with the statuesque form of another horse behind the figure of Ernst, this one frozen solid into the landscape. The portrait creates a powerful dissonance in which death and rebirth, stasis and energy evoke, for Carrington at least, the ambivalent collaborative relationship between her and Ernst. During their years at St Martin-d'Ardèche Carrington and Ernst frequently collaborated on both textual and visual work. For example, Ernst illustrated Carrington's first collection of short stories, producing in the frontispiece a collage of a detached Medusan evil eye, which appears to illustrate Carrington's short tale about a powerful anthropomorphic eye, which hovers throughout the narrative as solitary and enlarged. Carrington's influence on Ernst, however was also significant and as Martica Sarwin has argued it was in response to Carrington's presence and her own mythologically inspired work that Ernst's paintings became increasingly fairy tale-like and organic during this period, culminating in his experiments with dripping and blotting that resulted in the richly textured landscapes of his decalcomania series. In her overview of the Surrealists in exile in New York during and after the war, Sarwin suggests that under the influence of Matta and Kurt Seligmann, the movement became much more interested in magic and the occult: "References to alchemy abound in the artworks and in the pages of *View*, an interest reinforced by Jung's writings, which found in alchemy parallels for psychological processes" (197). As Jung replaced Freud, the Surrealist sensibility in these years became preoccupied with the process of morphology: "the form and structure of an organism considered as a whole, that is, inner and outer, as it evolves and changes …" (197). An emerging interest in morphology and anthropomorphism is certainly present in Ernst's paintings from this period, where human, animal and vegetable forms dissolve into each other producing fantastically detailed illustrations of strange hybrid creatures in hauntingly surreal landscapes. But long before Carrington arrived in New York, her painting and fiction had incorporated anthropomorphic and mythological elements largely as a result of her Irish background. But if Carrington's influence is reflected in Ernst's work from this period, Carrington would go on to borrow from Ernst's iconography by incorporating the surreal trumpet into her novel. The richly woven nature of Carrington's novel with its strange hybrid characters and surreal arctic underworld is also eerily reminiscent of Ernst's suite of decalcomania paintings as well as her portrait of Ernst from this period.

In his drawing, "The Lent Ear" Ernst reproduces the ear as an enlarged spiraling funnel form attached to a tiny bird-like head with a solitary beady eye. Within Surrealist aesthetics the ear often functioned as the morphological symbol of desire, as in Dali's *Phenomenon of Ecstasy*, in contrast to the eye, which is symbolic of reason. Indeed Bataille's own fondness for the labyrinth form signifies its status as "the antidote to the pyramid, that architectural symbol of solidity and substance, which was homologous to the optical cone" (Jay, 1994:

229).[19] The hearing trumpet motif, via its association with the ear, also evokes the underground cavern at the end of the novel as well as the labyrinthine structure of myth that permeates the entire narrative. But like the perversions associated with the eye, the ear motif in Carrington's novel operates at the level of scandal through its association with its eavesdropping heroine. Often seen as the feminine equivalent of the peeping tom, eavesdropping becomes the novel's central trope of perversion since it alone seems to be responsible for the narrative's vertiginous twists and turns. Rather than always providing Marian (or the reader) with the clarity that it should, it opens up a surreal and mythological wonderland where who is telling the tale to whom drives the machinations of the story as plots and subplots are executed and foiled. Here the roles of storyteller and listener, both active and interpretative, contrast to those of "looking" and "looked at"—a relationship constructed around the objectification of the passive other. But above all the hearing trumpet establishes the collaborative and conspiratorial relationship between Marian and Carmella, which seems to pay homage to a new kind of Surrealist collaboration—between women—moving beyond the eroticized dynamic of an older master and his young and beautiful protégé.

In her autobiography of Remedios Varo, Janet Kaplan writes of the mischievous and surreal sense of play that cemented the relationship between Carrington and Varo. Their delight in various games and pranks had been a staple in the Surrealist coterie in Paris, where Breton would cut short conversations with a "half-question, half-command: '*Alors, on joue*' (Well then, shall we play?)" (Sarwin, 1997: 124).[20] Carrington, already renowned for her spirit of revolt, enjoyed such occasions and together with Varo continued these games and practical jokes with the small group of Surrealist émigrés gathered in Mexico City after the war. The relationship between Carrington and Varo, however, was particularly intense; in each other they found a sympathetic and imaginative companion, creative and adventurous in all their endeavors whether painting, writing or concocting strangely bizarre feasts for the guests who flocked to Varo and Peret's apartment. Like many of the Surrealists influenced by Jung after the war, Carrington and Varo were also interested in the occult; in magic, sorcery and the tarot, which was no doubt enhanced by their presence in Mexico. Kaplan writes:

> They found Mexico a fertile atmosphere where magic was a part of daily reality: traveling herb salesmen would set up on street corners with displays of seeds, insects, chameleons … and neatly wrapped parcels with such mysterious labels as "Sexual Weakness"—all used for the practice of witchcraft by the *caranderas* (healers), *brujas* (witches), and *espiritualistas* (spiritualists) … (96).

Breton had described Mexico as "the Surrealist place, *par excellence*" (Polizzotti: 454) and Carrington and Varo were fascinated by the remnants of pre-Columbian culture that formed an archaic counterpart to the modern revolutionary political climate that welcomed Europe's avant-garde artists and intellectuals. Throughout the 1940s and 1950s both Carrington and Varo began to develop a more mature individual style of painting that still carried strong influences from Surrealism but which also included striking influences from their adopted country. Newly charged by the cultural paradox of their surroundings and each other's company, their painting began to share an ironic and fantastical whimsy which earned them high praise within the context of a Mexican modernist tradition: in 1956 Diego Rivera was moved to declare: "Mexico has the good fortune that among us live three women painters who undoubtedly are among the most important women artists in the world: Remedios Varo … Leonora Carrington and Alice Rahon" (Kaplan: 133). In Mexico, Carrington was no longer an eroticized *femme-enfant* confined to the status of Ernst's lover. As Rivera's praise suggests, Carrington and Varo had become significant figures within Mexico's flourishing modernist art community. While *The Hearing Trumpet* certainly memorializes the importance of their friendship and artistic collaboration, the novel still carries the traces of the personal and political convictions that had first brought Carrington into Surrealism's fold. Meeting Carrington for the first time during the early 1940s, the art collector and Surrealist patron, Edward James, described her as "a ruthless English intellectual in revolt against all the hypocrisies of her homeland, against the bourgeois fears and false moralities of her conventional background and sheltered upbringing" (Sarwin: 282). While the novel celebrates a newly expanded sense of the marvelous, one saturated in the patina of Mexican culture and female collaborative friendship, its overall stylistic and thematic eclecticism also connect it to an earlier Surrealist political sensibility.

As an overdetemined iconic object, the hearing trumpet is perhaps the most significant motif of the novel's recurrent obsession with the fetishistic collection and display of objects and architectural forms, again reminiscent of the poetic intensity brought to the Surrealist object as well as its radical transformation of the exhibition space. The description of the architectural structure of the nursing home at the beginning of the novel brings to life the themed spaces of the Surrealist exhibition in which paintings, performances, objects and audio recordings transformed an otherwise neutral gallery space into an uncanny *mise-en-scène* suffused with anxiety and desire:

> First impressions are never very clear, I can only say there seemed to be several courtyards, cloisters, stagnant fountains, trees, shrubs, lawns. The main building was in fact a castle, surrounded by various pavilions with incongruous shapes. Pixielike dwellings shaped like toadstools, Swiss chalets, railway carriages, one or two ordinary bungalows, something shaped like a boot, another like what I took to be an outsize Egyptian mummy. It was all so very strange that I for once doubted the accuracy of my observation. (29)

In evoking the iconography of the nursery rhyme, these bizarre architectural forms ironically reverberate Marian's infantilization, initially by her family and later by the Gambits, the repressive and pecuniary caretakers of the home. The fetishistic detail of the institution's architecture also forms a parallel to the excessive decoration of the Abbess's monastery and her incorporation of the external ethnological world into her private gaze. Her bizarre collection of objects and domestic items reinforces the significance of the flea market and the shop window as modernist loci of desire and the concomitant Surrealist fascination with the psychological, primitive and erotic underpinning of the object:

> Relays of foreign craftsmen came to the convent to redecorate the sumptuous apartments of the Abbess ... Scarlet silk studded with little purple and gold Griffins constituted the wall hangings ... The furniture ... was carved like all the beasts in creation ... . The Bishop himself brought gifts from the East. These included the embalmed head of a white elephant (and) all sorts of organically embroided apparel. (97–8)

The Abbess's collection of souvenirs and precious objects heralds a peculiar reification of the animal and the ethnological which is part of the novel's microscopic world, the domain where the artefact or primitive and esoteric object is domesticated, removed from its natural origin or location and fashioned into a commodity. Again we are reminded of the Surrealists' love of arcane collections and ethnographic objects, in particular the collection of primitive masks and other objects by both Breton and Ernst.[21] By transporting and reifying the ethnological world into the realm of her private gaze, the Abbess, like the Surrealist collector, collapses the public into the personal, the macroscopic into the microscopic. The objects thus come to attain their value both because of their connection to the other world and by their very removal from that world. Susan Stewart has analyzed the way commodity collection signifies our longing for origin and authenticity, represented as a contradictory desire for a distance that is collapsed into proximity. She argues that

> Like the collection, (the souvenir) displays the romance of contraband, for its scandal is its removal from its "natural" location ... . The souvenir generates a narrative that reaches only "behind," spiralling in a continually inward movement rather than outward toward the future. (139)

While Carrington's fascination with the souvenir is highlighted by the novel's "collection" and display of arcane material objects, the temporal schema of the souvenir as an inward spiraling allegorizes the belatedness of Carrington's own narrative. As Stewart argues, the souvenir represents "not the lived experience of its maker but the 'secondhand' experience of its possessor/owner" (135). Spliced into the text's play of fantasy and mythology are highly self-conscious autobiographical moments, what the narrator calls "[s]ouvenirs of the past," which rise up "like bubbles," and float randomly in and out of the narrative:

> The Luxembourg Gardens and the smell of chestnut trees, Paris. St. Germain des Prés, having breakfast on the terrace of a café with Simon ... Simon talking like the Arabian Knights. Love and Magic. Then I dreamt I was preparing lunch in the summer house

> in the hollow of a large garden with Simon… He had beautiful eyes like a Siamese cat. Simon lost in interminable gardens, never getting free, and he knew so much. Simon. Perhaps I would still be in Paris, oh the joy if I could walk along the quais and admire the books, or look at the Seine from the Pont Neuf. (76–7)

The nostalgic longing in this passage is contrasted with more satirical and self-conscious passages:

> … in Lancashire [where Carrington grew up] I got an attack of claustrophobia and tried to convince mother to let me go and study painting in London. She thought this was a very idle and silly idea and gave me a lecture about artists … Your Aunt Edgeworth wrote novels … but she would never have called herself "an artist" … Art in London didn't seem quite modern enough and I began to want to study in Paris where the Surrealists were in full cry. Surrealism is no longer considered modern today and almost every village rectory and girl's school have surrealist pictures hanging on their walls. Even Buckingham Palace has a large reproduction of Magritte's famous slice of ham with an eye peering out. It hangs, I believe, in the throne room. Times do change indeed. The Royal Academy recently gave a retrospective exhibition of Dada art and they decorated the gallery like a public lavatory. In my day people in London would have been shocked. Today the Lord Mayor opened the exhibition with a long speech about twentieth-century masters and the Queen Mother hung a reef of gladioli on a piece of sculpture called "navel" by Hans Arp. (85)

These "souvenirs" of the past randomly floating in and out of the text reflect the narratorial incontinence often associated with the reminiscences of the elderly and which the narrator herself sardonically draws attention to: "How my mind runs on, or rather backwards, I shall never get on with my narrative if I can't control those memories, there are too many of them" (85). Frequently throughout the text Carrington ironically solemnizes the figure of the strolling Surrealist, whose own meandering narrative becomes a moment of heroic self-analysis, allowing both the exigencies of chance and the historical unconscious to leak into the narrative. Through this kind of revisionist parody or "souvenirs of the past" Carrington's novel expresses a simultaneous nostalgia for the past and a celebration of the present. As Stewart suggests "the souvenir displaces the point of authenticity [here high Surrealism] as it itself [Carrington's novel] becomes the point of origin for narrative" (138). Self-consciously nostalgic and belated, *The Hearing Trumpet* displaces a traditional Christian past—and a masculinist Surrealist past—in order to celebrate feminist mythmaking and a Surrealist female collaborative tradition. But the text's self-irony, represented by the Abbess' iconographic wink, reminds us that Carrington's parodic feminism also has its use-by date. While the reference to Magritte reinforces the scopophilic theme played with throughout the narrative, it also illustrates the incongruity of Magritte's painting in the throne room; an *in situ* pun on the Surrealist's penchant for striking juxtapositions. But it also points to the domestication of this once scandalous work and its incorporation into the most conservative and traditional institution in England. The outmoded nature of Magritte's painting therefore reminds us of the belatedness of Carrington's own Surrealist text, and its attempts to rejuvenate a Surrealist aesthetic through its incorporation of feminist parody.

Guiding much of the narrative is Marian's nostalgic memory of the northern hemisphere, in particular her English childhood as well as her fantasy land, Lapland, which she connects to her childhood reading of "The Snow Queen." Indeed "The Snow Queen" is one of the many references framing the novel's quest theme and Carrington's feminist intertextuality. The first reminiscence in the text centers on Carrington's/Marian's adolescent awakening to the power of imagination and fantasy, discovered through the solitary act of reading:

> Strangely enough I was in England and it was Sunday afternoon. I was sitting with a book on a stone seat under a lilac bush .... My long dark hair is soft like cat's fur, I am beautiful ... Beauty is a responsibility like anything else, beautiful women have special lives like prime ministers but that is not what I really want, there must be something else ... The book. Now I can see it, the Tales of Hans Christian Andersen, the Snow Queen .... The Snow Queen, Lapland. Little Kay doing multiplication problems in the icy castle (20).

When we first encounter Carrington's narrator reading "The Snow Queen" in the garden, we are transported into her own fantasy world. This moment of imaginative reflection, however, is abruptly broken by the intrusion of a young suitor, who chastises the narrator for reading fairy tales and ignoring her guests (21). The trope of the woman reader seduced by the romance plot surfaces again in Carrington's work. As in "The Debutante," reading signals a rebellious withdrawal from social interaction; one which always takes place, significantly, on the threshold between childhood and adulthood. Andersen's story of the brave young Gerda, who sets out on an intrepid journey to free her beloved Kay from the cold-hearted Snow Queen and the world of detached reason, is set in the snow-bound regions of Scandanavia, a landscape that is described as desolately beautiful and foreboding, not unlike the frozen landscape in *Portrait of Max Ernst*. A tale about desire and longing as well as the loss of childhood innocence, "The Snow Queen" is divided into a series of chapter headings that chart the cast of characters that Gerda meets on her journey to free her friend; many of which are loosely taken up in Carrington's own text.

The opening chapter of Andersen's tale, "The Mirror and Its Fragments" recalls Marian's epiphanic moment with the old crone in the underground cavern as she looks at herself in a broken piece of mirror and sees a splintering of herself into three characters. In "The Snow Queen" the metaphor of the distorting mirror that splinters into tiny fragments registers the fusion of Christian and pagan elements in the folk tale genre as well as the sinister breaking up of the innocent world of childhood, as Gerda's journey leads her into a world of frightening adult encounters. In the chapter, "The Little Robber Girl," Gerda meets a gruesome old hag, the robber woman, who kills all her coachmen and wants to eat Gerda; the robber woman's daughter, however, intervenes, wanting to keep the young Gerda as her play friend. Once the little robber girl hears the story of Kay's imprisonment in the Snow Queen's palace, she assists Gerda in her escape, lending her the precious reindeer she keeps by her bed. In Andersen's story the robber girl and her mother are grotesque feral characters that exist on the borders between the animal and the human world, reminiscent of the many semi-wild and hybrid characters in Carrington's early fiction. Their thieving profession, however, and the robber woman's monstrosity, allude to the Abbess's own grotesque appearance and her theft of church paraphernalia, as well as Carrington's theft and reappropriation of various stylistic and narrative devices. The final chapter in Andersen's fairy tale, "What Happened In the Snow Queen's Palace and Afterwards" recalls the final scene in Carrington's novel in which a new ice age is brought about by the restoration of the Holy Grail to a female pagan tradition. In Andersen's story the palace is entirely made of snow, beautifully lit by the northern lights. In the middle of the palace is a frozen lake called the Mirror of Reason upon which resides the Snow Queen's throne. Here Kay sits trying to solve the puzzle of how to write Eternity with the fragments of ice, just as Marian has to solve three riddles in order to free the mysterious figure (perhaps herself) trapped in the tower.

The novel's pastiche of myth, fairy tale and biblical story as well as its inclusion of autobiographical and historical material celebrates the belatedness of all "pasts" and a Surrealist process of making something "new" out of a collection of outmoded objects. Myth and history (both cultural and individual) take on the status of the found object and Surrealism's fetishization of history's discarded bric-a-brac. Like Marian's hearing trumpet that Carmella finds at the market and which eventually transforms Marian's world and the narrative events of the text, the category of the outmoded is celebrated for its nostalgic effects as well as its new contextual value.[22] Carrington's "souvenirs" of the past make explicit the link between her feminist parodic narrative and the novel as autobiographical pastiche. Many of the characters in the text are recognizable from Carrington's own life in Mexico: while Carmella commemorates her close friend, Remedios Varo, the appearance of Marlborough at the end of the novel celebrates Carrington's eccentric friend and patron, Edward James. In a recent review to mark the reprinting of *The Hearing Trumpet*, Carrington's novel itself was described as a "lost classic" and Marian as "one of literature's most endearing and colorful characters, all the more remarkable for belonging to a demographic category novelists usually slight" (Wren, 2000: n.p). In her introduction to the Virago edition of the novel, Helen Byatt reflects on the incongruity between Carrington's relatively youthful age and Marian's elderly status: "It seems perverse that a beautiful and resilient woman in her early thirties or forties should identify with a 'drooling sack of decomposing flesh'"(Marian's grandson's description of her in the novel) (1996: v). If we read the novel as loosely autobiographical then Carrington has cast herself and Varo in the role of slightly senile, though intrepid, old women. Having gone beyond society's determined use-by date—and certainly the use-by date of the *femme-enfant*—Marian and Carmella constitute the text's central preoccupation with the old and the new, the modish and the outdated. Beyond a Surrealist interest in the reliquary status of the found object and other cultural detritus, the tension between the old and the new seems to prefigure a concern with appearance and reality. Throughout the narrative we are constantly witnessing the contradiction between how her family and the rest of society see Marian (as a dependent, senile old woman) and the mastery and wit of her narrative voice. In what sense might this be an explicit comment on the contradiction of women's roles within Surrealism? Frequently represented as the visible sign of its radical aesthetic practice, women Surrealists were caught in the web of appearance and reality: as the objects of a representational practice that gave them a degree of visibility that also threatened the very agency of their own critical voice.

And yet the novel is not solely interested in exploring the past. As well as evoking the past through her collection of souvenirs, in the very act of imagining herself as an old woman, Carrington brings the future to the present in what is an overall strategy of playing with the boundaries of distance and proximity. By employing satire and parody, Carrington necessarily demarcates her own narrative from a high Surrealist discourse, but also reactivates that discourse, bearing out what Naomi Schor has described as the homology between irony and fetishism: "just as the fetish enables the fetishist simultaneously to recognize and to deny woman's castration, irony allows the ironist both to reject and to reappropriate the discourse of reference" (1993: 98). The narrative's double strategy of co-option and transformation is registered by the events of the inset narrative—the story of Dona Rodalinda, the winking Abbess—in what becomes a literal doubling of the narrative. Alongside Marian's quest to overthrow her corrupt institution for old women, is the unfolding story of Dona Rosalinda's attempts to steal the Grail from a male hierarchical Christian tradition and restore it to an underground pre-Christian world. The salient feature of the Abbess's directorship of the Convent of Santa Barbara is her continued theft of church information and paraphernalia, including the Musc Madelaine, the powerful aphrodisiac that allows her to perform strange rituals and miracles and which seals her reputation as perversely sadistic. The Abbess's repeated theft of all things (like Carrington's borrowing of Surrealist aesthetic devices and themes as well as various versions of the Grail myth) signals a kleptomania that was marked by early psychiatry as the female equivalent to male fetishism. The fetishistic detail of the Abbess's interiors and her vast array of exotic objects unfold her own obsession with souvenirs and collections. While her dual perversions remind us of her ambiguous sexual status, the allegorical nature of her monstrosity reinforces Carrington's textual parody as also doubly perverse: as both kleptomanic and fetishistic.

Myth and Laughter: The Hybrid and Grotesque Body

Mythopoeia occupies a central place in the novel, as different versions of the same myth compete with each other and combine to form new ones. Michael Bell suggests that the structure of myth is not unlike the uncanny; just as the uncanny is both familiar and unfamiliar or hidden, myth "means both a supremely significant foundational story and a falsehood" (1997: 1). Looking at the narrative strategy in the novel, Renée Riese Hubert argues that Carrington offers us realistic details only to constantly subvert them: "The way that the narrative proceeds actually discourages ordinary causality and prevents us from forming a coherent view of unfolding events" (1994: 136). Carrington's use of myth unfolds a contradictory dynamic of significance and falsehood. The Grail legend, the defining myth of the quest for knowledge, is explored through competing interpretive permutations: pagan, Christian, literary and finally feminist. In presenting a hybrid collection of different versions of the Grail legend, the text draws attention to the way myth presupposes a relationship between the ancient and the modern as well as the past and the present. According to Bell "modernist mythopoeia is a way of combining radical relativity with the aproditic nature of conviction" (4). Carrington's mythopoeia thus registers the playful and subversive elements of her story.

Through its incorporation of the many partial versions of the Grail myth, the novel registers the all-pervasive cultural desire for sacred and esoteric knowledge. But throughout the text the attainment of sacred or pure knowledge is constantly thwarted by a multitude of profane and satirically banal details that get in the way; as such the novel does not simply celebrate a utopian vision of a feminist quest for self-knowledge. As Helen Byatt argues, *The Hearing Trumpet* "is like a series of Chinese boxes, each containing another version of the myth … . Though on one level Carrington is undoubtedly out to reclaim its meaning for women, on another, she is a muse who has an eclectic eye for stories, references and allusions" (1991: xiv). But in the same way that myth evokes both the continuity and discontinuity of the past, the quest for self-knowledge is reduced to a series of random but interconnected events, parodying Breton's haunting "Who am I?" *and* the eternal wandering of the ghost figure in *Nadja*, as well as the role of chance in Surrealist aesthetic practice. At the end of the novel a terrified Marian descends into the underworld in search of who she is, only to experience a disconcerting sense of herself as a literal "double". Asked to jump into a pot of boiling broth by a menacing old crone, Marian takes the plunge only to find that she becomes both the person in the pot and the crone stirring it. Watching in uncanny horror her own limbs bobbing up and down, Marian informs us that

> From a speculative point of view I wondered which of us I was. Knowing that I had a piece of polished obsidian somewhere in the cavern, I looked around, intending to use it as a mirror. First I saw the face of the Abbess of Santa Barbara de Tartarus grinning at me sardonically. She faded and then I saw the huge eyes and feelers of the Queen Bee who winked and transformed myself into my own face …

> Holding the mirror at arms length I seemed to see a three-faced female whose eyes winked alternatively. One of the faces was black, one red, one white, and they belonged to the Abbess, the Queen Bee and myself. This of course might have been an optical illusion. (176)

Marian's presence both within and outside the pot, ironically reflects Carrington's own relationship to Surrealism, as the object in the frame and as the subject outside the frame watching her own objectification. Marian's obsidian mirror also references both a Surrealist and psychoanalytic preoccupation with the mirror as a symbol of feminine narcissism and subject formation. Here the image of the mirror—and its splintering—metaphorizes the spectral quality of female identity, but rather than reflect back a framed and idealized *femme-enfant*, the image in the mirror reflects the novel's trinity of transgressive female figures—Marian, the Queen Bee and the Abbess. The mirror also represents the world of dream and imagination, of desire and becoming, referencing here Lewis Carroll's Alice stories and their own preoccupation with optical illusion; the symbolic nature of the looking glass thus represents the threshold between the self one thinks it knows and the self opened up to the terrain of imaginative reverie.

The Abbess's wink, a performative gesture of irony, reinforces Carrington's comic tone throughout the novel, reminding us of Breton's description of Carrington's "smooth mocking gaze" and a Surrealist conflation of visual and textual modes of expression.[23] The Abbess's wink, first encountered by Marian in the portrait of her that hangs in the dining room of the home, signals Carrington's evocation of the detached eye and its ubiquitous presence within Surrealist iconography. Underscoring the novel's unrelenting perversion, the Abbess's pose in the portrait is described as leering and sinister:

> The face of the nun in the oil painting was so curiously lighted that she seemed to be winking, although that was hardly possible. She must have had one blind eye and the painter had rendered it realistically. However, the idea that she was winking persisted, she was winking at me with a mixture of mockery and malevolence. (36–7)

And later, still obsessed with the portrait, Marian inquires:

> "Do you suppose she is really winking, or is she blind in one eye?" I asked, anxious for Georgina's opinion on a more personal aspect of the lady.
>
> "She is definitely winking; the bawdy old bag is probably peeking at the monastery through a hole in the wall, watching the monks prancing around in their knickers." (53–4)

The Abbess's voyeurism, alluded to throughout the narrative, is contrasted with Marian's constant eavesdropping. As a character who assumes both male and female identities, the Abbess represents the possibility of erotic transgression beyond the often prescribed sexual roles frequently deployed within Surrealist work. Invited by Breton to participate in an exhibition on eroticism in 1959,

Carrington responded with her own enthusiastic rendition of such an exhibition, reinforcing the comic nature of her erotic vision:

> I've longed dreamed of a similar show, but I must confess that I see it as comic eroticism … Among the most sublime American inventions, it seems that there exists a huge apparatus in the shape of an organ, which giggles across forty different octaves … With this apparatus in mind, I visualise a room—somewhere between a cathedral and a Swiss [cuckoo] clock—equipped with an organ of peals of laughter multiples through the octaves … A very rich bestiary of erotic appliances would furnish the room. Thus, mermaids of inflatable rubber, choirboys made of chocolate, steel nuns for the masochists, giraffe-lavatories in pastel-coloured glass for the voyeurs … bearded corpses in jars of alcohol for the necrophiliacs, velvet spiders with hundreds of vaginas for orgies, etc. etc. etc., all this to the sound of the organ … . (letter to Breton in Warner, 1991: 11).

The catalog of perversions in Carrington's imagined exhibition of erotica mirrors the collection of fetishistic objects and cast of transgressive characters littered throughout the novel. The comic-erotic excess in Carrington's work thus provides an explicit disruption to a Surrealist location of transgression in the eroticized body of the *femme-enfant*.

Frequently in Carrington's fiction and visual work, the body is represented as interchangeable, between male and female as well as between the animal and the human or as a hybrid of both.[24] The feral women in her early fiction critique the production of bourgeois femininity, in particular the cultural codes of feminine propriety.[25] While within much Surrealist textual and visual practice sexual transgression is located at the site of the violated female body, in *The Hearing Trumpet* it is located in the body of the maternal crone, variously signified throughout the narrative as the Queen Bee, Hecate, Marian and the Abbess. The gigantic Queen Bee and the Abbess—who when pregnant inflates to an enormous size—occupy a central place in the novel's mythological network. By incorporating the gigantic and the grotesque into her novel, Carrington effects a disruption of the socially contained bourgeois body, which echoes a Surrealist dismemberment of the body, but also significantly transposes the terms of this figurative disruption. As Stewart argues "the grotesque body, as a form of the gigantic, is a body of parts … the grotesque presents … a dismantling and re-presentation of the body according to criteria of production rather than verticality" (1993: 105). While the grotesque body is invariably achieved through an emphasis on the internal elements of the body, a corresponding sense of disorder is achieved through "an exchange of sexuality and an exchange between animal and human" (104). In Carrington's narrative the exchange of sexuality is represented through a number of cross-dressing and sexually ambiguous characters; the Abbess, Maude (Arthur) and Marian herself. When Maude, one of the residents of the home, is accidentally poisoned, it is revealed that Maude is really Arthur, a camp pun on Malory's Christian version of the Grail myth, *Le Morte D'Arthur*. Moreover, it is the daring Marian—sporting a gallant beard—rather than her feckless son, Galahad, who assists in the reclamation of the Grail. Within the novel the grotesque and the hybrid become significant sites of literary and cultural transgression.

Just as transgression exists through the awareness of the limit that defines it (the sacred and the profane, fascination and horror) the use of the hybrid form in the novel registers the imaginative process of combining disparate elements or planes of reality. The hybrid figure is the deviant subject par excellence: a subject represented as a subject *of body*. In the work of many Surrealists the exploration of the disintegration and perversion of the psyche is often mapped onto the body so that the blinding and dissection of an eye—say in both *Un chien andalou* and *Story of the Eye*—may be read as a celebratory displacement of the conscious by the unconscious. In Carrington's novel, it is the hybrid wolf woman, Annubeth who represents the figure of the female artist, and embodies the text's overall strategy of transgressive displacement, employing techniques of collage and embalming in the creation of her art objects:

> Anubeth growled and reached up to get a very strange animal from the ceiling for my inspection. It was a tortoise with a baby's wizened face and long thin legs which were frozen in a gallop. "Annubeth says this kind of collage she made for fun when the keeper of the principal morgue in Venice gave her the present of the dead baby. The legs originally belonged to some storks that died of the cold. (193–4)

While collage dissects and displaces its material in order to create something new, embalming preserves the integrity of the body, albeit as a static and lifeless object. Here the dual strategies of dissection and preservation suggest an aesthetic practice grounded in both tradition and innovation. Anubeth's taxiderm collage provides a literal example of the figurative violence of collage, with its strategies of displacement and rearrangement. Her embalmed "exquisite corpse" is fashioned from the body parts of animal and human, from the process of art and chance and paradoxically evokes both life and death through its foregrounding of the body as a site of death *and* preservation. This figure marks the novel's overall use of the hybrid form—stylistic and thematic—and works to decenter a single subject and generic position as well as highlighting the often visceral materiality of Surrealist representation. Here the hybrid explicitly disrupts the law of non-contradiction (that something is either *a* or not *a*) in its production of disparate combinatory systems, producing the discordant effect so privileged within a Surrealist aesthetic praxis. Derived from the latin *hybrida*, which was used to refer to the offspring of a tame sow and a wild boar and to one born of a Roman father and foreign mother or a freeman or slave, the hybrid is that which both insists on, and confounds, taxonomic identification.[26] Through its figurative deployment of the hybrid, Carrington's novel continually foregrounds questions of origin, miscegenation and classification, if only to mock our obsession with them.

Conclusion

In the work of both Bataille and Carrington, parody functions as a literary form of transgression, one that performs a Surrealist violation of form but also redirects the possibilities for literary perversion outside of it. While Carrington parodies Surrealism's cult of the beautiful, young muse by replacing the figure of the *femme-enfant* with a plethora of geriatric and monstrous heroines, Bataille challenges the purity of Breton's idealistic conception of love with his excessively perverse sexual quest. The presence of the "double" in their fiction, worked through the relationship between literary narrative and autobiographical reflection, attests to the duplicitous nature of the unconscious mind—the privileged site of creativity—in its relation to the everyday. But if transgression and taboo are formulated through a relationship that is symbiotic, their work makes clear how parody itself is indebted to the very ideology it attempts to disrupt; while their work may be contaminated by the very discourses and ideologies they critique, it also opens up the possibility of wider political and social meaning for the Surrealist project. Like many of the hybrid characters in her novel, Carrington's text ruptures thematic and generic unity, producing in the texture of its narrative a strange hybrid of feminist and Surrealist ideological positions. As Suleiman has argued, the novel is "both a prolongation of and a (feminist) divergence from Surrealist aspirations" (1990: 173). As the bastard offspring of feminism and Surrealism, Carrington's novel explicitly challenges the privileging of literary transgression as a male avant-garde practice.

Notes

1 See my discussion of Breton's description of Carrington in Chapter 2.
2 In his recent biography of Bataille, Michel Surya reminds us "1928 was the year that Abbé Bethléem updated the 1905 edition of the compendium *Novels to Read and to Forbid (since 1500)*" (104).
3 Surya quotes Bataille's response to Breton's charge against him in the Second Manifesto: "I have nothing much to say about the personality of André Breton since I hardly know him. His police reports don't interest me" (132).
4 Surya writes: "… Georges Bataille made *Document* the instrument of the marvellous. Monstrous is the 'play of mankind and its own decay,' and it is cowardly that this game 'continues in the most dejected condition without one having the courage to confront the other … .' Love of the marvelous says, profoundly, *No*, to existence: it bears witness against it. True to himself and to the project he discussed with Leiris and Lavaud in 1924 to form a *Yes* movement, involving a permanent acquiescence to everything …" (2002: 124).
5 There seems to be a great deal of confusion as to when the novel was actually written. Suleiman suggests that it was written in the early 1950s when Carrington was in her early thirties (1990: 144), while Helen Byatt suggests sometime in the late 1940s or early 1950s. In her interview with Paul de Angelis for her catalog, *The Mexican Years*,

Carrington dates the novel from the 1950s, suggesting that she wrote it when she was in her forties (1991: 40). For Carrington to be "about forty" when she wrote the novel, it would have to have been in the late 1950s since she was born in 1917.

6 Gabriele Annan in the *Times Literary Supplement* sympathetically reviewed *The Hearing Trumpet* on May 27, 1977.

7 While Breton quietly admired Bataille's novel, by the time he came to write the Second Manifesto he had become increasingly hostile to Bataille's dedication to a transgression which manifested itself in terms of all things vulgar and base (Bolt-Irons, 1995: 3).

8 My title references Barthes' reading of the chain of metaphor that the eye instigates in Bataille's text, and the way in which it unfolds in the manner of the haruspex (121).

9 For example, Eliot's "The Lovesong of J Alfred Prufrock" uses the trope of lepidoptery to convey an image of the lover's sense of a violent scrutiny.

10 Within Surrealism the alter-ego became an important facet of identity and self-representation and were cultivated by Ernst, Carrington, Cahun and Duchamp, among others.

11 See my reading of masculine trauma in relation to Breton's *Nadja* in "Surrealism's Banging Door," *Textual Practice*.

12 Although Buñuel has consistently refused a singularly symbolic interpretation of the film, he suggests that psychoanalysis may be an appropriate tool for analyzing some of the film's meaning (Jay, 1994: 257).

13 Surya writes: "Élisabeth Roudinesco cast some supplementary light on the practice of Adrien Borel which gives some idea of how he could have been compatible with Bataille's intractable spirit. With him, treatment was above all else 'therapeutic, adaptive and founded with attention to suffering' … It was, in short, 'not very rigorous' and not 'ritualized', *a fortiori* with creative people (Borel had several in analysis, mainly surrealists) who, she says, he allowed to struggle with the violence of their unconscious" (97).

14 An interesting contemporary comparison to Carrington's revisionist novel is Kathy Acker's *Pussy, King of the Pirates*, which tells the story of a group of prostitutes who set fire to their brothel, destroy the city and incite revolution.

15 Critical readings of this work have tended to stress its feminist mythological framework. While I concur that this is certainly present, I also want to suggest that the novel has a dark comic edge that resists a purely celebratory feminist reading. Of course my own reading emerges from a moment in which feminism itself has taken on a self-critical approach in terms of its acknowledgement of its own privileged institutional authority.

16 The heroine of Bataille's later novel, *Madame Edwarda*, also shares similarities with Carrington's representation of femininity. In this novel Edwarda, the prostitute and madwoman, triumphs over the world of the novel. For a counter reading of Bataille's representation of women, see Susan Rubin Suleiman's "Bataille in the Street: The Search for Virility in the 1930s" (1995). Suleiman critiques Bataille's essentially conservative obsession with virility arguing that "(a)s a concept, virility took shifting forms in Bataille's thought. His continued use of the word, however, locked him into values and into a sexual politics that can only be called conformist, in his time and ours. Rhetorically, 'virility' carries with it too much old baggage. Bataille's male protagonists may be sexually equivocal, possessing feminine traits and female soulmates; but his rhetoric of virility does not follow them" (43).

17 Suleiman defines Bakhtin's carnival as "the heterogenous, multivoiced, multilingual ... discourses of medieval and Renaissance popular culture, and their gradual integration into the high-cultural genre of the novel" (142).

18 Susan Stewart suggests that "the literary's nostalgia for oral forms is a nostalgia for the presence of the body and the face-to-face, a dream of unmediated communication that, of course, could never be approximated even in the oral—a dream of an eternalized present, a future-past" (1991: 90).

19 Jay reveals the importance of the labyrinth for modernist writers such as Joyce and Borges as well as postmodernist theory; primarily Derrida and Irigaray who have both associated it with different parts of the body, the ear and the labia respectively (229). See also André Masson's 1938 painting, *Labyrinth* in which the inner organs of a strange hulking mass are a series animate and inanimate labyrinthine forms and which capture the full horror of the war to come and the very real destruction of physical form. The family connections between Bataille and Masson are, ironically, also considerably labyrinthine: Masson was closely connected to Bataille through his marriage to Rose, who was Bataille's wife's sister. Bataille's wife, the actress Sylvia Makles, would later marry Jacques Lacan.

20 Sarwin suggests "To play, to really play, for Breton, was a special way of galvanizing the mind to make sorties into the unfamiliar and the adventurous in spirit would usually fall in with his challenge ... . Charades by analogy, Murder, and a game in which a person takes on the identity of an object, as well as the exquisite corpses—these were some of the forms of serious play to which Breton invited his friends" (124).

21 In her autobiography, Peggy Guggenheim records Max Ernst's obsession with collecting Kachina dolls and masks (1987: 265).

22 Carrington's love of the outmoded reminds us of Benjamin's comments on Breton in his essay on Surrealism: "[Breton] was the first to perceive the revolutionary energies in the 'outmoded' ..." (1978: 182).

23 Probably the most familiar example of this is Magritte's paintings in which text and image are used to create meaning as well as draw attention to the discrepancies between different mediums of representation. Other examples include Ernst's collage novels.

24 Carrington's use of the hybrid form, in both her painting and fiction, forms a striking parallel with Masson's late New York works, which Sawin argues replaces a more explicit violence with "a morphology of nature and the theme of regeneration" (114). Although there is a lot of violent imagery in *The Hearing Trumpet* its dominant mood as I have suggested is one of regeneration, a celebration of Carrington's new collaborative relationship with Varo.

25 See Rachel Carrol's "Something to See: Spectacle and Savagery in Leonora Carrington's Fiction" for an illuminating discussion of the feral woman in Carrington's fiction.

26 *The Oxford Dictionary of English Etymology*. Ed. C.T. Onions. Oxford University Press, 1985.

Chapter 4

Disturbing the Photographic Subject

> The arts in which Surrealism has come
> into its own are prose fiction … theatre, the arts of assemblage,
> and—most triumphantly—photography.
>
> Susan Sontag, *On Photography*

Introduction

The self-portraits that Claude Cahun produced over a twenty year period—across the 1920s and 1930s—together with her prose poems, political tracts, journalistic essays, photo-collages, sculpture-objects and theater sets, register the extraordinary range of media with which she worked. While this varied critical and creative practice was indicative of the interdisciplinary nature of the avant-garde itself, there is an acute restlessness in Cahun's movement between different modes of articulation that resonate with the immense scope of personae staged for the black-and-white snapshots produced from this period.[1] The small and intimate size of these images as well as their private circulation among Cahun's closest friends—very few were ever published—necessarily complicates their connection to Cahun's more public political and critical work. And yet, there is a consistency in the themes Cahun explored across the full range of her work that necessitates a reading of the portraits as an extension of the political and creative ideas that preoccupied her for most of her life. Indeed Cahun's active role in revolutionary politics and her desire for broader social and political transformation cannot be separated from the radical reconfiguration of the self that emerges in the self-portraits. As Laurie Monahan suggests: "For Cahun and other leftist intellectuals … a potential space of disruption was the subject transcending its own bounds. In a society where the coherent subject was central to social stability—its structure, moral codes, rules—a radical reconceptualization of the self promised fundamental change" (1996: 132). As such the portraits form part of a sustained interrogation of identity across the boundaries of political activism, aesthetic practice and personal and erotic style. Within the context of an orthodox Surrealism, with its fetishization and dismemberment of the female body and its underlying homophobia, Cahun's work directly addresses the crisis of identity and self-definition for women (and) homosexuals. While Abigail Solomon-Godeau argues that "Cahun is an artist for whom sexual politics, as opposed to the sexual *body*, is a domain to consciously, deliberately, indeed intellectually investigate, a far different enterprise than surrealism's celebration of the anarchic and liberating potential of eros and eroticism" (1999 :119), I would suggest that the erotic is indeed an important dimension of Cahun's reconceptualized radical subject although I agree she was far more canny in understanding the sexual politics underpinning any such mobilization of the erotic. In Cahun's political and experimental writing at least, there is a bold attempt to reconcile Marx and Freud in a way that reflects her strong allegiance to Breton's own beleaguered struggle to define art and life as part of the same radical drive. However, the politics and aesthetics of identity that Cahun grapples with in her work might be said to extend the parameters of a Bretonian Surrealist investigation of the self by radically foregrounding Surrealism's own limited sexual politics.

Disturbing the Photographic Subject

In looking at Cahun's self-portraits one recalls the particular kind of awe Barthes invokes when he contemplates the obvious and obtuse essence of the photographic portrait; its necessary challenge to the reductive claims of authenticity; its disturbance of boundaries; its labelling and obscuring of the subject; its moments of loss and mourning; its uncanniness. For while the subject of photographic portraiture can be read as the index of the real, it also constitutes the dismemberment of the real, what Barthes calls "the advent of myself as other: a cunning dissociation of consciousness from identity" (1980/1993: 12). The instability of the photograph's essence is accentuated in the medium of self-portraiture since the very act of photographing the self confounds the roles of subject and object (of author and figure). In Cahun's self-portraits the constant interrogation of the self via disguise and distortion increases the intensity of this disturbance since it reminds us of the gap between the way Cahun *looks at* us (her gaze) and *to* us (her appearance). Rather than simply objectify her body as a static image, Cahun's self-portraits perform a series of visual tropes that continually renegotiate the boundaries of identification and subjectification. The variations of Cahun's vestimentary style, the use of mirrors to create illusion and fantasy, the employment of assorted photographic techniques to manipulate and distort the image and the use of dolls and mannequins to highlight the uncanny—all shape the complex representation of subject formation, of gendered and sexual identity in the portraits. For Cahun, the photographic self-portrait is itself a mask that extends and confounds the self as a subject in the making.

Given their overt themes of masking and performance, many recent critics have suggested that Cahun's portraits anticipate Judith Butler's work on the performativity of gender, in particular its emphasis on masquerade as the very sign which disrupts an established gender ontology.[2] Without completely disregarding the subtle ways in which Cahun's work might pre-empt many of the concerns of Butler's theory, here I want to frame my discussion around Sedgwick's interrogation of contemporary theories of difference as a way to think through Cahun's legacy in terms of a queer and feminist reading of identity and representation.[3] If, as Sedgwick suggests, much contemporary theory conceives itself as something of the present, its ideas framed within the rhetoric of the revolutionary and the utopic, how do we *read* these portraits without losing the force of their transgression? What constitutes a sense of *disturbance* in these portraits is their astute knowingness of the trajectory of theories of the modern subject in relation to technologies of representation. The assorted display of stylistic identities developed in the self-portraits, indeed the continual metamorphosis of the self through the photographic image, illustrates Sedgwick's axiom that "People are different from each other" (1990: 22). Beyond the self-evident banality of this statement is the underlying ambiguity of the self-portraits: that people are different from each other but also different from themselves. In Cahun's work the mask illustrates this aspect of internal difference by revealing the contradictions that inform the changing temporal, spatial and psychic structures of individual subjectivity. While Sedgwick argues that contemporary theory has put difference and the "deconstruction of the category of *the individual*" at the very center of its epistemological project, this has amounted to a certain banal representation of many of its critical insights:

> Deconstruction, founded as a very science of *différ(e/a)nce*, has both so fetishised the idea of difference and so vaporised its possible embodiments that its most thoroughgoing practitioners are the last people to whom one would now look for help in thinking about particular differences. (1990: 23)

If, as Sedgwick argues, difference has become so overdetermined within contemporary theory as to diminish the very possibility of a cogent articulation of its effects, what do Cahun's images offer us in terms of a theory of the subject conceived within the rubric of a radical otherness before the advent of what we might call a fetish of difference? Given the uncanny currency of Cahun's work, how do we read the past from the moment of knowingness in the present, and retain the sense of an emerging dialogue around the representation of sexual and political identity that we now take for granted? Many of the themes that Cahun explores—such as the performance of gendered identity and erotic style within a politicized commitment to social transformation—have resonances with queer theory's attempt to deconstruct identity politics in order to unsettle rigid categories of definition and self-definition, across political, aesthetic and theoretical domains. Of course there are important distinctions between Cahun's work and contemporary queer theory and aesthetics. If we want to situate Cahun as a pioneer of queer practice we need to recognize that queer itself is part of a larger distillation of modernity's attempts to formulate new ways of inscribing the relationship between politics, sexuality and artistic expression.

Sedgwick is useful for my reading of Cahun's work, not only because she draws our attention to theory's conception of itself as something always of the present, but because she locates knowledge in modernity around the question of sexual knowledge, around "the crisis of homo/heterosexual definition" (1990: 1). Like "the relations of the known and the unknown, the explicit and the inexplicit" (3) that structure epistemologies of sexuality, the photographic self-portrait is itself structured around a dynamic of what is revealed and what is concealed, which both promises the possibility of authentic presence if only to foreclose it at the point of its displacement through reproduction. In addition, Cahun's portraits continually play out a self-consciousness around the spectacle of identity; an erotics of appearance and disguise that disturb the clearly defined parameters of masculine and feminine and their concomitant binarized formations of sexual identification. As such the photographic self-portrait becomes an exemplary medium for representing a crisis of definition, both sexual and aesthetic. The crisis of definition that pertains to both the photographic image *and* sexual and gendered identity discloses the importance of fantasy as that which exceeds the ontological and representational "real;" that which allows the subject to imagine itself across the temporal and spatial coordinates that maintain its difference from itself as well as that which haunts the indexicality of the photographic image as it occupies a life beyond its moment of reproduction. It is this capacity of the photograph, its uncanny insistence on a crisis of identity that manifests the haunting effect of Cahun's images on the present.

The Captive Balloon

Cahun's interest in masking is expanded beyond the visual domain in a way that reinforces the mask as a more general trope for the specular conditionality of the subject. An analysis of some of her political and theoretical writing provides an important frame for understanding the politics of representation as it unfolds in her turn to the photographic self-portrait. In her 1926 essay, "Captive Balloon," published in *La Ligne de Coeur*, she writes:

> Masks are made of different quality materials: cardboard, velvet, flesh, the Word. The carnal mask and the verbal mask are worn in all seasons. I soon learned to prefer to all others these off-the-market stratagems .... You create for yourself several clearly defined vocabularies, several syntaxes, several ways of being, thinking and even feeling—from which you'll choose a skin the color of time .... (Quoted in Rosemont, 1998: 52)

For Cahun, the mask represents a complex grammar of identity that refuses an instrumental distinction between appearance and reality, a performative and a "real" self or indeed a material and theoretical understanding of the subject. Rather, the temporal skin of the mask becomes a captive balloon that encloses the ontological, affective and intellectual "materials" that form the subject over time; and like the inflating and deflating balloon, it represents the subject as continually under construction and erasure. Here the emphasis on the materiality of the mask, alongside the vast array of costumes and props used in the self-portraits, highlights the significance of commodity culture to the very representation and construction of the body, in a way that reveals both commodity and erotic fetishism as itself a fantasy of presence. In performing and representing a series of fetishized personas in the portraits—the dandy, the sailor, the aviator, the boxer, the vamp, the exotic oriental woman, the actress or female performer, the Aryan blonde maiden and so on—Cahun discloses the centrality of commodity fetishism to a social and cultural reading of the body. Each persona, each mask, represents a culturally performed social identity, coded through the detail of its costume and props. As such the mask discloses the operation of both Freudian and Marxist fetishism; revealing the erotic allure of commodity culture and the fantasmatic projections it allows as well as the commodification of the body enacted through the reifying effects of fetishistic desire.

In this essay Cahun also emphasizes the importance of psychic repression to the mask's conditions of success and failure:

> I remember, it was Carnival time. I had spent my solitary hours disguising my soul. Its masks were so perfect that when they happened to run into each other on the plaza of my consciousness, they didn't recognise one another. I adopted the most surly opinions, one after another: those that displeased me the most were the most certain of success … . (52)

Since the contingencies of knowing the self are fraught with the risk of misrecognition, the unconscious undermining of everyday consciousness and aims, the mask, as an internal and external mechanism, both marks the inevitability of classification as a socially constitutive endeavor as well as the impossibility of its coherence for self-knowledge. But here the materiality of the mask is inseparable from its "carnal" and verbal" variants in a way that underscores the subject as the necessary product of a symbolic, psychic and bourgeois social economy.

The private and undisclosed world of the self-portraits forms a striking contrast with Cahun's extremely active role in left-wing political groups throughout the 1930s and the publication of several important political and theoretical texts. Her meeting with André Breton in 1932 crystallized her association with the Surrealist circle, and led to her involvement with the anti-fascist political group, *Contra-attaque*, formed by Bataille and Breton in 1936. Throughout this period, Cahun was prominent in the Association of Revolutionary Artists and Writers (*Association des Artistes et Ecrivains Révolutionnaires*), producing a number of reports and essays that were eventually published as part of *Les Paris sont ouverts* (1934). In a section from this work, pointedly titled "Poetry Keeps Its Secret," Cahun provides a defence of poetry in order to counter a vulgar Marxist dismissal of its non-utilitarian and bourgeois status, and hence its inadequacy as a means of propaganda. In providing a passionate plea for the importance of avant-garde art within a communist political program, Cahun claims that it is precisely the self-reflexive quality of poetic language that makes it an important revolutionary practice but also an unpredictable medium for political propaganda:

> Here, we need to recall the distinction made by Tzara between the *manifest content* of a poem and its *latent content*. The manifest content of a poem, in my view, cannot be revolutionary, in the sense that we normally understand it here ... However, poets in their own way act upon people's sensibility. Their attack is more cunning; but even their most oblique blows can be fatal. (Quoted in Rosemont: 54)

In taking up Tzara's Freudian reading of the poetic image, Cahun emphasizes the necessary asymmetry between the manifest and latent content of a poem; while the manifest content is available to the reader or critic for interpretation, the interpretive act itself, akin to the operation of displacement and condensation in the "dream work," may reveal "all sorts of unconscious reticences" (55). Cahun concludes that it is precisely the ideological tensions in a poem that make it difficult to determine its "*propaganda* value" (55). While she argues that "Communist propaganda should be entrusted only to the *directed thought of conscious prose* writers, journalists, orators" (54), she does not rule out the revolutionary potential of poetry, or avant-garde art in general, but suggests their effects are far more "cunning." Defending what she calls "the dada-surrealist experiment," Cahun argues for a more nuanced category of revolutionary art, one that recognizes the effects of chance and desire in the construction and reception of the aesthetic object. She thus concludes that it is impossible, except very crudely through psychoanalysis, to gauge the revolutionary "effect" of a poem since its "effects" will always produce individual affective responses. Here Cahun's analysis of poetry discloses the clash between individual and collective desires as they unfold in the antinomies between bourgeois and socialist values.

The tensions inherent in identifying a revolutionary aesthetic plagued the Surrealists throughout the 1930s as Breton attempted to justify the revolutionary goals of art in broader terms than those offered by the French Communist Party (PCF). As Robert Short reveals, by 1934 "the dogma of 'socialist realism'" imported from the USSR into the PCF had seen an escalation in the differences between Breton and the Surrealists on one side, and Aragon and the communists on the other (2003: 29):

> For Breton, a writer's "meaning" lay in the words he wrote and the intention behind them; their subversive value was latent within them. For Aragon, meaning lay solely in the interpretation made by the reader or the majority of society at any given time. (Short, 2003: 30)

Cahun's essay responds to this crisis, or what became known as the "Aragon affair," by reframing the question of form and content in terms of poetry's "diverse manifestations" against Aragon's aesthetic positivism:

AVANT

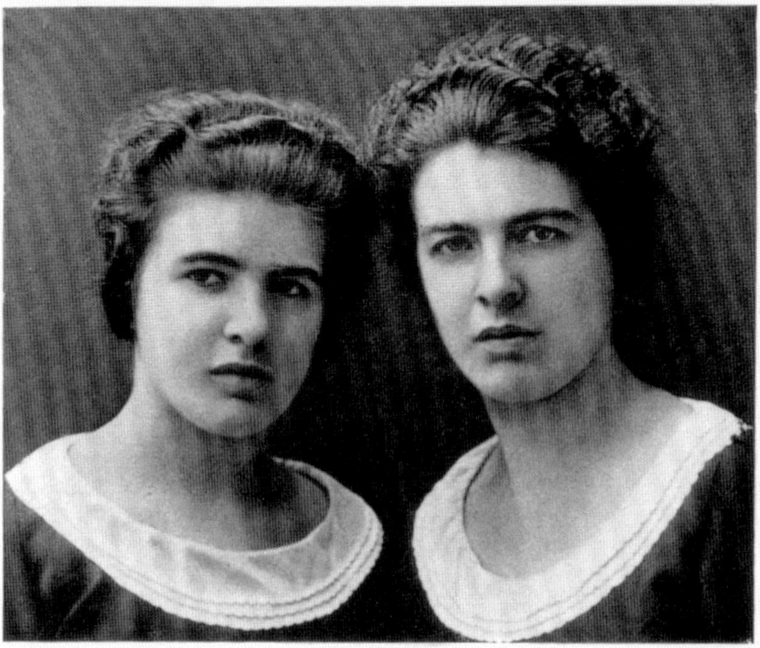

APRÈS

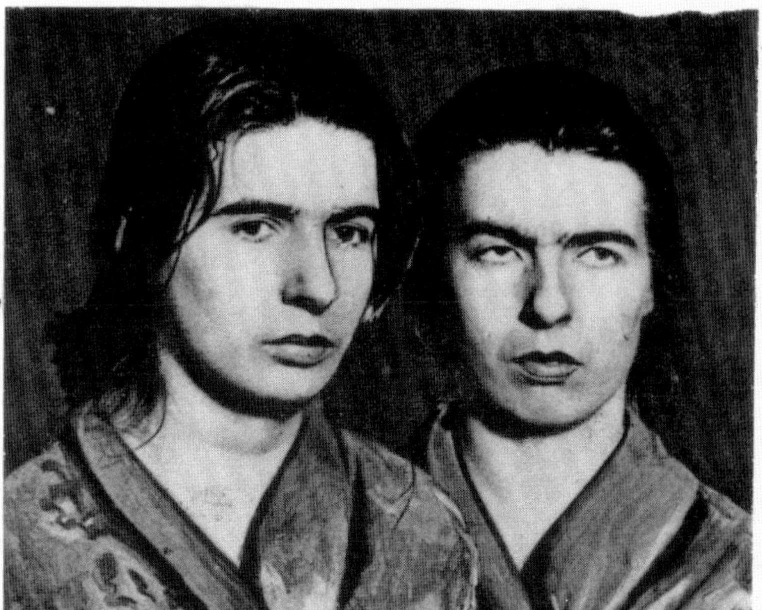

1 Anonymous. Photograph of The Papin Sisters: "Before" and "After", *Le Surréalisme au service de la revolution* no. 5 (15 May 1933)

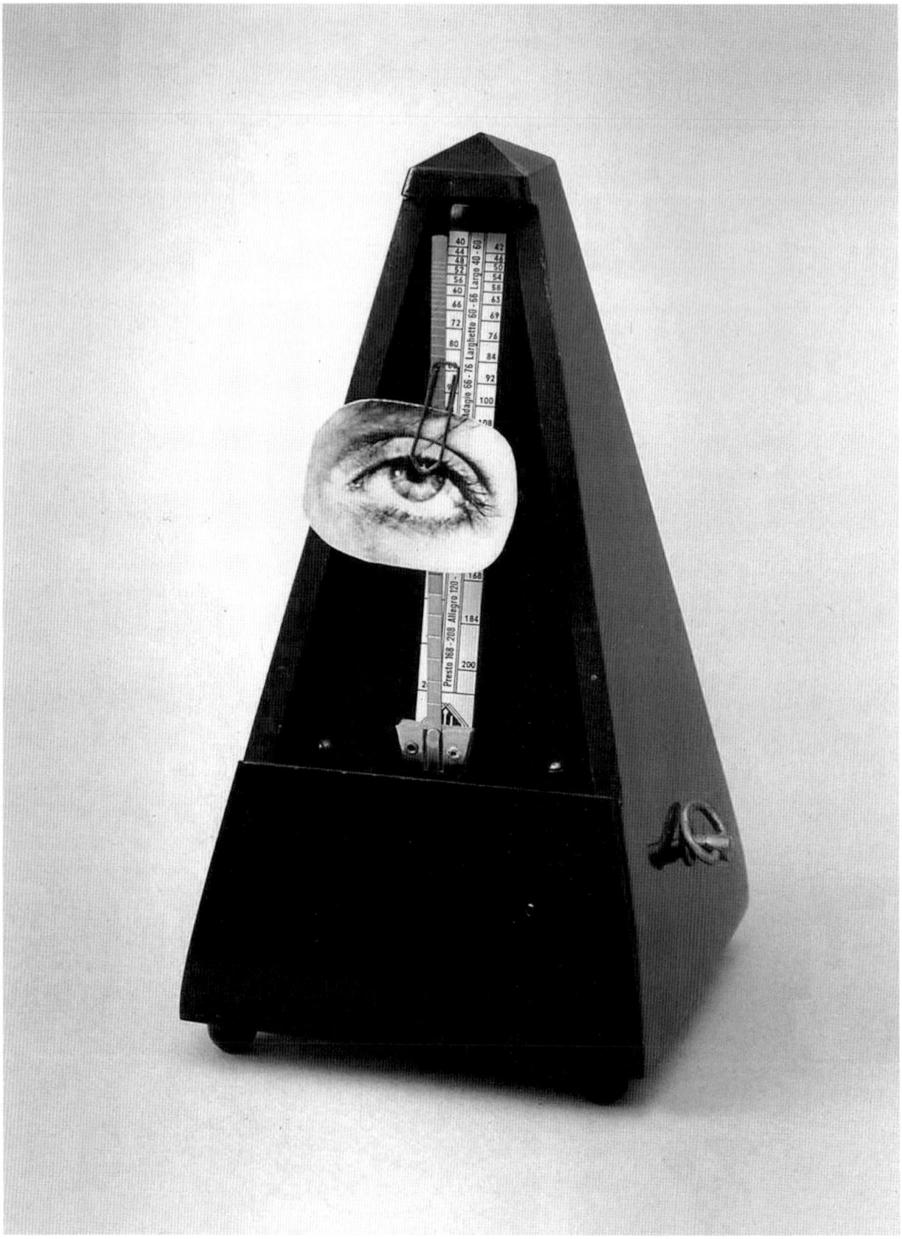

2 Man Ray. *Object to be Destroyed* (1932). © Man Ray, Licensed by VISCOPY, Australia, 2006

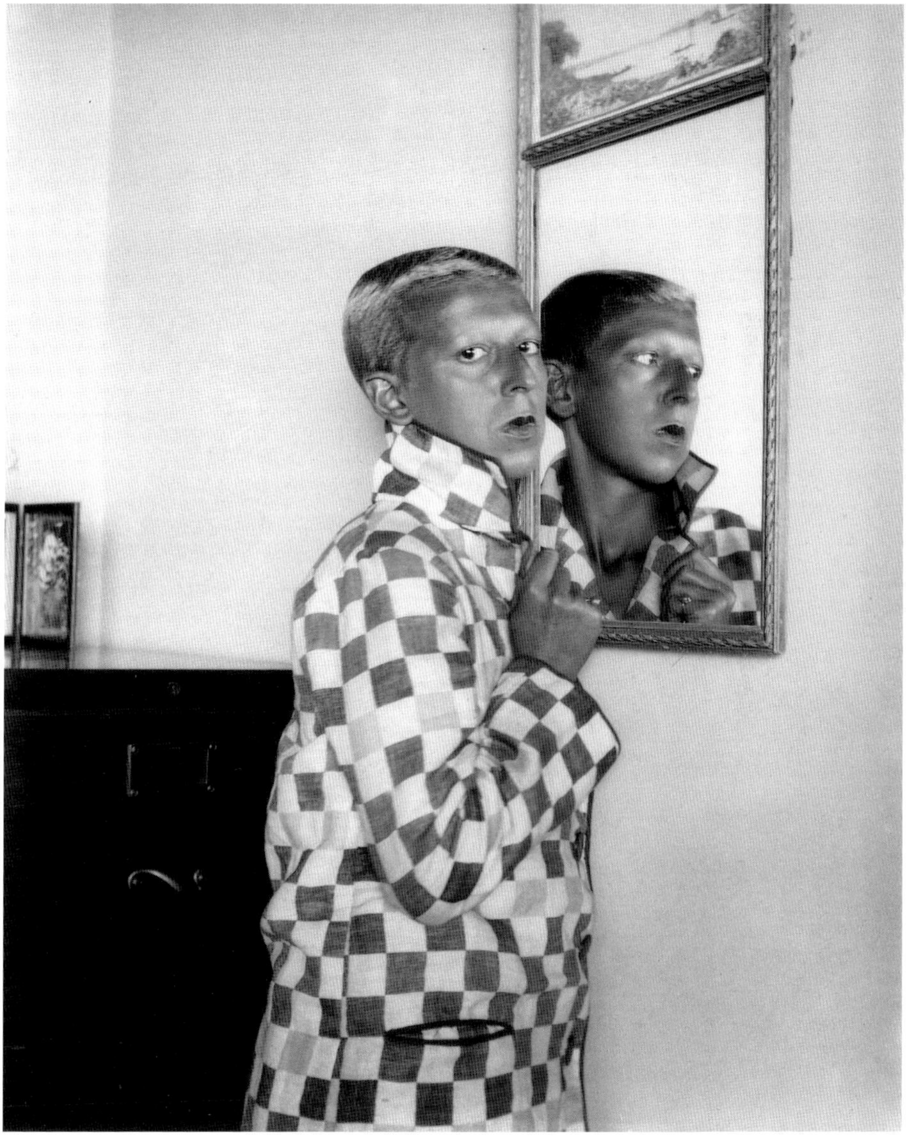

3 Claude Cahun. *Self-Portrait* (1928). Courtesy of the Jersey Heritage Trust Collection

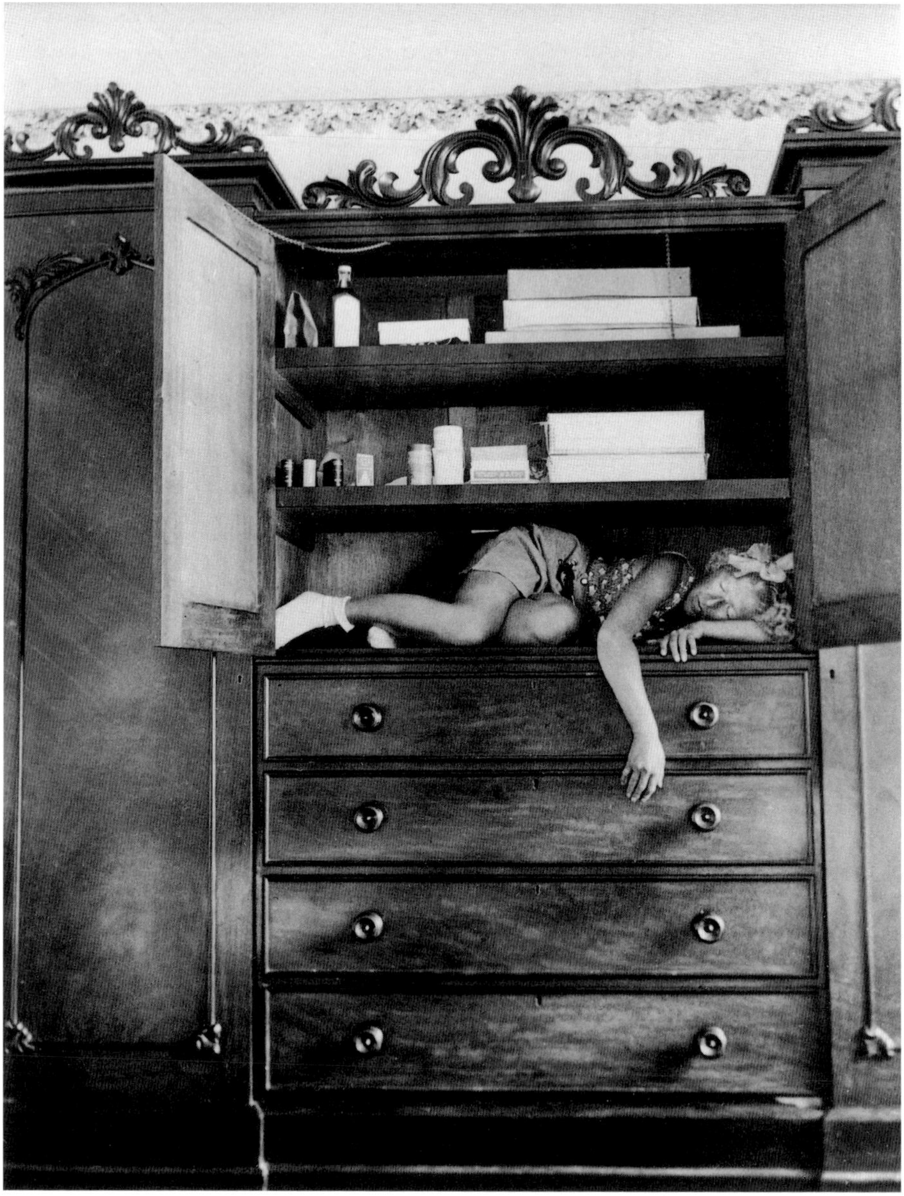

4 Claude Cahun. *Self-Portrait* (1932). Courtesy of the Jersey Heritage Trust Collection

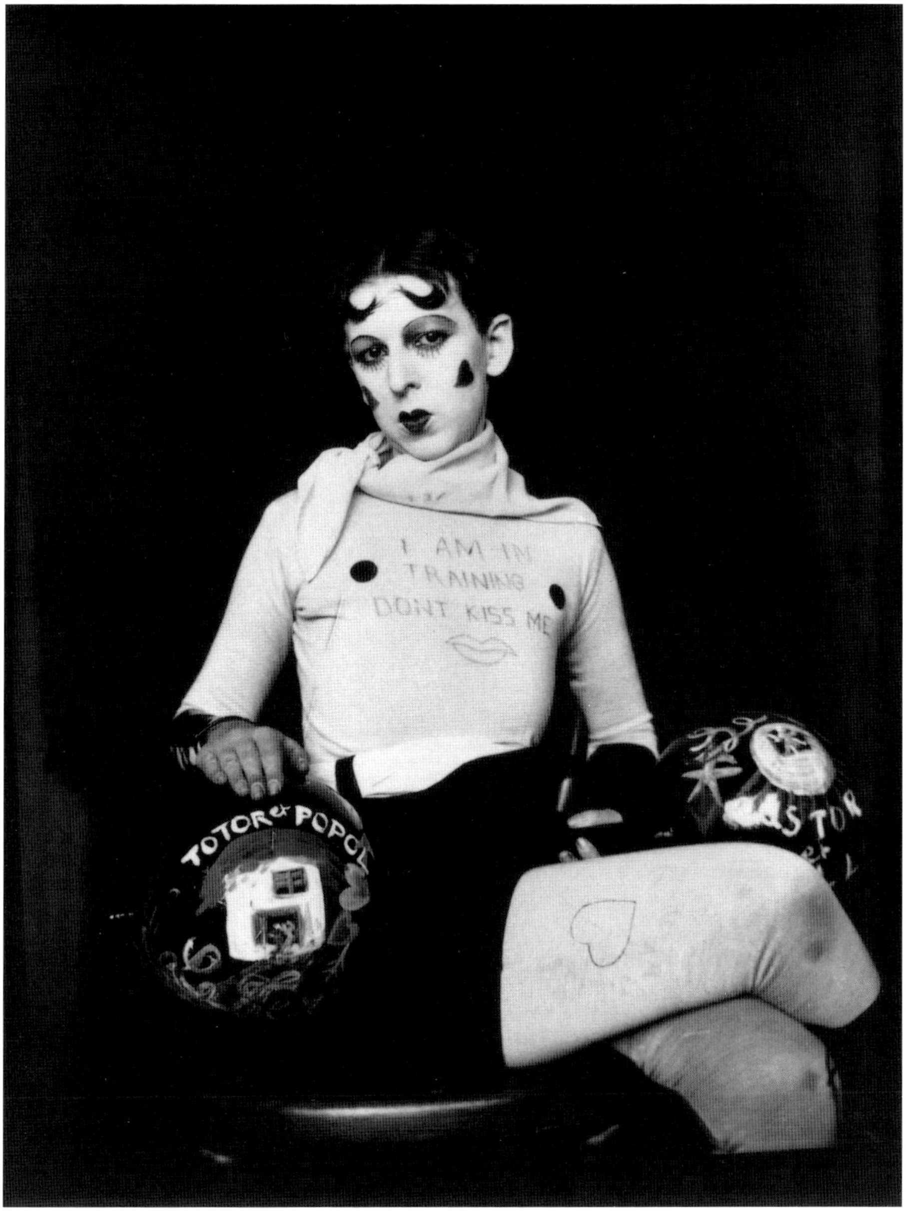

5 Claude Cahun. *Self-Portrait* (1927). Courtesy of the Jersey Heritage Trust Collection

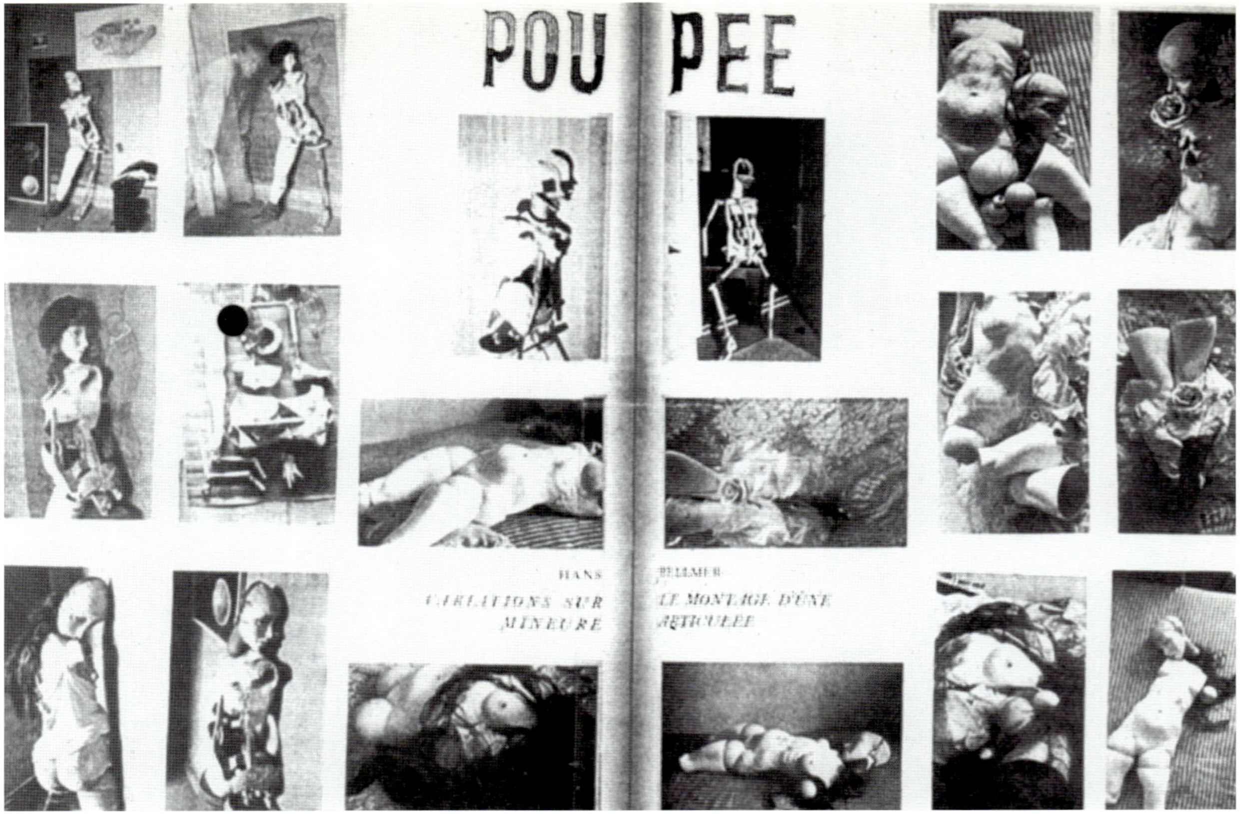

6 Hans Bellmer. "Variations sur le montage d'une mineure articulée", *Minotaure*, 1934–1935. © Hans Bellmer, Licensed by VISCOPY, Australia, 2006

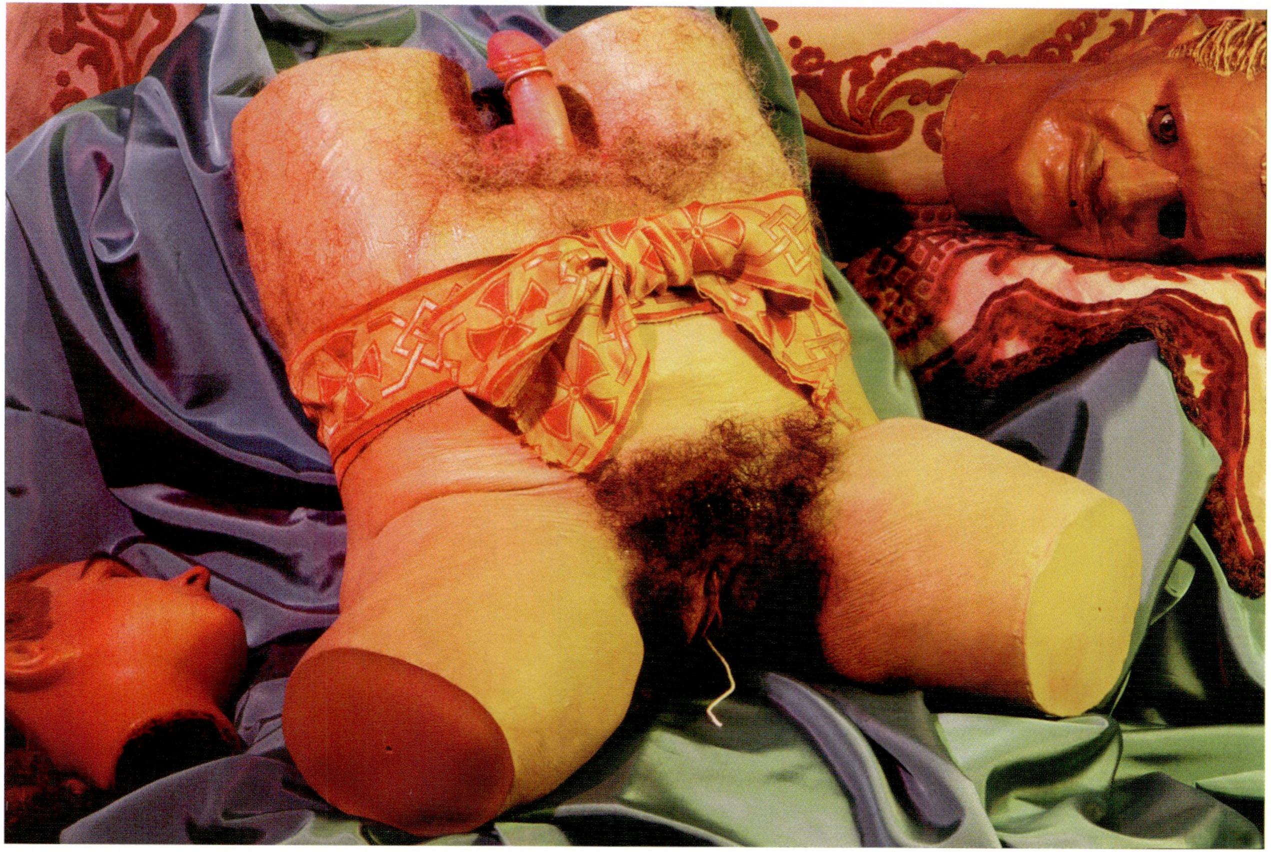

7 Cindy Sherman. *Untitled #263*. Courtesy of the artist and Metro Pictures

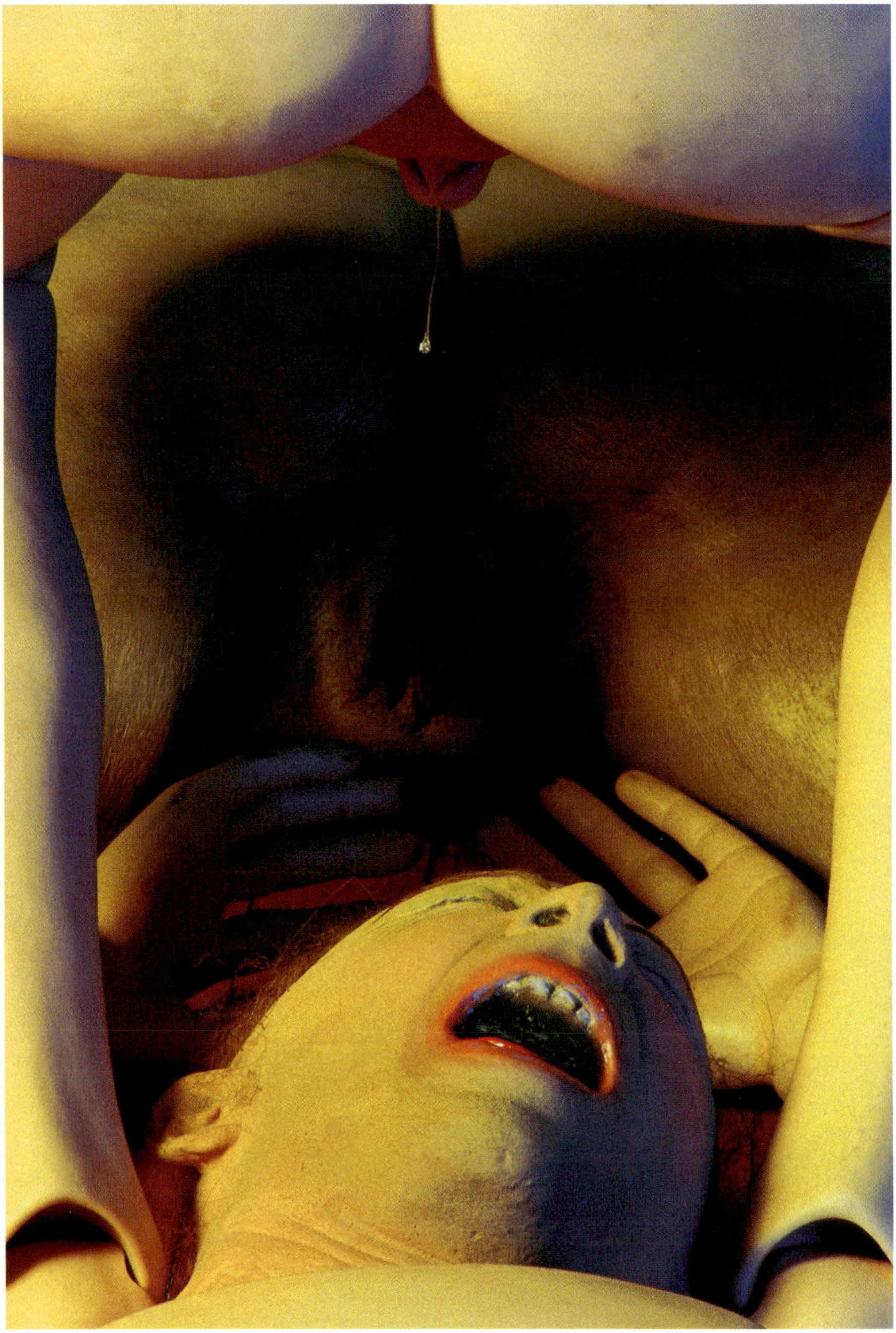

8 Cindy Sherman. *Untitled #257*. Courtesy of the artist and Metro Pictures

> Liberation from formalism is precious because it prevents poetry from being reduced to games for the literate. On the other hand, the demand for ideological conformity would lead to the very suppression of all poetry ... For if it is impossible to keep consciousness completely out of the picture, it is impossible as well to avoid absences, a slackening of surveillance, and, consequently, latent content. (Cahun, quoted in Rosemont: 55)

Having begun the essay with the emphatic declaration that poetry "seems undeniably an inherent need of human ... nature, undoubtedly linked to the sex instinct" (54), Cahun challenges poetry's bourgeois frame by stressing its innate universal function, establishing a fundamental connection between human creativity and sexual desire. In line with Surrealism's privileging of content over form (through its incorporation of the psychic and material traces of the everyday), Cahun resists a formalist reduction of art to "games for the literate" and extends the making of art to all. This emphasis on a non-professional and largely unmediated form of poetic expression closely aligns itself with the Surrealist experiments with automatic writing, though, as the above passage illustrates, Cahun seems to be as sceptical about a complete absence of consciousness in poetic expression as she is about the singularity of a poem's ideological expression. Nevertheless, Cahun's extraordinary creative and intellectual interdisciplinarity does indeed acknowledge her ideological resistance to *metier*.

While Cahun's focus in the essay is poetry, it is, significantly, through the description of the unconscious revelations inherent in the photographic image that she illustrates the effect of the manifest and latent content of the poem:

> A man believes he has photographed the hair of the woman he loves, mingled with bits of straw, as she sleeps in a field. But in the *developed* snapshot there appear a thousand divergent arms, shining fists, weapons; we see that it's a photo of a riot. (Cahun, cited in Rosemont, 1998: 55)

What is fascinating about this passage, in the context of Cahun's own photographic practice, is that in her rhetorical elaboration of poetry's secret she turns to an analysis of the latent content of the photographic image in a way that corresponds with Benjamin's own explication of the optical unconscious as photography's "secret:"

> Whereas it is a commonplace that, for example, we have some idea what is involved in the act of walking, if only in general terms, we have no idea at all what happens during the fraction of a second when a person *steps out*. Photography, with its devices of slow motion and enlargement, reveals the secret. It is through photography that we first discover the existence of this optical unconscious, just as we discover the instinctual unconscious through psychoanalysis. (Benjamin, 1968: 243)

For Benjamin, the optical unconscious registers the explosive moment in which the optical device renders the secret of the self-evident, what Tom Gunning describes as "a perceptual mechanism that takes in more than it can consciously account for" (2003: 126).[4] Benjamin's description of the optical unconscious lies close to a Surrealist suspension of the logical rules that govern the realm of empirical evidence, a mode of experience that splinters the apparentness of the everyday into a dialectic of canny and uncanny recognition. As Gunning argues,

> The surrealists offered Benjamin the glimpse of a method in which the mystery and its solution were not antithetical but mutually engendered each other. The flash of dialectical optics reveals both the solution of the mystery and the truth of the dream. One learns something from the flash of recognition, but one also discovers through it a mode of knowledge that exceeds logical categories of verification. (128)

For Cahun, the latent and manifest qualities of a poem correspond to the "secret" of the optical device that renders the image in excess of its indexical dimension; here the transformation of the beloved's hair into a riot of fists, arms and weapons reveals the eruption of the uncanny that engenders for the spectator the fantasy life of the image.

In Cahun's political tracts and theoretical writing, as well as in her self-portraits, there is a consistent approach to the treatment of subjectivity and representation in terms of a Freudian economy of conscious and unconscious desire. Like the optical unconscious, which presupposes the meaning of the photograph as a dialectic of the canny and the uncanny, the mask establishes a similar effect through its presentation of a "double" inscription. In terms of the broader intellectual and political scope of Cahun's life and work, this represents a tenacious desire to recognize the importance of inner psychic life to the external material world. This is, I would argue, at the heart of her exploration of the self as a subject-in-process and which closely corresponds with Breton's own vision for Surrealism in the 1930s, one which sought to configure political action and artistic expression as part of the same radical drive for emancipation.[5] But Cahun's interest in sexual politics, rather than, or alongside, the sexual body per se, extends the political scope of emancipation by driving home the destabilizing effects of sexual difference in a symbolic order whereby the identities woman and lesbian are already fake versions of masculinity. Like the refusal of the professionalized codes of artistic practice and identity, an aspect of Surrealism she extended to her political essays, Cahun's rhetorical elaboration of the mask in both verbal and visual contexts, points to the mimicry of authority, as a way to reinforce the provisional nature of all such claims to mastery. A close reading of the self-portraits will illustrate the ways in which Cahun used the medium of photography to extend her theoretical analysis of the psychic and material traces of subjectivity *and* representation.

What Do You Want From Me?

In a self-portrait from 1928 (see Plate 3), Cahun appears side-on in front of a mirror wearing a black and white checked shirt; her face, reflected in the mirror, is caught from two different angles, and is as strikingly chiselled and tonally contrasted as the geometric pattern on her shirt. The image plays with reality and illusion by revealing two different sides of her face; although both angles of the face represent the same temporally photographed subject, they appear as two distinct expressions, indeed different selves. While the image in the foreground directly engages the gaze of the viewer, the shirt and collar pulled up to conceal the neck and décolletage, the image reflected in the mirror furtively avoids our gaze, revealing the shirt open at the neck and chest. The appearance of two subjects in the portrait is an illusion since the furtive gaze is merely the "other" side of the subject staring directly at us, the side we wouldn't be able to see without the use of the mirror. So although the mirror provides us with a reality that would otherwise be lost in the two-dimensionality of photographic portraiture, it distorts that reality through its reflection of the other side of the face, so that Cahun becomes literally Janus-faced. In other words the mirror discloses the "secret" of the photographic image, and in the process deconstructs the ontological stability of the subject, since it simultaneously inscribes and splinters the singularity of the self. Here "the double" sets up a dialectic of self and other, of subject and object which is echoed in the black and white checks of Cahun's shirt, which functions as an apt homology for the photographic process itself: the positive and negative of a photographic image, one necessarily being the same but also the reverse of the other. This figurative doubling discloses the narcissism of the mirror and of photographic self-portraiture, underscoring the ambiguity of their status as mediums that confer authenticity.

The theme of the double returns in another portrait, dated from the same year, *Que Me Veux-Tu?* [What Do you Want From Me?], one of the few self-portraits to be titled. Here again we are presented with two images of the same subject, one looking over its shoulder at the other with an expression of self-observation, a haunting of one self by another competing self. Instead of a mirror, Cahun uses montage to duplicate the subject and in the process captures a surreal sense of the split subject, hinting at both its conscious and unconscious dimensions. In posing the question "What Do You Want From Me?" as a moment of self-interrogation, Cahun registers the opening words of Breton's own self-interrogation, "Who am I?," at the beginning of *Nadja*. But here Cahun shifts the question from "Who am I?," an interrogation that belongs in the case of *Nadja* to the uncertainty of the autobiographical project itself and the connection between subject formation and a Freudian understanding of the uncanny as the return of something familiar that has been repressed, to an awareness of the multivalency of the subject, and to a Freudian explication of narcissism as the subject's search for an ego ideal. In his essay "On Narcissism" (1920) Freud develops an account of the importance of narcissism to self-development, noting that "we must recognise that self-regard has a specially intimate dependence on narcissistic libido" (*PFL*, vol. 2: 1991: 93). Cahun's frequent use of the double as well as her development of a rhetoric of make-up and costume as central to the visual texture of the body's form and identity, suggests that narcissism functions here as a highly self-conscious practice of self-definition and self-creation, one which works against the ubiquitous Surrealist atomization of the female body. In many of the self-portraits costume and techniques of visual distortion reveal a phallic overdetermination of the body, a simultaneous assertion and deconstruction of identity. That is, "the double" highlights a self-conscious narcissism, what Cahun elsewhere alludes to as "sail[ing] ahead only in the direction of my own prow" (quoted in Rosemont: 53). The intensely private and intimate nature of these snapshots suggests that they might function in terms of what Shelley Rice calls "a parallel universe" that allowed Cahun to "live the imaginary life with a freedom that was denied her in the historical world" (1999: 23). And yet reading the self-portraits alongside her theoretical and political writing there is a sense in which the imaginary life was, for Cahun, not a parallel universe, but fundamental to the lived reality of the historical subject. As such the excessive desire for self-invention and renewal that we witness in the portraits mirrors a radical commitment to political and social transformation.

The dialectic of self and other, authenticity and copy produced in these images coincides with Cahun's experimentation with masculine and feminine costume, both before and away from the camera. As such the self-portraits read like a kind of visual diary, a collection of moods, erotic styles, favorite costumes, masks and identities which form a visual accompaniment to Cahun's anti-teleological autobiographical project, *Absent Confessions* (*Aveux non avenus*). Indeed many of the photographs that Cahun took of herself and other objects find their way into this work as photo-collages created by Suzanne Malherbe (née Suzanne Moore), Cahun's lifelong lover and stepsister. In *I. O. U (Self-Pride)*, a work that explicitly challenges the righteous fecundity of the bourgeois family, a series of cut-out heads of Cahun are stacked one upon the other, emerging from a single phallic-shaped neck. Around the edge of Cahun's cascading stack of heads are the words "Beneath this mask another mask. I will never be done lifting off all these visages" (cited in Blessing, 1997: 37). Here the self is constructed as an endless play of masks, reminding us of Riviere's suggestion that there is no difference between the mask and what lies behind it; that the mask itself is a trope for the very "absence" of woman from signifying cultural practices. But the subtitle of this piece, "Self-pride," suggests that the image might also function as a celebratory totem pole of identities that are both the same and different, a homage to the theme of narcissism that is at once antidote to, but also sign of, a crisis of self-definition. A reading of this work must be informed, in part, by the knowledge that Suzanne Malherbe played an instrumental role in facilitating and witnessing the creation of Cahun's self-portraits. Does the "I.O.U" of the portrait's title function as a homage to Malherbe, a recognition of the "other" in the collaborative act of these images as well as Malherbe's implicit presence in the autobiographical project?

Elsewhere in this image a pyramid structure encloses a father, mother and child, all joined at the stomach like Siamese twins; the father's hand violently holding the child up by the hair in a simultaneous embrace of the mother. A banner with the words "La Sainte Famille" hovers above them, mocking the deification of the bourgeois family in the face of the reality of its incestuous violence. Behind these figures is a further reference to the saintly family: a set of Russian doll-like figures, containing foetuses in various stages of gestation, invoke the narcissism of the bourgeois family and its desire to reproduce itself, over and over. Against the biological reproduction of the bourgeois family, Cahun insists on her own fecund powers of self-reproducibility and artistic creation. In the middle of the collage a tree sprouting from the navel of a naked torso gives birth to an eye, an ear, a nose, lips and a hand, a clear homage to the five senses that inaugurate both artistic creation as well as libidinal desire. In this work, the bracketed "self-pride" of the title demands the recognition of the subject beyond the confines of heterosexual reproduction and the bourgeois family.[6] Like other women couples of the period (Gertrude Stein and Alice B. Toklas, Adrienne Monnier and Sylvia Beach, Bryher and H.D., Natalie Barney and Romaine Brookes, Radclyffe Hall and Una Troubridge) who resisted the social and biological imperatives of traditional female roles and opted for same-sex partnerships, the relationship between Cahun and Malherbe signals the importance of female artistic collaboration as an alternative to bourgeois heterosexual marriage. As such creative self-invention and intimate artistic collaboration become important themes in Cahun's work, ones that register lesbian desire and artistic creation as alternatives to conventional social and sexual hierarchies and practices.

The theme of creative self-invention, and its Freudian associations with the fantasy play of childhood, becomes the focus of what is perhaps one of Cahun's most extraordinary portraits: the doll and dresser self-portrait from 1932 (see Plate 4). In this image Cahun becomes a life-size doll, lying on the shelf of a large open Victorian wardrobe (an image which renders literal Sedgwick's epistemology of the closet argument *avant la lettre*). Here Cahun's own body becomes an automaton-like creature, an Olympia yet to be woken by its master, one arm hanging limp over the edge of the dresser drawers ready to be brought back to life. In this image, Cahun's compact and fragile body contrasts with the ornate and imposing solidity of the Victorian closet, which partially conceals and frames it. This self-portrait forms an interesting comparison with an image from Hans Bellmer's *Poupée* Series, in which one of his mannequin dolls is placed in the open section of a kitchen dresser. In this image, which is dated a few years after Cahun's, we are confronted with the uncanny fusing of the domestic and the everyday, the arcane and perverse. The strangled torso and limbs of Bellmer's doll sit awkwardly with the domestic utility of the kitchen dresser, establishing a Surrealist sensibility of disjunction as well as the uncanny. Bellmer's doll series represents the return of the childhood nursery; as the ultimate plaything the doll signifies the world of desire in the childhood act of dismembering and assembling. In Cahun's image the doll-like figure within the domestic frame of the wardrobe symbolizes the child's love of self-transformation and dressing-up, suggesting death and self-renewal rather than sadistic violence. The strange serenity of the photograph invokes the sense of a child, exhausted by its masquerading reverie, having fallen asleep in the midst of play. The portrait's lyricism reinforces the memento mori effect of the photographic image, its ability to halt time and encrypt its subject in a death-like pose. The doll's limpness becomes a sign of impending rigor mortis; the closet shelves its coffin.

The Surrealist fascination with the automaton or doll is a fascination with the unconscious as well as with the uncanny. Hans Bellmer's *Poupée*, inspired by Offenbach's *Tales of Hoffman*—which itself forms a central part of Freud's essay on the uncanny—is a particularly striking example of the operation of the uncanny in Surrealism. Describing the uncanny as the return of the familiar in an unfamiliar form, Freud suggests that the uncanniest objects are "wax-works figures, ingeniously constructed dolls and automata" (1929: 347), precisely because they invoke an indeterminacy that unsettles our normal understanding of what they represent. Freud's elaborate discussion of the etymological significance of the term *unheimlich* reveals that "*heimlich* is a word the meaning of which develops in the direction of ambivalence, until it finally coincides with its opposite, *unheimlich*" (347). Heimlich, therefore, means not only homely and familiar but also hidden and secret. Freud suggests that automata are uncanny precisely because they remind us of the return of something from an earlier period of time, either an infantile narcissism or a primitive animism, which should have been overcome in the course of social and individual development. The uncanny is therefore that which should have remained repressed and part of the unconscious but which has resurfaced. In her reading of the importance of the uncanny to Surrealism, Elizabeth Wright suggests that the doll Olympia in Hoffman's story "serves as an ideal mirror image by means of which the suffering protagonist unsuccessfully tries to reconstruct his shattered self-image" (1990: 272). She argues that just as "the favored object turns into an object of fear … the beautiful Olympia … turn[s] into a rigid automaton which [is] dismembered before the protagonist's eyes" (272). The doll and the mask thus become harbingers of death: as inanimate objects that take on animation they remind us of our own trajectory toward death, thereby tracing the etymological trajectory of the word *heimlich* toward its opposite, *unheimlich*. It is within this schema that the familiar can become unfamiliar and terrifying.

Bellmer's dolls, as I have suggested, uncover the world of the imagination as a primordial return to the assembling and dismembering of childhood play, a kind of play, Freud reminds us, in which living and inanimate objects are not sharply distinguished (355). The indeterminacy of the living and inanimate, the familiar and the strange that define a Freudian uncanny are evoked in Bellmer's dolls through, what Hal Foster suggests, are a forcing together of a series of polar opposites: sex and death, the erotogenic body and a dismembered body, innocent play and sadomasochistic aggression (1993: 102). Foster argues that in working over cathected memories, Bellmer "restages primal fantasies and/

or traumatic events concerning identity, difference and sexuality" (102), and in so doing childhood fantasies become sadomasochistic events in which "construction as dismemberment"—Krauss's term—"signifies both castration (in the disconnection of body parts) and its fetishistic defence (in the multiplication of these parts as phallic substitutes)" (103). In suggesting that the key to his own work lies in the anagram: "The body is like a sentence that invites us to rearrange it" (cited in Foster, 1993: 103), Bellmer points to the significance of the uncanny in the very conception of his dolls; it is precisely their anagrammatic quality ("construction as dismemberment" and its opposite) that performs the trajectory of the *heimlich* into its opposite. In becoming the stage on which male aggression and sexual fantasy are performed, the shattered and reassembled female body serves as a reminder of the male subject's own fragmentation and the threat to his bodily boundaries. As phallic substitutes, the dolls reveal the threat of castration and the ambivalence of sexual difference, but in their unveiling of a castration anxiety they nevertheless reinforce stereotypes of women as masochistic, as infantilized objects of desire.

On the other hand, Cahun's human doll, through its memento mori effect, stages its own sleep/death as a reminder of renewed life, of the possibility of change and transformation. Like her masks and costumes, Cahun's human doll registers the active transformation of the self into a work of art and the fantasy of self-renewal this entails. If the uncanny represents the return of the repressed, its ultimate subversion lies in the possibility that the existing repression may be reconfigured. As Wright argues, the uncanny may represent that moment in which we come to the realization that the old repression has ceased to be of value and that a redirection of that desire is needed (1990: 275). In presenting us with a doll-like human, rather than the more ubiquitous human-like doll—the avatar of the uncanny—Cahun defamiliarizes the uncanny itself, redirecting our reading of it, away from a Freudian and Surrealist uncanny immersed in the violation of the female body. In both Freud and Bellmer's illustration of the uncanny, the doll represents the passive feminine object who merely reflects male desire and identity, albeit one in crisis. Cahun's Olympia, however, is no "object to be destroyed"; although fragile and vulnerable, she evokes the potential for self-transformation as well as self-mastery.

In the context of the other self-portraits from this period, which develop an elaborate rhetoric of costume, the closet or wardrobe in this image becomes symbolic of masquerade itself. The inert body of the doll-like Cahun is literally framed by the open shelves of the closet so that body and closet resonate in a series of binaries: photograph and frame, inside and outside, open and closed, concealed and displayed, familiar and strange, figurative and literal. Through the intimation of what lies hidden in its drawers and behind it doors and what lies outside the photograph—the masks and costumes, the secret desires and identities that will be constructed and reconstructed, performed and paraded in a myriad disguises and costumes, male and female, theatrical and workaday—the closet and its (hidden) contents become a trope for identity itself. So while many of the portraits shore up oppositional categories as implicit to identity formation, they also reveal the instability of those categories against the social imperatives to maintain them. As such Cahun's question, "What do you want from me?" stages the crisis of identity as internal as well as external to the subject: the self's internal drama between the narcissistic desire for an ego-ideal and the subject's sense of impending fragmentation in the face of material and social demands. Breton's question "Who am I?," framed as it is within the context of the great men of history as he ponders the similarities and differences between his and Rousseau's autobiographical projects, already assumes a certain stability of professional identity, if not notoriety, outside the text. For Breton the question is, who am I in terms of a writing self and what unique contribution, along with the other great men of history, can I make to the history of the self-examining writing subject? For Cahun, self-interrogation and self-invention operate as a dual mechanism that insists on the cycle of life and death in all aesthetic production. As an artist and writer, theater performer and political activist occupying multiple positions across disparate avant-garde and professional coteries, Cahun's self-portraits produce a rich archive of the subject that points to its mutability in life as it is in art.

Notes

1 My focus on Cahun in this chapter and the following one is confined to the period from the early 1920s through to the late 1930s since this was the period in which Cahun's interests across a range of artistic movements and intellectual disciplines coincided with her intense photographic scrutiny of the self. Cahun's move to the Isle of Jersey in 1937 reduced the range of these activities and subsequently marked a shift in the photographic work she produced. As Shelley Rice suggests, "These pictures are different from the earlier ones; focusing less on the body and more on landscape and the environment, the later works are transformations not of the self but of space … Unable to move, Cahun created a global space in her own backyard; her domestic environment is transformed in these tiny black-and-white snapshots into a world theatre" (1999: 23).

2 See Abigail Solomon-Godeau, "The Equivocal 'I': Calude Cahun as Lesbian Subject" and Katharine Conley, "Calude Cahun's Iconic Heads: From 'The Sadistic Judith' to *Human Frontier*."

3 See Eve Kosofsky Sedgwick and Adam Frank, "Shame in the Cybernetic Fold: Reading Silvan Tomkins" in *Shame and Its Sisters: A Silvan Tomkins Reader.*

4 Susan Sontag echoes Benjamin and Cahun when she suggests that "Surrealism lies at the heart of the photographic enterprise" because "Surrealism has always courted accidents, welcomed the uninvited, flattered disorderly presences. What could be more surreal than an object which virtually produces itself, and with a minimum of effort?" (1977: 52).

5 In the "Second Manifesto of Surrealism" Breton famously writes of "a certain point of the mind at which life and death, the real and the imagined, past and future, the communicable and the incommunicable, high and low, cease to be perceived as

contradictions" (1972: 123). This has been interpreted by Hal Foster as evidence of Breton's reinscription of the normative function of the aesthetic (1997: 111).

6 It seems that there is much work to be done on the collaboration between Cahun and Malherbe. Although there has been a great deal of emphasis on Surrealist collaboration, it has largely been in terms of the configuration of heterosexual partnership. See Suleiman (1994), Hubert (1994) and Chadwick and de Courtivron (eds) (1993).

Chapter 5

Fashioning the Lesbian Subject of Surrealism

> Hermaphrodite can visit the house of Narcissus—and introduce himself there on my behalf.
>
> —Claude Cahun, *Heroines*

Introduction

Rather than read Cahun's self-portraits as a straightforward engagement with avant-garde aesthetics, I want to suggest that they reflect other cultural, material and intellectual transformations within modernity; including the science of sexology with its labelling of new kinds of bodies and desires, the importance of fashion in shifting the appearance of women within metropolitan public life across popular and avant-garde cultural domains, and the central role of photography in making visible new kinds of modern identities. In 1922 Cahun moved to Paris with Suzanne Moore, setting up house in the Montparnasse quarter. Here she formed close associations with Adrienne Monnier and Sylvia Beach (of whom she produced a portrait), becoming a regular visitor to the *Aux Amis des Livres* on the rue de l'Odeon. Indeed before Cahun became involved with Surrealism and the AEAR, her interests were incredibly eclectic and included the world of journalism, publishing for both the literary mainstream and avant-garde press, and the world of experimental theater. As a translator of Havelock Ellis's work in the late 1920s and as a contributor to *L'Amitié*, France's first homosexual review, Cahun was also an important participant in the emerging debates around homosexual identity. In 1928 she completed a translation of Havelock Ellis's *Études de psychologie sociale*, publishing "La femme dans la Société. I. L'hygiène sociale" the following year in *Mercure de France*. As with other lesbian women of Cahun's generation—including Radclyffe Hall—photographic portraiture became an important mode of technological self-invention, one that reflected both the tumultuous transformation of women's fashion in the years following the war as well as the drive for a distinctive sartorial style predicated on a more radical sexual and political reconfiguration of the self. Cahun's appearance, like Hall's, thus produces a prescient account of how the relatively new technologies of photography and sexology coalesce in a striking way around the increasingly visible lesbian subject.[1]

Fashioning Modernity

In 1926 Janet Flanner wrote: "Women have looked the same for two years. By day they look like boys and by night they look like female impersonators" (quoted in Benstock, 1986: 111). Flanner's "Letter from Paris," published fortnightly in *The New Yorker*, from 1925–39, was remarkable for its wide-ranging chronicle of the social and cultural landscape of Paris between the wars. Alongside astute observations about the changing economic and social conditions for ordinary French women, including a lengthy piece on French feminism in the year that the suffrage vote went before the French Assembly, were reviews of fashion shows and couturiers, art openings, automobile shows, the ballet, cinema, as well as her intimate and often wry portraits of the various literary and avant-garde figures who had made Paris their home. Flanner's eclectic eye revealed the subtle ways in which everyday modern culture and the concerns of literary and artistic coteries were never as discrete as they often appeared. For example, in her 1927 profile on the dancer, Isadora Duncan, Flanner observed how artistic style and performance had influenced women's sartorial decorum: "A Paris *couturier* once said women's modern freedom in dress is largely due to Isadora. She was the first artist to appear uncinctured, barefooted, and free" (1972: 29). In her observations on the *garçonne* look and women's new sense of sartorial freedom, Flanner documents the momentous changes in women's fashion since the war. It is surely no coincidence that Cahun's most extensive body of self-portraits was produced throughout the 1920s—the period in which the instability of gender identity finds its full expression in various sites of consumer culture.

The variety of costumes in Cahun's self-portraits reveal a fascination with the way in which clothes themselves can consciously create gendered ambiguity and which reflects a widespread shift in women's fashion and the confusion of reading dress codes as signs of sexual identity. During the 1920s female fashion garments and style were increasingly masculinized so that by the late 1920s the figure of the masculine woman had become a prevalent style among fashionable heterosexual women. As Laura Doan has noted, female masculinity was not always linked or associated with same-sex desire or lesbian behavior. In "Passing Fashions: Reading Masculinities in the 1920s," Doan reveals how style and fashion for women in the decade after the war became particularly ambiguous. Looking at a fashion spread from a 1926 issue of *Eve: The Lady's Pictorial* Doan writes:

> *Eve* depicts a virtual panorama of what might be called the "passing fashions" of the 1920's: active women moving into the once exclusively masculine preserve of motorboat racing and yachting, rakishly boyish society women, a cross-dressed artist, and an actor posing as a tomboy. (1998: 667)

Doan, therefore, warns against interpreting the performance of masculinity within fashion culture as necessarily a sign of sexual subversion since many fashion-conscious women of all sexual persuasions were obliged to "cross-dress" to a certain extent by cutting their hair short and donning boyish or mannish attire. However, the panorama of "passing fashions" available to the readers of *Eve* strikes a powerful chord with Cahun's own use of recreational and sporting costumes, many of which appear to play up the ambiguity of gendered identity informing consumer and print culture throughout the 1920s. In a portrait from 1920, Cahun appears in the costume of a sailor; wearing wide-leg trousers, a white polo-neck jumper and a sailor's hat, her legs solidly astride and her hands on her hips. In this portrait it is unclear whether Cahun is simply masquerading as a sailor, her costume and stance performing the concomitant masculine attributes of freedom and independence, or simply exploring the new kinds of "fashions" and "roles" now available to women? In another series from 1927 (see Plate 5), Cahun camps up the professional costume of the boxer or gymnast. Appearing with a hand painted dumb-bell, kiss curls framing her face and love hearts painted onto her cheeks, the words "Do not kiss me, I am in training" written across her chest, Cahun, in camp theatrical style, masquerades as the "show-off" boxer or sporting man.[2] In another portrait Cahun dons a pair of aviation goggles, revealing a wry similarity to Man Ray's portrait of Breton in aviation goggles, as well as recalling images of pioneering women such as Amelia Earhart and the frequency with which Earhart appeared in the daily press, in her flying suit and goggles. Women's increasing participation in a wide range of recreational activities—such as motoring, boating, tennis and walking—contributed to the development of women's sports or leisure wear and which accounted for many of the "passing fashions" of the 1920s. Earhart herself attempted to market her own line of leisure wear, including a version of the black cotton flying suit she wore in her flight across the Atlantic in 1928.[3] While Cahun's parade of costumes might borrow from the visual language informing the Modern Woman's burgeoning spirit of adventure and the ambiguity of gender that accompanied her new self-image, they also reveal a sardonic use of quotation and mimicry that is a unique expression of her experimental "theater" of gendered and sexual performance. The appearance of a cross-dressed artist in the pages of a mainstream fashion magazine, however, illustrates the cross-fertilization of popular and avant-garde culture through the medium of fashion. Certainly not all fashion conscious Parisian or London women replicated the "passing fashions" which appeared in magazines throughout the 1920s, nor was cross-dressing always a sign of radical gendered or sexual expression. The widespread consumption of such images, however, significantly expanded the visual rhetoric of clothing, making fashion an important site for women's cultural and individual expression.

As a powerful visual language as well as an important cultural commodity for women, writers such as Janet Flanner and Gertrude Stein saw fashion as an important subject for their journalistic forays. Radclyffe Hall and her partner Una Troubridge were both avid readers of fashion magazines while Stein in her later years was dressed by one of the leading couturiers of the day, Pierre Balmain. Attending one of Balmain's shows, as if it were one of the many exhibition openings she had attended throughout her life, Stein was moved to write rapturously of his costuming genius for *Vogue*. As a young writer, practicing the craft of journalism, Cahun also produced essays on fashion for the consumption of her family members and friends. Far from being seen as a frivolous interest or as a straightforward sign of sexual orientation, lesbian women in Paris and London were often keen consumers of fashion, though the styles they adopted were as diverse as their literary or artistic tastes. Within both Cahun's self-portraits *and* the pages of fashion magazines as well as in the observations of women's sartorial style made by Flanner, Stein and others throughout the 1920s, fashion signals complex questions around the performance of gendered and sexual identity between the wars, reflecting the association of the changing style of women's fashion with her newfound political freedom, social independence and visibility.

If writers such as Stein and Flanner took the subject of fashion seriously, this more or less reflected wider sociological interest in reading discreet cultural formations such as fashion as an important lens through which to chart social change; in this sense clothes were increasingly seen as a prosthetic extension of the rapidly changing modern subject. Georg Simmel, writing against the backdrop of the suffragette movement, for which he had great sympathy and support, as early as 1905, provided an important correction to the pervasive correlation of women's oppression and "weak sensibilities" with a narcissistic love of clothes. Contrary to these prevailing sentiments Simmel suggested that women's avid interest in clothes served "a kind of mask;" a creative subterfuge that could act as either an important supplement to women's lack of social standing or similarly demonstrate their newfound social mobility and visibility (1997:197–8). In providing a more subtle account of women's attraction to clothes, Simmel demonstrated the underlying contradiction of fashion's propensity to individualize and homogenize, which precipitated a rethinking of the psychological vicissitudes of clothing rituals in the context of the rapidly changing roles men and women performed within modernity. It was, however, J.C. Flugel, whose important psychoanalytical study of clothes and fashion was published in 1930 by the Woolf's Hogarth Press in association with the Institute of Psychoanalysis, who developed the most systematic account of fashion and sexual difference. In *The Psychology of Clothes* and his later work, *Men and their Motives* (1934) Flugel provided an analysis of the way in which political and social change effect vestimentary codes and how clothing produces and reflects both somatic and psychic traits within the individual. For Flugel, sexual difference is created in part through men's and women's different habits and conventions with regard to clothing or fashion. In fact, the strength of Flugel's argument lies in his observations that in the process of socialization, as the human infant moves from its sexually undifferentiated state into one in which he or she is marked culturally through the successful attainment of masculinity and femininity, clothes become one of the means in which the reality of sexual difference is experienced, as both a somatic disposition and as an internal drama of the psyche. In other words clothing and fashion play a key role in the construction and maintenance of both gendered and sexual identity. Likening fashion to a neurotic symptom, Flugel claimed that the wearing of clothes becomes a perpetual compromise between modesty and eroticism. Since society represses overt sexuality, fashion becomes one of the mediums in which to reveal it covertly. Implicit in Flugel's analysis is the increasing awareness of the way in which clothes become codes for both gendered differentiation as well as sexual desire.

In its time Flugel's work was the definitive study of sexual difference and fashion, which was not only the most extensive work to incorporate Freud and psychoanalysis into its focus but was also framed within a wider social reformist agenda, including the reform of anti-homosexual laws and men's clothing styles. Inspired by the great change in women's clothes between the wars, Flugel noted how sartorial extravagance and variability is encouraged in women but not men. Tracing the decline in male sartorial display from the end of the eighteenth century under the label, "The Great Male Renunciation," Flugel observed how men's clothes have become increasingly uniform and sombre; a shift he links to the democratization of the social classes since the industrial revolution. But perhaps the most interesting aspect of this thesis is his account of the psychoanalytical vicissitudes that have resulted from this renunciation, insisting that men's new plainer style of dress has suppressed or at least diverted his narcissistic tendencies:

> Certain changes that have taken place during the last hundred years or so point to a remarkable repression of Narcissism amongst men—a repression that has at any rate not taken place to a corresponding extent among women … all originality or beauty in clothing (to say nothing of the even more direct gratification of narcissism in actual bodily exposure) being reserved for women. (*Men and their Motives*, 1934: 65)

In his extremely savvy account of the decline of male sartorial display, Flugel reveals how previous exhibitionistic and narcissistic desires which were expressed through the sumptuousness of aristocratic costume, are now channeled into a professional display of "showing off"—through spectator sports such as boxing in which the power and display of the masculine body becomes a vicarious form of exhibitionistic behavior. As a result, Flugel argues, men's psychoanalytical make-up has shifted from "(passive) exhibitionism to (active) scopophilia (pleasure in the use of vision)—the desire to be seen being transformed into the desire to see" (*Psychology of Clothes*, 1930: 118). Flugel's argument that men now gain pleasure through looking at women (and at certain types of men, such as the sporting hero), rather than in their own self-display, offered a fairly radical reading, for its time, of scopophilia; one that suggests a phallic overdetermination for women at the expense of phallic loss for men. Like Simmel, but far more radically, Flugel refuses the more ubiquitous reading of fashion that explicitly denigrated women's propensity for adornment. Rather, he suggests that it is men who have experienced a far greater sense of psychic loss in having to give up sartorial display. Women, on the other hand, he implies, have newly acquired a sense of how clothing functions as a sign of originality and self-invention rather than simply one of feminine lack.

In striking ways Cahun's portraits seem to explore the relationship between narcissism, clothing fetishism and subject formation in a way that corresponds with Flugel's radical social critique of gender, sexuality and fashion. For Flugel, clothes become a way of supplementing or extending the self; in this sense women's avid interest in clothes assumes an authority of self-invention, not so readily available to the male subject for whom narcissism has been repressed. While a number of critics have connected Cahun's work with Riviere's account of feminine masquerade,[4] Cahun's performance of a range of masculinities and femininities as well as her public cross-dressing, functions very differently to Riviere's reading of feminine masquerade as a ruse to hide the possession of masculine authority. Riviere's notoriously opaque contention that there is no difference between the mask of womanliness and what lies beneath, suggests on the one hand that femininity is performance rather than essence but on the other it also hints at the intractability of the feminine mask. Flugel's argument, I would suggest, more directly implies that femininity and masculinity are equally forms of masquerade, their difference residing in the production of either narcissistic or voyeuristic pleasure. That an early version of Flugel's argument appeared in the same issue of the *International Journal of Psychoanalysis* that carried Joan Riviere's essay, "Womanliness as a Masquerade," underscores the anxieties around women's professional and public performance during a period, the late 1920s, in which clothing styles for women increasingly conveyed ambiguous gendered and erotic codes. In Cahun's self-portraits clothing fetishism reveals the arbitrary signs attached to fashion statements and indeed the very codes of gendered identity they supposedly reflect.

Photography, Sexology and the Visible Lesbian Subject

In tracing the rise of photography in the late nineteenth and early twentieth century, John Tagg points to the contradiction between photography as a technology of surveillance and its more democratic presence in an ever-wider amateur market. Increasingly portrait photography became a new form of consumption, one, which conferred particular kinds of social status. Tagg suggests that the photographic portrait functioned as "a sign whose purpose is both the *description* of an individual and the *inscription* of social identity" (1988: 37 [my emphasis]). Similarly, Elizabeth Wilson argues that the widespread consumption of fashion photography through magazines as well as the ubiquitous rise of the snapshot in amateur photography contributed to a more self-conscious individual, one who was ultimately more attuned to her or his appearance, self-presentation and performance in public life (1985: 158). At the same time the consumption and circulation of sexological material by literary and artistic women in the decades following the publication of Havelock Ellis' *Sexual Inversion* (1897) and Edward Carpenter's *The Intermediate Sex* (1908) contributed to a greater self-consciousness around lesbian identity.[5] The emergence of a visible lesbian subculture can thus be connected to both the rise of sexology, which mapped in detail the visible somatic signs of what Havelock Ellis called female sexual inversion and the widespread use of snapshot and studio portrait photography as a means to record and extend the subject's individual and social identity.[6] Cahun's interest in debates about same-sex desire, including her journalistic account of the British controversy over Maud Allan's performance of Oscar Wilde's *Salome* in 1918 and her involvement on the fringes of the lesbian coteries of Paris, provide an important context for situating her public cross-dressing and her increasingly theatrical performance of gendered identity in the self-portraits.

The fashionable figure of the lesbian was immortalized by Radclyffe Hall throughout the 1920s and 1930s through a series of photographic portraits she commissioned of herself dressed in a manner reminiscent of the nineteenth-century figure of the dandy. These portraits came to represent a uniquely flamboyant style which was read at the time as a sign of her increasingly public lesbian persona, what Terry Castle calls Hall's "lesbian high style," one which is in many ways not dissimilar to Cahun's own use of the dandyesque effect, particularly in the early self-portraits. Cahun's own Anglophile upbringing as well as her participation in the lesbian literary scene in Paris, would have brought her into contact with Hall's world, if only tangentially. Like Cahun, Hall was immensely interested in the work of Havelock Ellis, whose attempts to provide a congenital explanation of homosexuality paved the way for a scientific justification for the rights of homosexual men and women. In preparation for her novel, *The Well of Loneliness*, Hall read the work of contemporary sexologists which confirmed her view of her own sexuality as in-born rather than acquired. Her novel explicitly takes up the theories of both Ellis and Kraft-Ebbing, at times almost reproducing particular descriptions of lesbians from their case studies: "the air of degradation and vice that hangs over the lesbian fraternity in Stephen's story is a vision of homosexuality which smacks strongly of Kraft-Ebbing's morbid case histories" (Baker, 1985: 218). Kraft-Ebing appears in the novel as the distinguished father of sexology; his work, *Psychopathia Sexualis*, discovered by Stephen in her father's study after his death, her name inscribed by him in the margins of the text in what is clearly a signal to the reader of the didactic element of Hall's novel. Indeed as Laura Doan has shown, a primary motive for writing *The Well*, was Hall's desire to popularize sexology by making it available to the public in a more easily digested form (2001).

The central argument of Ellis's "Sexual Inversion in Women" is the assumption of "a certain degree of masculinity" in all female inverts as well as "a disdain for the petty feminine artifices of the toilet" (1897/1936: 94). But tellingly, Ellis also noted "a woman who is inclined to adopt the ways of men is by no means necessarily inverted" (94). In arguing that female inversion was congenital, and therefore incurable, Ellis associated female homosexuality with a set of clearly defined cross-gendered characteristics. Despite Ellis's tendency to eclipse a multivalent notion of homosexual desire (for example he failed to account fully for masculinity that is present in non-homosexual women or those inverts who although not masculine themselves are nevertheless attracted to masculine women), he was sympathetically viewed by many homosexual men and women, including Hall, who found in his work an important rationalization for legal and social tolerance of homosexuality. By incorporating the work of the sexologists into her novel, Hall hoped to give it a verisimilitude that would ultimately serve its polemical purpose. In a letter to her editor, Hall defended her manuscript in terms of its groundbreaking and didactic importance: "So far as I know, nothing of this kind has ever been attempted before in fiction … I have treated it as a fact of nature—a simple, though at present, tragic, fact. I have written the life of a woman who is a born invert …" (Baker, 1985: 202). Intent on cementing the ties between her didactic lesbian novel and the semi-respectable science of sexology, Hall asked Ellis to provide a preface for the work. Although Ellis was at first reluctant since *Sexual Inversion* had been banned for obscene libel in 1898, he finally consented to writing a "Commentary" to the novel, which forever connected Hall's novel to the wider project of sexology, in particular Ellis's account of sexual inversion:

> I have read *The Well of Loneliness* with great interest because—apart from its fine qualities as a novel by a writer of accomplished art—it possesses a notable psychological and sociological significance. (1929: n.p.)

It was, however, this very emphasis on explaining her character within the terms of late nineteenth- and early-twentieth-century sexology that caused such a hostile reaction from otherwise sympathetic contemporary reviewers, including the derision of Bloomsbury and the Parisian lesbian literary scene. Reflecting on the novel in later years, Janet Flanner described it as "a rather innocent and confused book" and remarked that Hall's "whole analysis was false and based on the fact that the heroine's mother, when expecting her, had hoped for a baby boy, which as a daughter, Miss Hall interpreted literally" (1973: 48). Flanner's comments reinforce the difficulty, for readers then as now, of Hall's essentialist argument but nevertheless glosses the historical importance of the work.[7] In her analysis of the hostile reaction to Hall's novel, Esther Newton has suggested: "by endowing a biological female with a masculine self, Hall both questions the inevitability of traditional gender categories and assents to it" (1989: 291). While critics have taken issue with Hall's essentialist construction of female homosexuality, Hall's portraits of lesbians in *The Well* provided a degree of verisimilitude that contributed to the visibility of the lesbian subject, both inside and outside the text. As well as drawing on the work of the sexologists, Hall had experienced first hand the lesbian artistic scene in Paris and included in her novel thinly disguised portraits of both Romaine Brooks and Natalie Barney. After the publication of *The Well* and the ensuing controversy over the obscenity trial, Hall's sartorial style became the tangible sign of her lesbian sexuality.[8] Just as Stephen's sexual attraction in the novel is mediated through her masculine clothing, her "well-tailored clothes and black slouch hat" (1929: 372), Hall's own sexuality becomes readable through her costume: in both fiction and real life masculinized sartorial style increasingly became the visible sign of lesbian sexuality, one that was afforded semi-scientific status through the widespread consumption of sexology by the literary and artistic coteries in London and Paris.

The conflation of the novel's central character with its author meant that Hall herself became the prototype of the "mythic mannish lesbian," a description that is often at odds with actual photographs of her from the 1920s and 1930s and indeed published accounts of those who met her. In recalling Hall's attendance at one of Natalie Barney's salons, Flanner in a postscript to an entry on the availability of the novel in France after it had been banned in England, provides a somewhat different portrait:

> Miss Radclyffe Hall was a strange but impressive-looking woman, short of stature, with a disproportionately large but handsomely shaped head and always with a perfect haircut. Her hands and feet were also large, as were the beautiful sapphires which she wore, one as a finger ring and one each as a cuff link. She wore beautifully tailored English suits, tight-fitting across the bosom and shoulders. In her tailoring she was indeed *une grande dame*. The Paris Latin Quarter denizens first met her at a tea (with wonderful cucumber sandwiches) at Miss Natalie Barney's, heavily attended, since *The Well of Loneliness* had aroused a great deal of curiosity, if very little admiration as a literary or psychological study. (1973: 48)

Beneath the acerbic tone of Flanner's description is a portrait of a woman, who, far from being overtly masculine, demonstrates a discriminating attention to the detail of her appearance, one that, as Flanner notes, gave the impression of a grand dame rather than a mannish lesbian. Indeed Flanner's observations of Hall's impeccable grooming and style counter Ellis's own account of the invert as someone who disdained "petty feminine artifices." While critics have noted Hall's identification with aristocratic values, including their dress, manners and politics[9], her cultivation of a masculinized flamboyant sartorial style and her avid interest in the details of fashion suggest a far more complex subversion of gender and sexuality than mere inversion. The air of aristocracy that shaped Hall's public demeanor is perhaps more closely associated with the late-nineteenth-century figure of the dandy, a figure in which the cultivation of a pseudo-aristocracy was based on personality and style rather than money and ancestry.

While the dandy was not an inherently politicized figure Baudelaire reminds us that the dandy was nevertheless a rebel since his entire modus operandi was defined through its opposition to utilitarian bourgeois values such as marriage. The dandy's increasing connection to a literary form of male homosexuality also produced a connection between the narcissism of his sexuality and a Decadent aestheticism defined in opposition to conventional bourgeois aesthetics; the dandyism practiced by Oscar Wilde was read precisely in these terms. But more generally, for Baudelaire, the figure of the dandy is a prototype of the modern cult of the self, one that sought to define the body and its everyday existence as a work of art. In this sense the dandy is both the creator of a work of art as well as its object; as pure artifice, the body of the dandy is represented as a blank slate that becomes a site for invention and performance that encapsulates the coding of modernity itself as a site of flux and innovation. In locating the figure of the dandy at precise historical conjunctures, Baudelaire points to the historical conditions that necessitate the inauguration of an autonomous social subject: "Dandyism appears above all in periods of transition, when democracy is not yet all-powerful, and aristocracy is just beginning to totter and fall" (1964: 28). In other words the dandy represents the disorder of his age, a moment in which the old has been destabilized but the new is yet to be fully coherent. Within the illegibility of social roles and norms that mark the transition of one historical period to another, the dandy uses his own "native energy" to reshape the self as an aesthetic category, a self that appears to be no longer chained to the political, social and economic conditions of his day. And yet the dandy is a figure in which paradox abounds. While on the one hand the dandy typifies the social transformation of the self within modernity, seemingly disturbing the binary conditions of gender behavior by highlighting men's capacity for artifice and self-display, his very construction, at least in Baudelaire's terms, demarcates him from an innate "natural" femininity tied to the uncontrolled forces of women's sexual appetite and desire for immediate gratification. For Baudelaire, women's inclination toward artifice highlights the natural imperfection of women's beauty which is why he so famously insists on women's incapacity for dandyism: "Woman is 'natural', which is to say abominable, therefore she is also always vulgar, which is to say the opposite of a dandy" (cited in Garelick, 1998: 34).

If Baudelaire defines women as the very opposite of the dandy, what are we to make of the similarities between this iconic figure and the masculinized self-fashioning by lesbian women such as Hall or Cahun? Given women's so-called natural love of clothes and the masculine woman's dislike of the feminine, I would argue that the figure of the female dandy disturbs both masculine and feminine stereotypes, including Baudelaire's misogynist classification of the male dandy as the very opposite of the "natural" feminine as well as sexology's straightforward portrait of the mannish lesbian. While Hall's novel internalizes to some extent a stable portrait of the mannish lesbian straight out of the textbooks of Ellis and Krafft-Ebing, her photographic appearances disrupt any singular legibility of lesbian identity since they convey the double ambiguity of gender and sexuality inherent in the figure of the female dandy; precisely because the female dandy neither completely erases the biological female body nor does it completely conform to hegemonic masculinity. While Cahun and Hall found in Ellis and the project of sexology an important and lively debate on same-sex desire,[10] in refashioning the figure of the dandy, a figure already associated with aesthetic self-invention, they contributed to the growing visibility of a lesbian self-image, albeit one that unsettles any straightforward relationship between the sexed body and gendered performance.

In a number of her self-portraits (most of them from the very early 1920s), Cahun adopts a more overtly masculinized pose and sartorial style, and which are decidedly different from the more satirical or Surrealist inflected portraits of the late 1920s and early 1930s. In these images Cahun conveys the perfected elegance and imposing attitude of the decadent dandy figure, not dissimilar to Hall's own commissioned portraits of herself as well as Romaine Brooks' painted self-portraits and portraits of friends. Without wanting to completely collapse the range of female masculinities exhibited across these portraits, there is a shared sartorial code and demeanor that persistently reminds us of the various incarnations of the dandy figure. In an early self-portrait dated from 1921, Cahun appears in a dark, almost funereal suit, its black intensity broken up by the brilliant white of a cravat and pocket-handkerchief. With close-cropped hair and a powerfully intense gaze, her masculine pose framed by a dark piece of rectangular cloth, Cahun conveys a self-conscious intensity reminiscent of Baudelaire's description of the dandy as someone who transforms their body into a work of art. Indeed the phallic power of her pose, its refusal of any association of passivity associated with being the object of the gaze, is most strongly registered by the intensity of her own gaze which confronts the viewer with an almost ironic acknowledgement of the perfection of her self-invention.[11] While there are marked differences that separate the aesthetic and political sensibilities of Hall and Cahun, their construction of a masculinized subject through photographic portraiture reveals the degree to which this medium was used to *inscribe* a particular kind of social identity. As Tagg argues photographic portraiture did not merely describe an authentic self but celebrated the subject's visible social identity through its status as a commodity. To be able to purchase such an object conveyed the sense of social mobility that the photograph also might describe. Like the dandy, the photographic portrait functioned to extend the individual and social possibilities of the self, one that opened up the fault lines between commodity and aesthetic culture.

Given the association of the dandy with male homosexual literary culture and the relative invisibility of lesbian sexuality up to this point, is it possible that lesbian women artists and writers found in this figure a socially recognized marker of gendered ambiguity, one that also more covertly registered the conflation of artistic and homosexual identity as marginal and deviant. The very public trial of Oscar Wilde had left a powerful residue of anxiety around deviant aesthetic culture that continued to be played out in the decades following his trial and imprisonment. In the lesbian circles of London and Paris, the spirit of Wilde lived on in the personality of Dolly Wilde, whom Flanner, a close friend and admirer, described as appearing at a Parisian party dressed "in the habiliments of her uncle, Oscar Wilde, looking both important and earnest" (1930/1972: 69). Evidence of Cahun's own identification with Wilde is signaled by her early adoption of the journalistic pseudonym, Daniel Douglas (a homage to Wilde's lover, Lord Alfred Douglas). It is, however, through her coverage of the sensational Billing's Trial in England in 1918, for *Mercure de France* that Cahun witnessed first hand the public and political controversy still surrounding the name of Wilde.[12] The Billing's Trial was sparked by the controversy over Maude Allan's private performance of Oscar Wilde's play, *Salomé*. Under the infamous and inflammatory heading, "The Cult of the Clitoris" the right-wing publisher and independent Member of Parliament, Noel Pemberton-Billing had linked Allan and her audience to a list of 47,000 perverts contained in a secret black book, purported to be in the possession of a certain German prince. For a nation at war, the supposed existence of the "black book" in the hands of the enemy was enough to create public hysteria over an imagined homosexual plot that threatened national morality and security. When Allan sued for obscene and criminal libel, Billing went on trial but as in the trial of Oscar Wilde, it was Allan herself who was left to defend her personal reputation and that of her art.

The parallels between Allan's failed suit against Billing and Wilde's earlier failed libel case against the Marquess of Queensbury are highlighted in Cahun's account of the trial through her focus on those aspects that concern the personal and literary reputation of Wilde. Indeed in the first few paragraphs of Cahun's editorial, she repeatedly mentions his name, rather than that of Allan, and justifies her actions by pointing to the already public scandal that has once again used Wilde's name to attack freedom of thought and literary expression.[13] Likewise the very title of her article, "La *Salomé* d'Oscar Wilde. Le procès Billing et les 47,00 pervertis du 'livre noir'" concentrates the subject of her piece with Wilde's play and *its* connection to Billing's fantasy of a homosexual conspiracy, rather than the accusations of female homosexual perversion levelled against Maud Allan. Similarly the bulk of the remaining article consists of the reproduction of direct transcripts of the cross-examination of Lord Alfred Douglas, who was produced as an expert witness by Billing. As Wilde's former lover and translator, but having subsequently converted to Catholicism and repudiated all former association with Wilde, his work and homosexuality, Douglas was constructed as an expert, though redeemed and therefore reliable, reader of Wilde's work. Claiming to have particular knowledge of what Wilde meant by his play, but shielding his own reputation by claiming to have been under the youthful influence of Wilde, "the greatest force of evil that has appeared in Europe during the last 350 years" (1918: 76), Douglas informed the court that the perversion of the play rests entirely on Wilde's use of a veiled language to convey explicit homosexual themes; and that it was customary for the sexually perverted to "dress-up immoral actions in beautiful and flowery terms" (78). The example cited to justify these claims was Wilde's use of the moon in *Salomé*, which Douglas testified was "a canvas" on which to depict "indecent and abominable pictures." Indeed Douglas concludes his testimony by claiming that whenever Wilde wanted to depict anything "horrible," he always justified it in terms of "Art" (78). After further questioning by Billing regarding Wilde's knowledge of sexology, Douglas concluded that a work such as *Salomé* could not have been written without the author having closely studied Krafft-Ebing or other such texts on sexology. Cahun further reports that in addition to Douglas, an expert witness, Dr Serrell Cooke, claiming to have been familiar with the work of sexology, in particular Krafft-Ebing's *Psychopathia Sexualis*, testified that Wilde's use of the moon in the play was designed to connote sexual perversion since he would have known that certain phases of the moon produce certain types of erotomania (1918: 79).

In focusing on the "Cult of Wilde" (Cahun includes a rather wry footnote explaining the word play on "Cult of Wilde/Wilde-Cult"), rather than the "Cult of the Clitoris," Cahun demonstrates how the trial itself, while introducing for the first time in Britain public discussion of female homosexuality, was not in essence about lesbian sexuality since its very unrepresentability, as a legal, linguistic and anatomical enigma[14], meant that the initial scandal over Allan's performance was merely a pretext to resurrect the ghost of Wilde as the most potent and public symbol of the link between sexual deviancy and aesthetics. In the fantasy of contamination and national danger that the trial enacted, Allan becomes a mere stand-in for Wilde, her sexual perversion (lesbian sexuality) subsumed under the "Cult of Wilde." In the transcripts selected by Cahun for her article, she makes apparent how the trial renders sexual and linguistic inversion a mirror image of the other, one that conjures the figure of the homosexual as narcissistic. In constructing the indecipherability of Wilde's work through the metaphors of display and artifice ("dress-up," "disguise," "flowery," "art"), Cahun reveals how Douglas produces for the court a visual reminder of Wilde's decadent dandy aesthetic, which had become, since his trial, the most legible sign of his acts of "gross indecency." But rather than provide clarity around what is or is not a homosexual text or indeed a homosexual, Cahun ironically reveals how the trial renders homosexuality as always coded and indecipherable and at the same time obvious and everywhere, producing in the process a circular argument around visibility and invisibility. Similarly, she demonstrates how the trial rendered the taxonomies produced by sexology, not as an expert knowledge, but rather as a primer for the perverted artist, a virtual glossary of "sodomite" behavior. Cahun's coverage of the Billing's trial, early in her career, brought her into contact with many of the issues—sexology and lesbian sexuality, the relationship between homosexuality and aesthetics, censorship and the freedom of artistic expression—that would resonate in her own work for many years to come. But what it also demonstrates is the degree to which her interest in and knowledge of sexual politics was inseparable from her wider political and aesthetic interests.

Investigating Sex

Mary Ann Caws presents Claude Cahun as a Surrealist heroine, who, like Nadja, is ultimately too strange and confronting for canonical Surrealism, her polymorphous unpredictability as well as her lesbian sexuality at odds with Breton's almost homophobic idealization of heterosexuality (1998: 95). However, Cahun's own work suggests a rigorous exploration of the discursive and libidinal conditions informing the theater of sexuality, which correspond in striking ways with Surrealism's own investigations into sexuality and desire. Originally published in *La Révolution surréaliste* (Nos 10–11, 1928), the "Recherches sur la sexualité" provided formal evidence of the movement's attempts to collectively formulate knowledge of the self and its "experience" of everyday practices. But while its aim was to open up discussion on sexual practices and experiences, to gather some kind of material evidence around this subject, the scientific terms of its inquiry were thwarted by the impossibility of gathering any such evidence. As such the discussions soon collapsed into disagreement over the appropriateness of certain topics; in particular, it is on the subject of "normalcy," in terms of sexual practices and desires that the discussion began to splinter. And it is Breton who defends most vehemently the concept of "a normal man." In the initial stages of the discussion, many of the participants, led on by Breton, expressed moral repugnance toward homosexuality, especially in men. But when some of the members of the group attempted to defend the moral right of homosexuals and describe their own "imagined" homoerotic desires, Breton threatens to abandon the discussion altogether. Aragon responded to Breton's threats by asking him if he condemns all sexual perversion to which Breton replies that he condemns no form of sexual perversion other than homosexuality. In other words the purported "openness" of the discussions very quickly collapsed into a rigorous policing of the terms of the inquiry. As Dean suggests

> [Breton's] problem with bourgeois morality was that it was not moral or pure enough, and he countered it with an idealized, liberated, natural heterosexuality purged of the tainted, repressed, and hence compromised bourgeois ideal of love that produced adultery, treachery, and presumably homosexuality. (78)

Michael Richardson (1998: 390) has also noted that since homosexuality in this period was defined in terms of its opposition to normative bourgeois sexuality, Breton pitted a Surrealist notion of purified heterosexuality directly against homosexuality. In essence, then, the Surrealist's, or at least Breton's, revolutionary concept of sex hinged on the way in which they came to define the notion of purity. Dean reinforces this when she argues that "Purified magical heterosexuality (Breton termed it *l'amour fou*) replaced homosexuality as the site of opposition to bourgeois culture" (1996: 78). While there is some semblance of a discussion on the nature and types of sexual perversion experienced by the participants in Breton's circle, what the discussion soon reveals is an overriding obsession with establishing "evidence" of romantic love between a man and a woman, including how to establish evidence of a woman's orgasm and whether a man is able to tell if she is faking. Although perhaps unique in its inclusion of desire and sex in its efforts to create a link between creative practice and the desiring subject, the discussions reveal a level of homophobia that diminishes the terms of the inquiry—that of radical investigation.

Michael Richardson, however, argues that Breton's homophobia was directed not so much against particular sexual acts but against the lifestyle of homosexuality:

> [I]t should be pointed out in all fairness that Breton's attitude is in part to do with the fact that during the 1920's homosexuality was a fashion among the modish set that Breton despised—his rejection of it is not so much a rejection of a particular sexual activity but lies in an equation he made between it and attitudes of superficiality and affectedness which he loathed. (390)

Richardson thus usefully points out that the slippage in translation between *homosexualité* and *pédérastie* makes our reading of Breton's homophobia more complex than it first appears:

> What is discussed is not *homosexualité* (that is homosexuality as a sexual penchant) but *pédérastie*, which has a wider range of associations than in English, meaning both pederasty and more specifically the culture of homosexuality which also identifies homosexual behaviour with superficiality and which was a prevalent attitude among French intellectuals at the time. (390)

I would suggest, however, that what Breton expresses in these discussions is disgust at the very thought of the homosexual act; a disgust that certainly may have coincided with his dislike of the cultural manifestations and institutions of homosexuality, indeed what he perceived as its widespread contamination of aesthetic culture.[15] Richardson's point, however, reminds us of the complexity of Surrealism's—in particular Breton's—attitude to sexuality. While Breton's views on sex, generally, tended toward the puritanical, as evidenced by his call for the closing of all brothels, the investigations nevertheless reveal an opening up of discussion on sexuality, one which removed love and sexuality from the sole confines of the bourgeois family. Moreover, the discussions actually revealed a great deal of disagreement among its participants over experiences of and attitudes toward sexuality, suggesting that the Surrealist's attitudes to sexuality were far more diverse than the official line put forward by Breton.

In this sense the Surrealist's investigations into sexuality disclose an ongoing discussion of sex that had been formally precipitated by both sexology and psychoanalysis, even if the terms of its inquiry revealed a much more poetic interest in the relationship between sexual desire and creative production. The rise of a sexual science at the end of the nineteenth century and at the beginning of the twentieth reflects what Foucault calls a discursive explosion on the subject; in charting the appearance of "peripheral sexualities" at the beginning of the nineteenth century, Foucault suggests that sexual practices began to be "entomologized," labelled and classified. This focus on new kinds of sexual practices aimed not simply to repress them but to give them "an analytical, permanent reality … to incorporate them into the individual" (1976: 44). Sexuality came to be redefined as central to our experience of modernity, indeed to the concept of ourselves as modern enlightened subjects. In the *History of Sexuality, Vol. 1* Foucault explores how the detail of sexual activity came to dominate not just our experience of sexuality but the core of our identity; the detail of descriptions of sexuality, the labelling of bodies, the will to knowledge about sex became integral to the concept of the modern subject. Alongside attempts to pathologize and fix sexual identity, there emerged, according to Foucault, counter practices and discourses which incorporated but also destabilized these new classificatory labels:

> There is no question that the appearance in the nineteenth century psychiatry, jurisprudence, and literature of a whole series of discourses on the species and subspecies of homosexuality, inversion, pederasty, and "psychic hermaphrodism" made possible a strong advance of social controls into this area of "perversity;" but it also made possible the formation of a "reverse" discourse: homosexuality began to speak in its own behalf, to demand that its legitimacy or "naturality" be acknowledged, often in the same vocabulary, using the same categories by which it was medically disqualified. (1984: 101–2)

Foucault's argument suggests ways in which the often prescribed discourses on sexuality—by Ellis and the Surrealists—were reinscribed by artists such as Hall and Cahun, according to their own desires and political aspirations. It also allows us to see Hall's work as both conservative and radical. As Newton cogently argues, Hall's heroine is "a double symbol, standing for the New Woman's painful position between traditional political and social categories and for the lesbian struggle to define and assert an identity" (1989: 289). While there are marked differences in their understanding and representation of sexual identity, what connects Cahun and Hall is their utilization of both sexology and photographic portraiture as a way to make visible new kinds of erotic styles and sexual identities, ones that I think, in the end, both conform to but also resist sexology's portrait of the mythic mannish lesbian. The shift in Cahun's self-portraits from a more sombre, dandyesque cross-dressing to a highly theatrical and often camp performance, one that destabilizes any clear masculine or feminine style, may indicate that Cahun was moving away from a model of sexual identity simply based on "inversion." Therefore the project of sexology and the broader discourses of sexuality that emerged in response to it, underscores Foucault's central premise that knowledge operates as both a repressive and libratory mechanism.

It is in the context of a sustained and complex exploration of the self in relation to sexual politics that Cahun's work needs to be read. Rather than associate her with the abjected figure of Nadja or the reviled homosexual figure of Bretonian Surrealism, I want to suggest that her work inserts into the Surrealist project an important rethinking of gender, sexuality and representation, interrogating the rigid categories that often define and implement a Surrealist politics and aesthetics: the polemical categories of male and female as well as heterosexuality and homosexuality. Cahun's interdisciplinary concerns around the relationship between art and sexuality self-consciously play out what Eve Sedgwick has referred to as the fundamental concern of modernity, "the crisis of individual identity and figuration itself" (1990: 83). In connecting artistic production and sexual identity in her aptly titled essay "Poetry Keeps Its Secret," Cahun establishes her interest in philosophical debates on sexuality, in particular contemporary discussions on "sexual inversion" within the framework of her aesthetic and political allegiance to Surrealism. Given the extraordinary details of Claude Cahun's life, it is uncanny that her work, as well as the details of her identity passed into complete obscurity after the Second World War. It seems extraordinary that someone whose appearance was as remarkable as Cahun's and whose work engaged with some of the most important philosophical and aesthetic issues of her day, could pass into complete obscurity.[16] Of course this unfolds the historical removal of women in the Surrealist movement in the course of its institutionalization, in spite of their troubling and often very visible presence. Since the rediscovery of these works, however, Cahun has come to be recognized as one of the most important Surrealist photographers, as well as one of its most inspired female theorists and political activists.

By Way of Conclusion: Krauss and Cahun

In the last part of this chapter I want to take up Rosalind Krauss's attempts to situate Cahun's work within a Surrealist framework. Moreover, I examine why Krauss chooses Cahun to mount a defence of her own critical practices, in particular her reading of the violence of much Surrealist imagery within the rubric of an "ungendered sadism." While I agree with Krauss that Cahun's work occupies an important place within the Surrealist movement, I argue that it does so as part of a wider engagement with questions of sexual politics and erotic style implicit to and explicit in her own experience as a lesbian. As I have indicated, Cahun's life and work forms a matrix of varying discourses and competing narratives and cannot simply be read solely within the context of a Surrealist avant-garde aesthetic. But in order to understand Krauss's reading of Cahun's work, I think it is important to revisit her extremely finessed reading of Surrealist photography.

In taking up Benjamin's analysis of photography's disclosure of an optical unconscious, Krauss suggests that Surrealist photography introduces a kind of temporal deferral through its use of montage and other distorting techniques. In her discussion of the ubiquitous use of the double in Surrealist photography, she writes:

> The double is the simulacrum, the second, the representative of the original. It comes after the first, and in this following, it can only exist as figure, or image. But in being seen in conjunction with the original, the double destroys the pure singularity of the first. (1985: 109)

According to Krauss, the frequent use of "doubling" within Surrealist photographic images represents the "blind, irrational space of the labyrinth," an optical unconscious that goes "against the grain of modernist opticality" (1993: 21). In her later essay on Cahun, Krauss suggests that Cahun's frequent "doubling" of her various identities and personae represents a kind of Deleuzian "fold," whereby the process of masking and doubling interrogates both the gaze of the viewer as well as the static positioning of the subject (1999: 47). Although Krauss's words illuminate the wider project of Surrealist photography and at times Cahun's own photographic practice, I think that Cahun's use of "doubling" alongside other photomontage techniques such as blurring and distortion also reference a crisis of identity and representation, one that destabilizes the centrality of heterosexuality within Surrealist politics and aesthetics. What seems to be missing in Krauss's account of Cahun's self-portraits is Cahun's own attempts to situate the decentered subject within the framework of an explicit sexual politics, which alongside her interest in contemporary sexological discussions of "sexual inversion," contests a straightforward incorporation of Surrealist aesthetic practices and sexual ideology. Certainly there is a sense of gender fluidity at the heart of Cahun's aesthetic practice, one that refuses the static positioning of the subject. But Cahun's repeated construction and scrutiny of her own body infers a political and aesthetic reversal of the heterosexist eroticization and commodification of the female body within Surrealist art practice and its avowedly strong reliance on a Freudian psychoanalytical economy. In collapsing the relationship between artistic and bodily performance, Cahun demands that we address all that she is: photographer, Surrealist, lesbian, actress, political activist, journalist etc. and all that she possibly could be—sailor, aviator, wrestler etc.; that is, she demands that we attend to the shifting registers of identity and subjectivity and to the competing disciplinary boundaries of her art practice and intellectual and political concerns.

In reading Cahun's portraits as a strategy to "declassify," Krauss argues that they resemble Bataille's obsession with "formlessness," with "a kind of categorical blurring" (1999: 5). I would argue, however, that Cahun is acutely interested in the process of classification and photography's role in rendering the subject's proximity to the work of art and the consumer object. Although Krauss wants to render the violence of much Surrealist iconography—from the slit eye in Bunuel and Dali's *Un chien Andalou* to the repeated violent displacement of body organs in Bataille's *Story of the Eye*—as "ungendered sadism," particularly in relation to the violent and destructive nature of formlessness in Bataille's work, that is, the horror of "a labyrinthine loss of distinction" (7), there is a sense in which this reading does not hold up in relation to Cahun's self-portraits. Although Cahun's work points to a sense of crisis for the modern sexual subject, she does so without resorting to the violence implicit in more canonical Surrealist representations of the subject's fragmentation. Cahun certainly at times employs Surrealist techniques and subject matter, incorporating many of the techniques that Krauss suggests distinguish the Surrealist photographer—double exposure, montage, solarization, sandwich printing etc.—techniques that function, according to Krauss's now well-rehearsed argument, as the "other" of straight photography, what she calls "a perverse feminization ... of the masculinist values of 'straightness' itself: clarity, decisiveness, visual mastery—all of them the source of the photographer's authority" (1985: 95). But by incorporating the lesbian subject into her portraits, Cahun performs both "straight" masculine and hyper feminine roles before the camera, complicating any straightforward association between gendered identity and erotic style or indeed any straightforward opposition between "straight" and Surrealist photographic techniques. The early "straight" portraits of herself cross-dressed tap into a partially coded representation of lesbian identity through the historically specific category of the female dandy. Many of these early portraits do not employ Surrealist distorting techniques, rather they emphasize the importance of clothes and sartorial style in registering the subject's identity, thus retaining the "authority" (albeit transgressively since she is in drag) of traditional portrait photography. In particular, Cahun's self-portrait with cravat reveals a similar "classic" and formal quality to Berenice Abbott's portrait of Janet Flanner and the many classic-styled dandyesque portraits of Radclyffe Hall. Thus Cahun's portrayal of lesbian identity, through the figure of the female dandy, points to an inherently unstable representation of sexual and gendered identity; one that mimics straightness but also distorts that straightness. While some of Cahun's portraits "master" Surrealist photographic techniques, others "mimic" the authority of straight photography, suggesting that it is precisely the photograph's "realism" that marks its authority and not a celebration of "sur-reality." As such Cahun's photographs seem to question any complete loss of form, and any complete evacuation of subject/object boundaries, but dwell in the possibility of the subject's transformation, its difference from the other and its difference from itself over time. Thus, what they repeatedly play out is Sedgwick's prosaic axiom.

The portraits contest the purity of such categories as "masculine" and "feminine" as well as "heterosexuality" and "homosexuality" within the context of a movement that often defined itself in terms of the purity of the heterosexual encounter and the fixity of gendered identity. As a lesbian who adopted a non gender-specific name and frequently cross-dressed in both private and public, Cahun seems to imagine a world where identity does not fix the individual but radically transforms the culture that would define us. Krauss's refusal to read the politics of gender and sexuality in Cahun's work seems to foreclose the multivalent possibilities opened up by her self-portraits and their modifying presence within canonical Surrealist photography. Indeed Krauss appears to close down questions of gender and sexuality in much the same way that Breton attempted to suppress any discussion of homosexual desire among the participants of their round-table discussions of sexuality. And although I don't want to discount completely Krauss's otherwise inspiring account of Surrealist photography, I think it is important in the case of Cahun's work to place questions of sexual difference and sexual orientation, or at least the possibility that she was attempting to expand the very terms of a Surrealist heterosexualization of desire, at the forefront of an analysis of her work. The evidence of her own investigations into sexuality radically transform how we might read the sexual and aesthetic codes operating within the Surrealist movement and indeed how we might attempt to come to terms with a more nuanced understanding of the politics of the sexual within Surrealism. As Breton was boisterously "silencing" discussion of homosexuality, Cahun was determinedly working away at questions of identity and representation across sexual, political and aesthetic domains, sometimes within the framework of a Surrealist aesthetic and political practice and sometimes against it. For if we read anything into these portraits, it is their "investigative" properties, their extreme openness to the question, "Who am I?"

Notes

1 I agree with Carolyn J. Dean that lesbian sexuality forms an instrumental part of Cahun's critique of transcendental aesthetics and its concomitant categorization of pure and impure art, though my reading stresses that the fashioning of the lesbian subject as a visible, though mutable, identity, bears the traces of other discourses besides aesthetics.

2 Cahun's image reminds me of the Dada boxer and poet, Arthur Craven, whose performances inside and outside the ring, seems at once to satirize and celebrate the "showing off" capacity of the boxer. Craven's boxing matches were renowned for their performative, if not slightly satirical quality.

3 In her article on Amelia Earhart's flight into the world of fashion and her own creation of a fashion label, Karla Jay reveals how this little known detail of Earhart's life has been glossed over and forgotten in an attempt to mythologize her status as an intrepid heroine (or spy?). The incongruity to that mythology of her interest in developing a line of clothes for women that would be both fashionable and comfortable reveals the disjunction between Earhart as intrepid aviator and her indulgence in the "feminine" world of fashion and clothes consciousness.

4 See Laurie Monahan, "Radical Transformations: Claude Cahun and the Masquerade of Womanliness" and Abigail Solomon-Godeau, "The Equivocal 'I': Claude Cahun as Lesbian Subject."

5 For further discussions on the influence of Ellis see Jeffrey Weeks, "Havelock Ellis and the Politics of Sex Reform."

6 The legacy of the nineteenth-century psychomedical construction of sexual identity, exemplified in the work of Havelock Ellis, Edward Carpenter and Kraft-Ebing, left an important mark on the life and work of a generation of lesbian writers and artists, women such as Radclyffe Hall, Natalie Barney and Vita Sackville-West—and also Claude Cahun. Like many lesbian women of their generation, they included themselves as the subjects of photographic portraits dressed in a range of male and female costumes—from the famous dandyesque portraits of Radclyffe Hall to the highly lyrical costumes donned by Natalie Barney in her series of masquerades of heroes and heroines of history. While fashions of this period had become more masculinized, the portraits left by these women suggest the increasing visibility of a distinctive lesbian

style. However, as the very different styles of Barney and Hall indicate, there was also a degree of diversity in terms of a distinctive lesbian sartorial style.

7 In her reading of Flanner's treatment of Hall, Shari Benstock speculates that Flanner "was annoyed, perhaps embarrassed, by Hall's emotional and stylised reenactment of lesbian relationships" (115).

8 Doan notes that during the obscenity trial for *The Well*, "[d]etailed and explicit information on lesbianism—often illustrated with arresting photos of the author—became suddenly accessible in most major newspapers …" (2001: xiii).

9 In her excellent discussion of the role of negative affect in relation to Hall's novel and the history of its critical reception, Heather K. Love argues that Stephen's "disavowal of the community of inverts is in fact underwritten by her support of masculinist, aristocratic, nationalist norms—the very standards which she is judged an outcast and a freak" (489).

10 Dean notes that "Cahun (along with Havelock Ellis and others) contributed a response to a "poll" conducted in the first issue [of L'Amitié] that asked writers (rather ironically) if and why they found the review offensive" (77).

11 Breton shunned Cahun when she appeared like this in public, avoiding his favorite café so as not to be seen in public with her. Throughout this period Cahun frequently appeared in public in similar attire, suggesting that her cross-dressing was not confined to the more or less private theater of her self-portraits but used as a sustained and disruptive element of her sexual politics.

12 Around this time Cahun seems to have dropped altogether the pseudonym Douglas, adopting Claude Cahun for this piece.

13 "La *Salomé* d'Oscar Wilde. Le procès Billing et les 47,00 pervertis du 'livre noir'," *Mercure de France*, July 1, 1918.

14 Cahun reports that the word "clitoris" was not reported in the British press because of its obscenity (69), but which the court defined as "a medical term qualifying any person who takes part in or attends performances" (69). Laura Doan argues that the criminalization of same-sex relations between women first entered legal discourse in Britain through the official record of parliamentary proceedings in 1920 (1998: 200).

15 Martica Sawin reports an incident in which Breton struck Ilya Ehrenburg, the Paris correspondent for *Izvestia*, for referring to Surrealist activity as "péderastique" (55).

16 Dean notes Cahun's exclusion from Whitney Chadwick's survey of women surrealists, *Women Artists and the Surrealist Movement.* She also reveals that one of Cahun's pieces, which had been displayed in the 1936 Surrealist exhibition of objects in London, was attributed to "Anonymous" in the Exhibition *Dada and Surrealism Reviewed*, held at the Tate Gallery (London) in 1978. In their book on Surrealist photography, *L'Armour Fou: Photography and Surrealism*, Rosalind Krauss and Jane Livingstone speculate that Cahun may have died in a concentration camp since they could find little detail of her life. Dean concludes that Cahun's displacement (or misplacement) from feminist histories of the Surrealist movement stems in part from the fact of her lesbianism, which Dean argues sits awkwardly with a movement that tied many of its aesthetic ideas to the maintenance of heterosexuality (1996).

Chapter 6

Surrealism, Violence and Censorship

Introduction

In his attempts to define postmodernism's relationship to the historical avant-garde, Matei Calinescu suggests that if the avant-garde may be typically defined through its twin tasks of destruction and innovation, postmodernism, fueled by a sense of exhaustion and scepticism, has opted for a "logic of renovation rather than radical innovation," a move which has defined its central role in terms of "a lively reconstructive dialogue with the old and the past" (1987: 275–6). It is perhaps in and through this dialogue with the past that postmodernism has absorbed its characteristic ambivalent cast; an ambivalence often defined through a mode of articulation that might be best described as a knowing return to "the already said," making irony, pastiche, parody, self-conscious nostalgia and playfulness privileged features of its aesthetic practice. As such it is not surprising that ambivalence has also dominated the various theoretical assessments of postmodernism's critical value. Frederic Jameson's seminal essay, "Postmodernism and Consumer Society" encapsulated a neo-Marxist hesitancy toward the possibility of postmodernism's criticality precisely because of its absorption of and into the logic of consumer culture. Signaling the erosion of any formal line between high culture and mass or popular culture, Jameson wrote:

> … many of the newer postmodernisms have been fascinated precisely by that whole landscape of advertising and motels, of the Las Vegas strip, of the late show and Grade-B Hollywood film, of so-called paraliterature with its airport paperback categories of the gothic and the romance, the popular biography, the murder mystery and the science fiction or fantasy novel. They no longer "quote" such "texts" as Joyce might have done, or a Mahler; they incorporate them, to the point where the line between high art and commercial forms seems increasingly difficult to draw. (1983: 128–9).

Jameson concludes his essay by mourning the loss of the subversive potential of modernism's negative aesthetics, which, whatever the specificity of its political agenda, was always implicitly at least "dangerous and explosive" in relation to "the established order," whether that included dominant bourgeois aesthetics or capitalist ideology (142). Jameson is of course more tentative about postmodernism's capacity for socio-political and aesthetic critique.

Whether or not one sees modernism as the true hero of a radical political and aesthetic modernity, what these potentially moribund debates provide here is a conceptual historical frame in which to position the critical ambivalence that has defined the reception of Cindy Sherman's work. As one of the most successful artists of her generation, whose work engages with a vast topography of commodity and consumer culture (fashion, film, pornography) as well as the history of art from the Old Masters through to Surrealism, Sherman's work exemplifies "a lively reconstructive dialogue" with both high and low cultural forms within the history of visual culture. And yet one of the most frequently cited criticisms of the work (one which echoes Jameson's own early critique of postmodernism) is that it so successfully incorporates the stereotypical and mythical codes of femininity disseminated through commodity culture that it ends up imbibing the very logic it supposedly sets out to critique. The *Untitled Film Stills* and the "Centerfolds" continue to form the focus of critical work on Sherman, and not surprisingly have attracted more censure than any of her other series, reiterating the concern that these works are too close to the "real" thing, namely Hollywood film and soft-core porn. This begs the question; what kinds of reading practices are mobilized when one series is read in isolation from the others or perhaps more importantly in isolation from the critical horizon that shapes their production and reception? While I do not want to suggest that this is never a legitimate mode of critique as obviously each series requires its own set of critical and thematic tools, it has also become clear by now that each series in Sherman's *oeuvre* forms part of a discursive arc that shapes a much broader narrative about the relationship between the past and the present. The ever-changing idiom of the work's engagement with visual cultural artefacts, represented through the often-radical departure of each new series from the previous one, also suggests a desire for the new that is nevertheless fueled by a looking back to the past.

In providing a close reading of the "Sex Pictures" (1992) in the context of Sherman's entire *oeuvre* as well as their implicit engagement with Hans Bellmer's *Poupées*, I want to examine the relationship between the past and the present as it informs each of these works as well as the relationship between them. Central to my reading is the way that Sherman's engagement with Bellmer unfolds a kind of hermeneutic retrospection that links any interpretation of Sherman's work with the attendant ambiguities around nostalgia, violence and censorship informing the creation and critical reception of Bellmer's own work. In this sense it may be worth considering how Sherman's work, and the "Sex Pictures" in particular, exhibit a logic of renovation analogous to Surrealism's own fascination with the outmoded. As Hal Foster demonstrates, one of the primary features of the outmoded, in its Surrealist incarnation, was that it not only brought the present into contact with the past but also returned the past to the present (1997: 164). If the outmoded describes a critical relationship to history that signals the return of the repressed as a moment of representational crisis in the present, an analysis of Sherman's work in these terms may be one way in which to move beyond the current critical impasse that positions the work as either the consumption of myth or as a clever deconstruction of myth.

More recently Jameson has suggested that the "reinvention of the outmoded in full postmodernity" is perhaps the most paradoxical of all its features, one that suggests a far more inextricable link between modernism and postmodernism than we might have expected:

> a dependence of the postmodern on what remains essentially modernist categories of the new .... is indeed no small or insignificant contradiction for postmodernity, which is unable to divest itself of the supreme value of innovation (despite the end of style and the death of the subject), if only because the museums and the art galleries scarcely function without it. Thus, the new fetish of Difference continues to overlap the older one of the New, even if the two are not altogether coterminous. (2002: 5)

If the New is constructed around a conscious forgetting of the past in order to imagine the artwork as the very sign of a utopian future (remembering here Breton's claim that "The work of art is valuable only insofar as it is vibrated by the reflexes of the future" (quoted in Benjamin's "The Work of Art in the Age of Mechanical Reproduction"), a fetish of Difference could be said to foreclose a utopian sense of futurity by knowingly dislodging past and present fictions of identity and power. In either case there seems to be a certain temporal amnesia that inaugurates the narratives of innovation and renovation for the projects of modernism and postmodernism respectively. Of course for Jameson, the larger issue is how late capitalism, of which postmodernism forms its most potent cultural expression, continues its expansion in the face of the crisis of a potentially limited market; thus the need for a cannibalization of the periphery or marginal (here a fetish of Difference) as well the outmoded which becomes in consumer culture the generation of a nostalgia that guarantees an endless recycling of the past. And yet could it be that the category of the outmoded itself, precisely because it traverses the temporal distinction between past and present actively confuses the difference between innovation and renovation. For Benjamin the outmoded signaled, in both redemptive and nostalgic terms, an underlying uncertainty about the acceleration of temporal experience and the expansion of commodity culture in the face of the utopian narratives of progress that accompanied it. Surrealism, too, found in the discarded and obsolete bric-a-brac of history a way to register the dialectic of innovation and ruination that underwrites the project of capitalist modernity. And yet in mobilizing the repressed desires and energies of the past "to the point of explosion" (Benjamin: 1929/1999: 210) in the present, the outmoded comes close to a logic of renovation since it too turns to the past in order to recharge the present.

From the Outmoded Film Still to the Female Body in "Ruins"

Although I will primarily focus on the "Sex Pictures" and their relation to Bellmer's work, I want to briefly trace the trajectory of Sherman's work, including its critical reception, up to this point, in order to provide a sense of how an engagement with the past haunts much of Sherman's work. While the critical reception of Sherman's work has produced heated debates as to how her work engages with feminist theories of the body and subjectivity, I will explore more fully the contested readings of Sherman's work in relation to the female subject of feminism in the final chapter, though it will be necessary to touch on some of those debates here. Firstly, however, I want to examine Sherman's critical introduction to the art world as a pre-eminently "postmodernist" artist with her first series, *Untitled Film Stills*. As so much has been written about this body of work, and since much of the ensuing critical debate has become increasingly removed from a sense of the work's moment of impact, I want to go back and examine some of those original critical insights. In his 1979 essay, "Pictures," Douglas Crimp famously cited Sherman as part of a group of emerging artists whose initial work, the *Untitled Film Stills* exemplified the "stratigraphic activity" of postmodernism. In suggesting that the *Untitled Film Stills* evoke the fragmented quality of the ordinary snapshot and the narrative sequence of film, but are actually neither, Crimp highlights the spatiotemporal confusion that presents the film still as "a narrative ambience stated but not fulfilled" (1979: 80). Quoting Barthes on Eisenstein stills, Crimp concludes that Sherman's photographs fulfil the condition of the film still, "that fragment '*whose existence never exceeds the fragment*'" (83). The "psychological shock" (87) produced by Sherman's images therefore reside in the film still's capacity to simultaneously disrupt the presence of narrative while leaving the mythic trace of the diegesis intact: in resembling "quotations from the sequence of frames that constitutes the narrative flow of film … [t]heir sense of narrative is one of its simultaneous presence and absence" (80). Crimp, however, reminds us that the self-evident "staged" quality of Sherman's work borrows not from the medium of film but from the theatrical apparatus of performance art of the 1970s, though significantly it reverses the priorities of presence and duration in the performed event through the creation of "a tableau whose presence and temporality are utterly psychologized" (77). Crimp therefore concludes that "the process of quotation, excerptation, framing, and staging" in Sherman's work uncovers the stratiform nature of representation, privileging not some original to which they might refer but to the very structures of meaning that inform her images. Crimp argues that while this might constitute postmodernism's break with modernism, it also discloses how "a theoretical understanding of postmodernism will also betray all those attempts to prolong the life of outmoded forms" (87).

There are, I think, a number of important points here that seem to have been lost in subsequent readings of Sherman's work. In the rush to give the women in the film stills fully fledged characterizations (the teenage runaway, the bit-part actress, the young lonely librarian, and so on) critics end up restoring a narrative sequence that the film still, as a fragment, necessarily disrupts. Peter Schjeldahl's 1987 essay for the catalog of the Whitney Museum exhibition of Sherman's work is indicative of such a reading:

> I find these pictures sentimentally, charming and sometimes fiercely erotic: I'm in love again with every look at the insecure blonde in the night-time city … (1987: 7)

Even apart from the reductive assertion that the projection of female vulnerability is the defining topos of these images, Schjeldahl's construction of a familiar melodrama of the insecure woman in the city waiting to be ravished/rescued by her hero, restores a fully coherent diegesis to a fragment that contains only the suggestion of "narrative ambience." As Barthes showed, in his reading of the Eisenstein still, it is precisely the foreclosure of full narrative that offers new kinds of affective depth in the film still or still photograph, a depth not found in film because it declares up front its emotional register through the temporal continuity of its narrative. As such the film still as fragment allows the possibility of reading against the grain of the narrative ambience invoked by the image. Of course Barthes' reading gives over formidable power to the critic since an affective reading is necessarily defined through a subjective relation to the image at hand. In this sense we could say that Schjeldahl's longing for narrative, where there is only an ambiguous suggestion of narrative mood, discloses more about his own desires and insecurities as a critic than those of the woman in the image, reminding us of Sherman's own canny observation that with this series she was trying to make people recognize something of themselves, rather than herself (1986). Moreover, what such a reading forecloses is precisely their staged quality and the obvious fact that these are different self-portraits, different appearances, of a single woman, who is both behind and in front of the camera. This of course sets up a tension between subject and object, between self and image, which creates a disjunctive rupture between our immediate sense of the work, their staged, surface effect, and their ambiguous coding within a popular and aesthetic visual and cultural context. Just as Cahun's own self-portraits render Sedgwick's seemingly banal axiom that people are different from each other as a difference internal and external to the subject, Sherman's film stills reveal the ambiguity around the relationship between identity and image; their staged quality calls into question the authenticity of the photographic image as a medium that confers an accurate record of reality just as the many different appearances of the one woman, who is both subject and object, artist and model, disrupts the idea of an authentic or true self.

Laura Mulvey's reading of Sherman's work hinges on a conception of the female body in terms of its subjection to "the icons and narratives of fetishism" (1991: 150).[1] In tracing the process of metamorphosis in Sherman's corpus from the *Films Stills* to the detritus and disgust images, she suggests Sherman's work "dissects the phantasmagoric space conjured up by the female body, from its exteriority to its interiority" so that "once the process of bodily disintegration is established in the later work, the early, innocent, images acquire a retrospective uncanniness" (139). It seems to me that this kind of narrativizing tendency, one centered on finding a coherent relationship between these two series invariably privileges the latter work as more sophisticated, more feminist, thereby implying that the earlier work exhausts meaning when in fact it does not. In constructing a narrative trajectory of Sherman's work from its earlier representation of idealized femininity, here coded as "innocent," to the unveiling of the very mask which the fetishistic gloss and glamor of "female allure and elegance" (143) conceal, it is as though Mulvey in the rush to cohere the work into a neat topography of fetishism and its undoing, represses the very enigma of femininity she points to elsewhere in her reading of the film stills. While I do not necessarily have a problem with this kind of retrospective construction that positions one series as a reaction against or in dialog with another, or that some kind of larger narrative about the work necessarily diminishes the integrity of an individual series, the construction of the earlier images as "innocent," requiring a certain retrospective logic in order to become uncanny, positioned, it seems, as inferior or at least dependent on the more astute, defetishizing later work, requires a certain containment of the very ambiguity that Mulvey elsewhere suggests is intrinsic to Sherman's film still images:

> The lure of voyeurism turns around like a trap, and the viewer ends up aware that Sherman-the-artist has set up a machine for making the gaze materialize uncomfortably, in alliance with Sherman-the-model. Then the viewer's curiosity may be attracted to the surrounding narrative. But any speculation about a story, about actual events and the character depicted, quickly reaches a dead end. (142)

And further on:

> There is no stable subject position in her work, no resting point that does not quickly shift into something else. So the *Film Stills'* initial sense of homogeneity and credibility break up into a kind of heterogeneity of subject position that feminist aesthetics espoused in advance of postmodernism proper. (142)

By Mulvey's own astute account there is something in Sherman's images that we can never quite get our head around, an obtuse meaning which defies a certain kind of critical narrative; of course Sherman gives us stereotypes of femininity, familiar filmic styles, recognizable emotions but as soon as our curiosity is aroused enough to begin the process of speculation as to what is going on, we are shocked back into a state of confusion, of uncomfortableness. Such is Sherman's trap, which for Barthes accounts for the still image's capacity to be "at once parodic and disseminatory" (1977/1984: 67). If the wit in these images suggests a wry imitation of certain styles of femininity always coded through a social matrix of visual effects with their attendant perceptual and emotional responses, there is also the counter image of femininity as inscrutable, imaginary and fragmentary. It seems to me that the very ambivalence in Sherman's work—the promise and refusal of narrative, the self-portrait which is the same woman but never the same, the gaze which traps the voyeur into a dialectic of curiosity and anxiety—arouses a kind of affective ambivalence that translates into precisely the critical ambivalence that Mulvey's reading, or for that matter any reading, enacts. As Barthes suggests what the obtuse meaning of the image disturbs are certain forms of critical language which struggle to overcome the still's indifference to narrative logic or obvious meaning (1977/1984: 61).

The film stills are uncanny, not so much because they haunt the exploded, defetishized, internal body, but because they are familiar but outdated icons of "1950s-ness" femininity; here the return of the repressed in the form of an uncanny disruptive femininity signals the uncertainty around the sedimented social narratives of a mass cultural landscape saturated with the desires and anxieties of the past; remembering here that the feeling most associated with the uncanny is one of uncertainty. As Mulvey puts it: "In Sherman's early photographs, connotations of vulnerability and instability flow over on to the construction and credibility of the wider social masquerade"(148), one which reveals a tension between the success of American post-war mass culture but which was nevertheless undercut by a politically conservative regime. The pertinent question seems to be, what are the implications of Sherman's own recycling of the outdated film still, along with her use of retro clothing and artefacts to create highly charged, though ambiguous fragments of 1950s cinema? It is surely significant that Sherman creates her *Untitled Film Stills* at the precise moment in which the film still poster ceased to serve its original function as an advertisement for film, becoming instead an outmoded cultural icon, a collectable souvenir. As Sherman has suggested, her attraction to these artefacts resided not in the content of the images themselves, but in the "cheapness" of these "now out-of-date productions."[2] As outmoded objects, as "fetish objects and camp souvenirs," the film still poster signifies retro itself as a recycling of use value that is both antithetical to a capitalist drive for the New as well as just another form of commodity innovation. As such, we need to look to Sherman's critical approach to the film still genre, as a consciously belated reinscription of 1950s-ness, rather than to the woman in the image, for our reading of fetishism. Sherman's images resurrect the allure of 1950s-ness femininity as well as the film still poster's souvenir status if only to mark their metaphorical death. Here then, fetishism works not to congeal the signification of woman as appearance, as image, but to suggest that through its recycling, it may be resurrected, worked through and resisted—the very terms Foster uses to describe the critical function of the outmoded in Surrealism.

In the series of work produced by Sherman prior to the "Sex Pictures" we begin to see the emergence of an explicit engagement with the figure of the "ruined" female body and psyche underpinning cultural and aesthetic ideology, including Surrealist iconography. Although the "Disasters" series (running from around 1985 until 1991, if we include the series often called "Civil War"), is a varied and in some ways heterogenous body of work, many of the images from this period begin to experiment with the disjunctive effect, between fascination and horror, desire and disgust that I have already examined in relation to Bataille and which, as it will become clear, underwrites the work of Hans Bellmer. While the Surrealists mined the female body for its erotic and transgressive effects, Sherman reminds us that their transgressive forays were nevertheless aesthetically coded, since to produce an erotic female body is coterminous with a desirable and aestheticized one. In a notebook entry on the power of the Surrealist image, Sherman reflects on the relationship between her own work and theirs and also the effect that much Surrealist work produces for a contemporary audience:

> I don't want to be purely decorative and make pretty, odd images. If anything, that would be my criticism of much of the old Surrealist stuff. It is really about esthetics, which, at that time was groundbreaking in itself, but now looks merely beautiful and stylish. Whenever there is a female figure, she's still always beautiful. (*Cindy Sherman: Retrospective*, 1997: 180)

If the aesthetic concept of convulsive beauty came to define the particular disjunctive shock produced in much Surrealist imagery, then Sherman's comments here reveal the way in which traditional beauty and its counterpart, aesthetics, was still very central to much Surrealist revolutionary rhetoric and aesthetic practice. While these comments were made before her engagement with the more desublimated art of Hans Bellmer, that is, before the "Sex Dolls" series, we get a glimpse of Sherman struggling with the meaning of Surrealist art in its more sublimated form in relation to her own turn toward the grotesque. Moreover, Sherman reminds us of the way in which the avant-garde aesthetic object over time loses its shocking and confronting status, its politicized value as an object that shocks, which uncannily reflects back onto the reception of her own work.

In Sherman's "Detritus" images beauty is stripped of its surface effects, leaving us instead with the visceral products of the convulsing, climaxing or wounded body while in the later "Civil War" series, the wounded body is staged as a fetishistic tableaux of cropped body parts. But even here, there is a certain ambivalence undercutting what are always staged reconstructions of disaster scenes or wounded, traumatized bodies. In *Untitled #175* we are presented with a lurid scene of abandoned objects among scattered pieces of left-over cake, amorphous piles of vomit and cosmetic lotion oozing from a plastic bottle. On closer inspection the sunglasses reflect an image of a naked woman lying horizontal, her mouth agape as if screaming or vomiting, her nose possibly enlarged by injury or else the distortion of the reflection. Here the inside and the outside merge into a scene of domestic disaster; the sunglasses, rather than shielding the eyes, are abandoned in a heap of gunk, only to reflect back to us an image of a traumatized woman lying in a quagmire of her own waste. The disturbing nature of this image is its recreation of a scene of trauma, one that reinscribes the pervasive image of the "ruined" woman while archly demonstrating the pervasive cultural narratives that inscribe woman as abject other. In this image the categories of the natural and the cultural, the artificial and the real, the inside and the outside of the body, merge into an undifferentiated mass of cultural and bodily waste, reminding us of the cultural construction of "beauty" and its abject other—disgust. As an image of the grotesque female body it belies the transgressive "beauty" of much Surrealist imagery but is not altogether unaware of its status as art.

In *Untitled #153* (1985) we are presented with a close-up of a dead woman's face and left shoulder, her eyes wide open staring blankly out toward the viewer. While the image presents a disturbing scene of trauma, it also parodically reproduces the aesthetic detail of her "ruined" state as itself a spectacle of excess not dissimilar to the fully masqueraded female body: the slight grazing of her cheeks, the wet soil and gravel clinging to her skin, the crumpled blouse as well as the luminosity of the greens and blues saturating the image (evocative of the hues of bruising) strangely mirrors the cosmetic artifice of the fully masqueraded female body. The care and detail in re-staging this scene of trauma does not authenticate any number of imagined narratives of the murdered or raped woman, the woman as victim, but rather exposes the exaggeration, the allure of lurid detail that underpin all trauma or disaster genres or narratives. In this sense, to read the "Disasters" series as somehow closer to the "real" misses the way in which Sherman's work interrogates the appeal to transparency and identification underpinning trauma or disaster narratives. While the dejecta contained within these images reinforces the materiality of the body and the traditional association of the female body with degradation, pollution and defilement, it also disturbs the traditional aesthetic sublimation of the abject within both high and low art traditions. The feelings of disgust and repulsion that the images evoke as well as their lack of form or narrative function creates for the viewer a sense of their own impending confusion and fragmentation.

Censorship and Crisis: Bellmer and Sherman

Tracing Sherman's work from the *Untitled Film Stills* through to the "Disasters" series reveals the degree to which her work stages an ongoing crisis of representation for the female body and subject. Indeed as Mulvey has suggested Sherman's work arrived at a time—the late 1970s—in which the female body had become unpresentable within feminist art practice unless framed by dense feminist theory (1991: 138). According to Mulvey "the representability of the female body underwent a crisis" (138) during this period, so that Sherman's introduction of a heavily masqueraded and fetishized female body in a sense recuperated "a politics of the body that had … been lost or neglected in the twists and turns of seventies feminism" (138). While the *Untitled Film Stills* attracted scorn, confusion and praise from both feminist and non-feminist audiences,[3] it was the embattled controversy and censorship of the "Centerfold" series that reinforced the extent to which Sherman's work went against the grain of an orthodox feminist theoretical position in terms of the representation of the female body. Commissioned in 1981 to do a two-page color spread for *Artforum*, an art magazine committed to publishing and supporting artists who produced so-called difficult or controversial work, Sherman created images of herself in large close-up horizontal formats, using glossy, vibrant color and strong lighting. In these images the female subject is often represented in a state of reverie or confusion, which gives them a quality of ambiguity and uncertainty. This series, however, was twice rejected by the magazine on the grounds that the images could be misconstrued as "real" centerfolds.[4] While some of the formal properties of the images mine the formal features of the soft-core "centerfold" format, the emotional register of the women in the images seem to contradict any obvious reading of them as simply objectified objects, available for the consumption of a pornographic male gaze. Over twenty years later it is hard to believe that these images could have caused so much controversy. The fully clothed female subject in these images is often caught in a moment of domestic melodrama as though she has been literally stunned by the intrusiveness of the camera (see *Untitled #93* and *#96*). The air of surprise and confusion in these images provides an ironic commentary on the intrusiveness of the pornographic/photographic gaze, rather than capitulating to it. The rejection of the Centerfold series was in many ways a mark of the feminist cultural and political mood of the late 1970s and early 1980s as well as the climate of political correctness sweeping through art critical circles and the academy in general. This episode, at least for Sherman, would come to haunt the very public debates about censorship, "obscenity" and the increased restrictions of public funding of the arts, which reached a critical point around 1989–1990.

I want to argue that it is within this context that the dialogue between Sherman and Bellmer must be situated. In returning to the confronting nature of Surrealist art practice Sherman gestures toward her own—at times—problematic reception within a feminist theoretical framework as well as the larger debates about censorship that precipitated this body of work. In an interview in the late 1990s Sherman, reflecting on her career and the reception of her work, explicitly stated that the "Sex Pictures" were developed as a critical response to the increasing climate of censorship in the art world, in particular the proposed changes to the funding guidelines for the National Endowment for the Arts, which restricted funding to those artists whose work was deemed "obscene" (Fuku, 1997: 125). The issue of censorship that dominated the American art world in the late 1980s and early 1990s had an immediate resonance for Sherman insofar as it uncannily invoked the censorship of her Centerfold series in the early 1980s.[5] But in returning to the violently erotic themes in Bellmer's images in the context of her own desire to create disturbing images that challenge the restriction of "obscene" art in the present, Sherman shifts the focal point of the censorship debate from the "here" and the "now" to the "then" and "always," implicitly reminding us of the climate of censorship informing Bellmer's own work in Nazi Germany.[6]

In his analysis of the art world controversies that dominated the period of the "Culture Wars," from the late 1980s to the early 1990s in the United States, Steven Dubin points to a more widespread sense of political and social crisis during this period—"AIDS, homelessness, crime, drugs, a seriously overburdened health care system, the persistence of poverty as well as the economic squeezing of the middle class" (1992: 15)—so that the controversy over art became a politically strategic diversion from the real social problems facing American society:

> [W]henever a society is overwhelmed by problems and its sense of national identity is shaky or diffuse, a probable response is for states to attempt to exercise control by regulating symbolic expression. Whether the target is art or language, governments try to demonstrate their continued efficacy by initiating diversionary conflicts. Although such struggles do not always produce tangible results or clear-cut victories, they temporarily deflect attention away from other concerns. (19)

If the end of the cold war meant that Communism was no longer the dominant threat to American values and culture, a new scapegoat had to be found. Pornography and obscenity became the focus for renewed anxieties about the moral and psychic health of the nation. At the same time, as Dubin points out, the art market had experienced an economic boom throughout the 1980s which resulted in increased exposure for a select few artists and their work in mainstream media culture (24). This was offset by an increasing public incomprehension about contemporary art. Now under increased scrutiny from the public and the media, the successful or in anyway notorious artist often became a scapegoat for larger social anxieties. This reached a crisis point in 1989 when Andres Serrano's *Piss Christ*, after having won a prestigious award funded by the Rockefeller Foundation and the National Endowment for the Arts, and a traveling exhibition of Robert Mapplethorpe's work, ignited an intense censorship campaign by the religious right against artists, galleries and funding bodies such as the NEA.[7] The rhetoric around degeneracy and obscenity from the religious right was echoed by conservative art critics who similarly condemned the use of public funds to support work that the public would neither understand nor find morally acceptable.[8] As if in response to the alarming number of cultural critics willing to call for censorship of certain forms of art, in 1991 the Los Angeles County Museum of Art staged an exhibition, "Degenerate Art: the Fate of Avant-Garde Art in Nazi Germany," which was a reconstruction of the original "Entartete Kunst" show in Munich in 1937 and which went on tour around the United States before its final staging in Berlin. If the original "Entartete Kunst" exhibition was intended as an instructional and propaganda exercise to warn the mass public of the dangers of modernist art, its reconstruction in the early 1990s was similarly cast as an historical lesson warning of the parallels between the enemies of artistic freedom in the Mapplethorpe/Sarrano controversy and those responsible for organizing the "Entartete Kunst" exhibition in the late 1930s. While the political and social circumstances of the German paradigm are very different to the attempted censorship of works of art deemed "obscene" in late-twentieth-century America, there are nevertheless overlapping concerns about public or state funding in these two historical moments. In her catalog essay for the exhibition, the curator Stephanie Barron points to the sense of social crisis that precipitated the censorship of modernist art under National Socialism:

> The country had experienced a humiliating defeat and had been assessed for huge war reparations that grievously taxed its already shaky economy. Movements such as

> Expressionism, Cubism, and Dada were often viewed as intellectual, elitist, and foreign by a demoralized nation … Many avant-garde artists continued their involvement in Socialism during the turbulent Weimar years and made their sentiments known through their art. This identification of the more abstract art movements with internationalism and progressive politics created highly visible targets for the aggressive nationalism that gave birth to the National Socialist party. (1991: 23)

One of the first ever blockbuster exhibitions, the "Entartete Kunst" show was carefully staged so that the public would feel that they were determining what was good and bad art; the inclusion of a price tag next to each work of art, indicating how much museums and private collectors had paid for each item, intensified the atmosphere of shame that identified modern art as decadent and wasteful and in no way representative of the tastes and values of the German people. In both the early German and later American contexts, the ideological war waged on "Degenerate" or "Obscene" art was made in the name of the state's accountability of public funds in supporting works of art that are seen as both incomprehensible and antithetical to the moral sensibilities of a mass public. In pointing to a wider political and social sense of crisis that shapes all periods of controversy over art, Dubin highlights the way in which the arresting image is mobilized by artists, critics and right wing political groups to signal a sense of social crisis; while artists or curators invariably use such images to comment on prevailing social conditions or to deconstruct the taken-for-granted discourses around sex, race, religion and power, topics which in themselves are highly explosive, the reactionary right points to such images as the very sign of social malaise thus obfuscating very real social problems and the lack of remedies for them.

Sex Games/Doll Games

In suggesting that her exploration of aberrant and confrontational figuration was a counter response to the climate of increased censorship in the American public sphere, Sherman forces us to rethink the programmatic scripts of critical practice that have shaped the reception of both Bellmer's and her own work. While this is not to suggest that Sherman holds a privileged reading of Bellmer's work, her notebook entries on the creation of this body of work provide an important insight into what we might call the "complex structure of feeling" evoked by Bellmer's and Sherman's images—and indeed Mapplethorpe's—and out of which a critical reaction is formed.[9] In the creation of her sex dolls Sherman explicitly confronts the violent eroticism of Bellmer's own *Poupées*, unsettling his use of the ruined female figure as the privileged site of transgression. If a great deal of Surrealist work, including Bellmer's, implies a negation of what had come before it (modernist formalism, bourgeois cultural institutions of family and religion etc.), similarly the "Sex Pictures" confront the claims of Surrealist art practice through a direct engagement with its themes and forms. Indeed as Calinescu suggests, "there is a larger moral and aesthetic sense in which postmodernism's loss of innocence goes beyond 'the already said' to relate to the darker, savage, unspeakable side of a modernity" (277).

While the "Sex Pictures" series uncannily exhibit the process by which contemporary questions of desire, representation and subject formation have their antecedents in a modernist aesthetic practice and its incorporation of psychoanalytical theories of perversion, they also move beyond what we might call the utopian moment of perversion that signaled the modernist crisis of subjectivity. In producing work that is confronting and shocking, at the same time, comic and parodic, Sherman's "Sex Pictures" draw out the very nature of complicity and resistance that also haunt the critical responses to the construction of perversion in both Bellmer's and Mapplethorpe's work.[10] As we have seen in relation to Bataille, in some of the more dissident Surrealist work, perversion operates as a challenge to or twisting of the traditional function of both sexuality and literary or aesthetic style. In Bellmer's *Poupées* perversion becomes a strategy of resistance to cultural norms in an escalating climate of cultural conformity and censorship, one that unfolds the drama of filial rebellion against the fascist father and the violent and repressive surveillance of the Nazi state.

Throughout the 1930s Bellmer constructed two different dolls, which he photographed in over a hundred different poses and settings. Looking at the plethora of images of these dolls in various interior and exterior settings, one is struck by the range of atmosphere and emotion that they evoke. In one image the doll is completely disassembled, neatly laid out as a collection of fragmented body parts in the manner of a decorative still life. In another image, perhaps the most haunting of thc scrics, the doll is reassembled and propped up against a wall, her head turned so that she is coyly looking over one shoulder; rendered ambiguously as both victim and seductress. In this image it is the single upturned eye of the doll, caught at such an angle that it directly captures our gaze, which makes her appear at once coquettish and vulnerable, seductive and deranged. While the doll's surface is rough and brittle, evoking a sense of decay and ruin, the folded layers of her cotton undergarment pulled up over her buttocks, and the long tangled mass of hair draped over her back, give her a disquieting erotic and lifelike air. Despite or because of the crudity of the doll's form—her crumbling buttocks, her armless torso and a left leg composed of a metal rod—Bellmer's doll in this image incites the spectre of the uncanny, through its fusion of the animate and the inanimate. In other photographs the doll appears in various fragmented forms, surrounded by different kinds of fetishized feminine and domestic items: a cotton lace petticoat, tulle, muslin cloth, an embroidered lace bed cover, mattress ticking, artificial flowers, a female shoe and human hair. The display of the doll's sex alongside these fetish items flagrantly stages the themes of eroticism, death and fetishism as intrinsic to the artist's creative practice. Like the child at play, Bellmer rearranges and recombines the objects of his world, mastering a fantasy game of mutilation and destruction as well as its opposite, imagination and creation. The fascination and the horror that the dolls evoke reminds us of Bataille's rearrangement and substitution of objects in *Story of the Eye*.[11]

The photographs of Bellmer's first doll creation were published in 1934 as *Die Pupée*, a booklet of ten black and white images accompanied by a small essay "Memories of the Doll Theme." In this essay Bellmer transfers his own memories of childhood onto the fantasies of his alter-ego doll. The doll's construction becomes a conscious resistance to the normative codes of work and leisure underpinning the moral structure of Nazi Germany. According to Bellmer, the doll functions as both an object of joy and fear: "Would it not be in the very reality of the Doll that the imagination would find the joy, the ecstasy and the fear that is sought?" (cited in Webb, 1985: 34). The first doll series was also published in the Surrealist journal, *Minotaure* (December 5, 1934) (see Plate 6) under the more elaborate title, "Doll: Variations on the Assemblage of an Articulated Minor." Although still living in Germany, this event marked Bellmer's entry into the Surrealist movement and precipitated his eventual move to France and a lifetime association with the group. The Surrealists were very much taken with Bellmer's creations and what they revealed about the nature of desire. Likewise, Bellmer's doll photographs were perfectly suited to *Minotaure*, the most lavish of the journals associated with Surrealism. Originally founded in 1933 by Albert Skira, *Minotaure* from its inception had hoped to be an elegant artistic and literary review. Like *Document*,[12] the journal that it modeled itself on in many ways, *Minotaure* often included extravagant photographic reproductions of macabre and disturbing themes.[13] As such the journal was a perfect vehicle for Bellmer's photographs and one that he would frequently contribute to over the years. In the same issue that contained Bellmer's second doll series, in 1936, Maurice Heine published an imagined dialogue between the Marquis de Sade and Jack the Ripper, which was illustrated with graphic photographs of Jack the Ripper's disemboweled victims. In his history of Surrealism, Marcel Jean noted that Bellmer's dolls did indeed have "an air of lewd abandon that one might associate with a victim of Jack the Ripper" (1960: 241), therefore acknowledging the violent dismemberment of the body in Bellmer's dolls as uncannily evocative of a Surrealist interest in the violated female form.

In 1935 Bellmer constructed his second doll, utilizing a series of ball joints to give it added mobility and manipulation. Over a hundred photographs were taken of this second doll in a range of settings, both indoor and out. A few years later Bellmer wrote "Notes on the Ball Joint" which would accompany his series of hand-tinted photos of the doll as well as poems by Paul Eluard in the booklet, *The Games of the Doll*, not published until 1949 because of the war. The second doll series elaborated and expanded the terms of reference of the first but here the atmosphere becomes increasingly disturbing and sinister. In one image from this series a doll is propped against a stairwell, a piece of rope tied around its knee, one leg amputated and the fingers of a hand poking through the gaps in the banister. The head of the doll hangs down, exposing a giant hair bow which seems to intensify the forlorn expression on the doll's face; the doll's demeanor suggests complete exhaustion if not death while the body's twisted form as well as the ominous lighting of the photograph hints at torture and sexual violation. In many of the photographs from this series the doll's legs are splayed open, so that our gaze is directed toward her genital area; often lying twisted and deformed, the doll arouses feelings of empathy as well as sadistic fantasies of manipulation and violation. For this second doll Bellmer constructed a number of extra limbs and body parts so that they could be substituted and arranged, invoking uncanny double forms. In one image two sets of limbs and buttocks are joined at the torso and share a single stomach. Propped up against a tree in a forest setting with a dark male figure spying from behind another tree, she appears even more vulnerable in this sinister setting than in the interior scenes. Moreover, the bright hues of the tints used to color the photograph, together with the half-concealed male figure, create a lurid voyeurism reminiscent of the lewd fantasies used to illustrate pulp fiction covers.

While many of the photographs stage scenes of sadomasochistic fantasy and fetishistic desire, the doubling and rearrangement of the body also propounds a childhood world of games, of play and manipulation, of substitution and rearrangement. Bellmer's lifelong identification with the world of childhood emerges in both his doll constructions and photographs and in his drawings. Many photographs of the dolls include childhood toys such as spinning tops and hula hoops, while the doll's childlike status is further evoked through fetishistic details such as Mary Jane shoes and white ankle socks. These items contrast to the voluptuous, almost maternally round, body of the doll figure in other images and which reinforce the powerful effect of her sexuality. In striking ways Bellmer's images at times also capture the awkwardness of female adolescence, a reminder of the figure of the *femme-enfant* with its own childlike and seductive capacity. The inclusion of domestic items in many of the images similarly evoke a disjunction between adult fantasy and childhood play. In several images an ornate carpet beater appears across the photograph, suggesting both childhood fantasy games (akin to the witch's broom) as well as adult sado-masochistic play. As such many of these images collapse the imaginative world of the child into the sadistic sexual fantasy world of the adult. Moreover, the "game" in the collection's title suggests the world of childhood play as well as the Surrealist love of games, reminding us of the element of chance that games provoke. In this sense Bellmer's dolls are like three-dimensional exquisite corpses whereby the substitution and manipulation of the doll's body parts mirrors the manipulation of the customary lexicon of the body in the pictorial exquisite corpse. Perhaps the most famous of the Surrealist parlor games, the exquisite corpse created a hybrid metaphorical body that introduced a new kind of aesthetic language, a language of desire and chance that replaced mimetic language, formal structure and individual *metier*.

If, in aesthetic terms, Bellmer's dolls explore the terrain of chance and desire in the creation of the aesthetic object, there are nevertheless two very specific events that precipitated the construction of his first doll in 1933: the rise of Hitler and

National Socialism and Bellmer's attendance at a performance of Offenbach's *Tales of Hoffman*.[14] Before turning to the importance of the uncanny in Bellmer's work, I want to discuss the political and social context out of which the dolls emerge. This context is important because it serves to mediate the meaning of the work, directing it away from the immediacy of an affective response grounded in the sadistic violence of the images. While I do not want to expunge the possibility of the work's inherent misogyny, I do want to suggest that the complex range of emotions produced by the work reflects the competing identifications and narratives operating in it. Moreover, I hope that the process of contextualizing Bellmer's work within its complicated social, political and personal framework provides an insight into Sherman's engagement with these images in her own series of "Sex Pictures" and the context out of which they emerge. Bellmer's work and the critical responses to them also become an important optic through which to gauge critical responses to Sherman's own work.

In his rebellion from his father and the dominant Nazi culture of the period, Bellmer, through the creation of his doll figures, appears to identify with the female subject position.[15] This is made clear in his prose poem, "The Father," written in 1936 and later published in *Le Surréalisme, même* (1958). Here Bellmer recalls the gulf that lies between his father's power and austerity and his own world of childhood pranks:

> We learned quite early on how to protect ourselves, and, in fact, even more. What we thought of while our teeth chattered persisted until the onset of sleep: rebellion, defence, attack .... In fact we were probably rather adorable, more like little girls than the formidable boys we would have preferred to be. Yet, it seemed to be more fitting than anything else to lure the brute out of his place in order to confuse him. (Cited in Webb, 1985: 177)

In this piece Bellmer reveals the rigid and reactionary nature of his father, contrasting his unemotional and sterile world to his own sense of childhood imagination and play:

> It goes without saying that the pretexts of education, the principles of obedience and supervised work, all reinforced his attitude. And it was obvious that we vaguely questioned ourselves about the inadequacies of the entire class that he represented and that hindered him from understanding that the abolition of play is not beneficial to goodness and a sense of equilibrium. (176)

Here the world of the father and the world of the child elaborates a series of dichotomous terms and emotions, which Bellmer exhibits and explores in the construction of his dolls, and which in turn also structure the doll's relationship to the world: childhood exuberance and fantasy versus adult repression and rigidity, the unconscious and the conscious, masculine identity versus feminine identification, the inside and the outside, the whole and the part, construction and destruction, desire and prohibition, empathy and violence, and so on. This series of oppositional categories suggests a complex drama of filial rebellion that mirrors the operation of transgression and interdiction in Bataille's work. Sue Taylor argues that "a world of joy, games, song and laughter and that of obedience, supervision, oppression, and self-satisfied power—are conventional tropes of the avant-garde for the free-spirited artist pitted against the corrupt bourgeois" (2000: 21). Like Bataille, Bellmer uses the female body to stage his aesthetic and social rebellion against a repressive, autocratic, bourgeois father and culture. Their work reveals the degree to which the female body becomes the site on which male avant-garde culture exhibits its struggle for mastery. The gendering of violence in Bellmer's work also unfolds the complicated process of self-identification with the feminine other that was not dissimilar to the male fascist subject's feminized obedience and submission to Hitler.

In this sense the doll becomes both fetish object and alter-ego figure; an object that wards off castration but also allows those fears to be openly staged. The importance of Freud's theory of fetishism seems particularly pertinent to Bellmer's construction of the doll figure for it underscores the structure of perversion in relation to sexual difference and gendered subjectivity. In his essay "Fetishism" (1927) Freud notes that the fetish represents both the recognition and disavowal of the threat of castration for the male subject. Therefore the fetish object is both adored and abused since its status as a substitute serves to compensate for the threat of castration but also to act as a constant reminder of it. In its representation of a traumatic loss, the fetish is also imbued with the logic of nostalgia. In Bellmer's essay "Memories of a Doll Theme" (1934) the longing for the lost experience of childhood is made so explicit that the dolls function as souvenirs of childhood; here the doll as fetish object becomes both the adored and abused plaything of childhood fantasy. Like the actual souvenirs of childhood that Bellmer collected, the dolls represent both fetishistic desire and nostalgic longing. As Susan Stewart suggests the very nature of the souvenir itself discloses the origin of the fetish:

> The souvenir generates a narrative which reaches only "behind," spiralling in a continually inward movement rather than outward toward the future. Here we find the structure of Freud's description of the genesis of the fetish: a part of the body is substituted for the whole, or an object is substituted for the part, until finally, and inversely, the whole body can become object, substituting for the whole. (1993: 135)

The dolls become a projection of Bellmer's sadistic fantasies as well as a reflection of his vulnerability and sense of persecution. The aggression and hostility exposed in the doll's creation implies a narrative of deviant subjectivity and desire that registers a catalog of perverse desires and fears: sadomasochism, fetishism, castration anxiety, and incest. As in Bataille's exploration of transgression, Bellmer's dolls stage a rejection of bourgeois family arrangements and the procreative function of its sexuality, exploring instead the loss of self and the fusion with the other in both fantasy and eroticism. But since the dolls are also imbued with a powerful sense of nostalgia they also paradoxically invoke a longing for the familial arrangements of a bourgeois childhood.

While Bellmer self-consciously casts himself as the perverse, degenerate artist rebelling against the image of the healthy Aryan body that came to dominate German National Socialist cultural policy throughout the 1930s, the dolls also reflect in part the internalization of fascist ideology. The fascist celebration of the mechanical or robotic body suggests its own contradictory relationship with the feminine and with mass culture. As with the spectral figure of the zombie, the automaton or doll is also frequently associated with the mass political subject of fascism, a subject that came to define the Nazi propaganda machine with its reliance on public rallies and mass spectacles and its program of assimilation. Indeed the qualities used to define the mass political subject under Hitler were the explicitly feminized qualities of devotion, sacrifice, submission and a relinquishing of the self for the greater good, so that a fascist cult of masculinity acts as a compensation for feminzed obedience. Throughout the 1930s Nazi ideology was constructed around a dichotomy of normalcy and degeneracy, inclusion and exclusion, so that the healthy, robust Aryan body was pitted against the degenerate bodies of homosexuals, the insane, Jews, blacks, avant-garde artists and communists. The ideals of femininity were embodied in the figure of the modest Gretchen maid, the very icon of a "natural" and girl-like femininity with her clean scrubbed features, simple dress and long blonde plaits, as well as the maternal house Frau, the child bearer who would guarantee the continuation of the Aryan race. As Terri Gordon has argued in her analysis of the use of the female form in dance during the Third Reich,

> The body became a social site onto which political ideals were mapped. The notion of the healthy body as a microcosm of the healthy state was reiterated in the images of the "sacred wife and mother" in officially sanctioned art and promoted in a vast propaganda campaign enjoining women to lend their bodies to the movement to maintain the vitality of the race. (2002: 164–5)

Often depicted as fragmented and in decay, or in surroundings that are themselves suggestive of ruin, Bellmer's dolls explicitly reject the ideals of the healthy Aryan body. And yet while the violence exhibited toward the doll figures suggests a partial identification with his feminized dolls, it also invokes the contradictory forces of submission and aggression that came to define the masculine subject in fascist culture.

In addition to his construction of a three-dimensional doll-figure, Bellmer explored the body's interior in a number of detailed drawings. For Bellmer such drawings allowed him to explore the bodies interior in a way that marks a violent penetration of the visceral cavities and organs, an externalization of the interior that unearths the structures of manifest and latent content: "I want to reveal scandalously the interior that will always remain hidden and sensed behind the successive layers of the human structure and its last unknowns" (Bellmer in Webb,

1985: 11). Throughout his life Bellmer was also obsessed with the image of the little girl and in a drawing from 1935/6, *Rose ouverte la nuit*, Bellmer depicts a prepubescent girl folding back the outer layer of her skin to reveal the internal organs and rib cage. Peering inside of herself with a curious expression, the image of the self-flaying child creates a haunting quality that disturbs her otherwise embodied innocence. In this image the girl's innocence is literally torn away in a moment of self-obsessed curiosity and sadistic voyeurism so that her curiosity for the unknown becomes a narcissistic desire to see inside herself, a move which will also ultimately destroy her. In this image, Bellmer projects his own curiosity and desire to penetrate the surface onto his girl subject so that she becomes a representation of sadomasochistic desire. In a curious way this image operates as a metaphor for Bellmer's own art practice; in his desire to penetrate the surface of the body and reveal its latent content, he must destroy something of its wholeness, its innocence, its identity, revealing in the process his own desires and fears.[16]

In reflecting on his doll constructions Bellmer has suggested that he was attempting to explore "the physical unconscious" (Webb, 1985: 38). Like the psychic unconscious, the physical unconscious in Bellmer's works reveals a disturbing undercurrent to the sealed and contained body of idealized bourgeois femininity so that the somatic structure and surface of the doll suggests a series of encrypted signs that uncover a narrative of libidinal desire.[17] The notion of the physical unconscious is elaborated through Bellmer's comparison of the rearrangement and deconstruction of the doll figure with the anagrammatic quality of a sentence:

> I tried to arrange the sexual elements of a girl's body like a sort of plastic anagram. I remember describing it thus: the body is like a sentence that invites us to rearrange it, so that its real meaning becomes clear through a series of endless anagrams. (Cited in *Hans Bellmer: Photographs*, 1991: 42)

Here the comparison between anatomy and syntax recalls Bataille's perverse play of metonymic and metaphoric objects in *Story of the Eye*. As in Bataille's use of transgression, Bellmer's dolls stage the familiar Surrealist representation of the female body as both transcendent and debased, a contradiction which Sherman's work explicitly takes up. The doll's uncanniness evinces its liminal status on the border between life and death, the real and the imagined, staging the enigma of femininity as both an image of revulsion and an image of desire, as passive victim and as enchanting seductress. Like the photographed hysterics in Charcot's hospital, the dolls are at once disturbingly vulnerable and enchantingly desirable. Bellmer's dolls thus raise complicated questions about male fantasies of erotic domination and manipulation that are central to a more general Surrealist aesthetic practice.[18]

The significance of the uncanny in much Surrealist art becomes especially evident in Bellmer's work. While Bellmer's visit to a performance of Offenbach's opera, *Tales of Hoffman* inspired his creation of his first doll, Freud's development of the uncanny hinged around his reading of the doll Olympia in the tales of Hoffman, whom he regarded as "the unrivalled master of the uncanny in literature" (1919/1985: 355). According to Freud the automaton or doll figure unsettles our everyday expectations of the real and the imagined, the living and the dead. Therefore the uncanny is evoked when "there is an intellectual uncertainty whether an object is alive or not, and when the inanimate object becomes too much like the animate one" (354). The uncanniness of Bellmer's dolls thus lies in their capacity to evoke human emotion: degradation, humiliation, shame, vulnerability, and exhaustion. But Freud goes on to complicate this first assumption about intellectual uncertainty by reminding us that the "living doll" is not really a fear of childhood but rather a desire:

> We remember that in their early games children do not distinguish at all sharply between living and inanimate objects, and that they are especially fond of treating their dolls like live people .... The source of uncanny feelings would not, therefore, be an infantile fear in this case, but rather an infantile wish ... . (355)

In connecting our adult fear of the automaton with our childhood desire that the inanimate come to life, Freud encapsulates the ambiguity of Bellmer's doll: the fascination and the terror that they evoke for the viewer. This ambiguity is reinforced by Freud's conclusion that

> we can understand why linguistic usage has extended *das Heimliche* ["homely"] into its opposite, *das Unheimliche*; for this uncanny is in reality nothing new or alien, but something which is familiar and old established in the mind and which has become alienated from it only through the process of repression. (363–4)

In staging the return of childhood play in the form of sadomasochistic desire, Bellmer's dolls reveal the subject's experience of imaginary identification embedded within the trajectory of the uncanny. As Elizabeth Wright argues, what gives much Surrealist art its "shock" effect is the return of the (un)familiar fantasy world of childhood into the domesticated world of familiar objects and things. But here fantasy is not understood as a straightforward wish-fulfilment but rather "as something that a subject constructs in order to get closer to what it desires or dreads" (1990: 273). The uncanny is important to Surrealist and postmodernist aesthetics because it contests the instrumental function of representation, and "makes us see the world not as ready-made for description, depiction, or portrayal (common terms used to say what an artist or writer does), but as in a constant process of construction, deconstruction and reconstruction" (265).

In the "Sex Pictures" Sherman creates graphic and disturbing images of anatomically detailed mannequin dolls, often with enlarged or distorted genitals and hybrid male and female body parts. Employing plastic mannequins purchased through medical supplies' catalogs as well as props and prosthetic devices from sex shops and novelty stores, Sherman conflates the pornographic and medical gaze in a way that unsettles any easy codification of the body in either scientific or sexual terms. While the work restages the psychosexual drama of Bellmer's work, Sherman's use of objects invariably work to unsettle the fetishistic nostalgia for childhood invoked by Bellmer's incorporation of childhood paraphernalia. In *Untitled #263* (see Plate 7) Sherman produces a parodic replica of Bellmer's doubled pair of legs and torso. Like Bellmer's doll the two sets of legs and genital areas are joined at the waist but in fusing male and female forms and truncating the legs so that our gaze is fixed to the genital regions of either mannequin, Sherman introduces the figure of the double as a hybrid of sexual difference. In contrast to the smooth pre-pubescent genital region of Bellmer's dolls, the genital region of Sherman's female mannequin is excessively hairy; out of its vagina hangs the string of a tampon, which serves to remind us of the bleeding and wounded body, the body of a woman rather than a girl. While Bellmer's hybrid doll image, with its half concealed male voyeur peering from behind a tree, conveys a pulpy psychosexual melodrama, by contrast Sherman's image is disquieting and unerotic. As Suleiman argues, "Sherman's truncated, parodically androgynous doll repulses any attempt at penetration or phantasmatic possession" (1998: 139). Moreover, the elaborate ribbon tied in a bow around the figure's torso, decorated with a swastika pattern, references Bellmer's own use of the ribbon motif as well as his incorporation of the swastika configuration in his arrangement of a double pair of his doll's legs. In Sherman's image the sumptuousness of the ribbon is further enhanced by an abundance of draped shiny fabric surrounding the hybrid mannequin. Draped silk or satin fabric or an abundance of long draped hair are frequently used in this series in a way that signals the boudoir effect of the pornographic mis en scene as well as highlighting Bellmer's own use of cloth and hair to give his dolls their disturbingly animate effect. By including two decapitated heads, each gazing at the genitals of the opposite sex, Sherman appears to complicate any straightforward reading of the male gaze as exclusively voyeuristic. However, the very fact that their heads have been removed seems to ironically restage the "money shot" in pornographic tableaux as that moment when the camera metaphorically decapitates the body in order to pursue the close-up of the sexual organs.

In *Untitled #258*, the metaphorization of the female genitals as wound or "hole" is made literal. Lying face down, a plastic mannequin is positioned so that she reaches back behind her, framing the large open gaping hole that stands in place of more detailed anatomical representation of the anus and vagina area. The dark genital hole at the center of the image suggests that something is "missing." Here the missing female genitals in the narrative of sexual fetishism are parodically displayed as a sign of the "artificial" status of female identity and embodiment within a masculine and heterosexual economy of sexual desire. In this sense Sherman's work reveals strategies of critical subversion that Judith Butler locates in the process of staging the parodic:

> The critical task is ... to locate strategies of subversive repetition enabled by ... constructions, to affirm the local possibilities of intervention through participating in

> precisely those practices of repetition that constitute identity and, therefore, present the immanent possibility of contesting them. (1990: 147)

In recontextualizing Bellmer's construction and manipualtion of his dolls, Sherman uses the deviant body of avant-garde aesthetic practice in order to reveal the historical authorization of transgression as a male avant-garde practice. Moreover, the "nothingness" of the genital region is uncannily repeated in minute form as a single eye peering out at us from the top right hand corner of the image. The lighting in the photograph produces a stylization of the eye that renders the iris area as a stark black void. The vagina as eye, a ubiquitous Surrealist pornographic trope, and a constant theme in Bellmer's work as well as central to Bataille's *Story of the Eye*, reminds us of Freud's suggestion that the female genitals may invoke uncanny feeling. Indeed Freud likens our relationship to the uncanny with the adult male's relationship to the female genitals: once the birth canal and origin of the self, they embody the uncanny's development in the direction of ambivalence by becoming the primary sexual object and staging the objectification of the other. The eye as vagina is again taken up in *Untitled #261*. Here a partially decapitated mannequin lies with its head upside down, one eye staring from the bottom of the image directly into our gaze. The partial decapitation of the head is mirrored by the amputation of the legs, at the genital region. On top of the mannequin sits a pair of detachable breasts. The fragmentation and displacement of the bodily forms explicitly mirror the effects of displacement and disintegration in Bellmer's dolls. But again Sherman makes much more explicit the sexual manipulation and decapitation of the doll; in draping red silk fabric beneath and around the doll, she parodically highlights the fetishistic status of the image while the doll's partial decapitation and amputation reminds us of the structure of the fetish as substitute for, protection against and continual reminder of castration.

Sherman's monstrous hybrid sex dolls parody the hermaphroditic body and its attempts to obscure sexual difference while also disclosing gender and anatomical difference as specific operations of the cultural construction and manipulation of sexual bodies, be they grounded in pornography, medicine or art practice. In a series of notebook entries, Sherman reveals how she began to think of ways in which to disengage her own physical presence from the camera lens, which coincided with an escalating interest in Dada and Surrealist photography. In an entry about her "Sex Pictures" Sherman discloses her unfolding frustration and ambivalence in relation to this body of work:

> Should move towards terror. The shock (or terror) should come from what the sexual elements are really standing for—death, power, aggression, beauty, sadness, etc ... It's easy to make a funny or shocking picture based solely on the appearances or revelations of the sex organs (esp. these organs). The difficulty is making poignant yet explicit imagery. ("Notebooks": 1987: 180)

Attempting to eke out the distressing nature of her subject matter and her desire to produce a range of emotions within the images, Sherman constructs some hauntingly surreal images. In *Untitled #257* (see Plate 8) the parodic tone of earlier images is replaced with a scene of sordid horror. Here the head of a female mannequin, again cropped at the neck to suggest decapitation, lies below a pair of buttocks which appear to be squatting over her open mouth. From between the buttocks of this squatting figure the light faintly captures a drop of clear bodily fluid falling from a shape that suggests either a penis or a nose. The expression on the mannequin's face is similarly ambiguous, suggesting terror and/or sexual ecstasy. Behind her head lies the dark genital region of another body, the texture of its artificial skin also caught in the light. The use of stark lighting in this image produces an ambiguity of bodily forms and emotions which together with the presence of bodily fluid and the textures of skin, hair and teeth, create a powerfully uncanny ambience. In this image Sherman produces a disturbing atmosphere of violence, desire and sexual trauma as well as disgust and repulsion.

While Sherman's work explicitly confronts the pornographic gaze of Bellmer's work, it does so by reflecting on the complicity of our own gaze. In his *Poupées*, the doll becomes a kind of alter-ego, an erotic object on which Bellmer's sadistic fantasies are played out. In imitating this process Sherman makes us reflect on those strategies of desire and complicity in Bellmer's images and in our own viewing of them. But rather than reveal a narrative of identification, as Bellmer does in relation to his dolls, Sherman evokes an "ambivalent structure of feeling"[19] that reverberates with the viewer's fascination and disgust at her parodic versions of Bellmer's images. The comic and grotesque effect produced in the "Sex Pictures" invokes what Butler calls "a subversive laughter in the pastiche-effect of parodic practices in which the original, the authentic, and the real are themselves constituted as effects" (1990: 146).

While Bellmer's use of the doll figure captures both the Freudian and avant-garde representation of the automaton as a category of ambiguity and contradiction, Sherman's sex dolls stage a postmodernist investment in parody. In Sherman's graphically sexual images, there is a sense of self-irony and comic manipulation that moves beyond Bellmer's aesthetic construction of transgressive eroticism. But in the very act of parody, Sherman imparts a dynamic of complicity and resistance that constitutes all actions of transgression and parodic subversion:

> I can't seem to keep from making everything have a sexual, "political," or 'heavy" edge, which I don't exactly want. If anything, I'd rather make the work seem politically <u>in</u>correct. I was thinking how the surrealists were very much into de Sade and thus misogynistic which rather intrigued me, I guess because the main thing that bothered me with their work was in the beautification of the women used, not how they were used. (Not to mention however, how these men, themselves seemed rather piggish the way girlfriends, wives, etc … seemed to have been treated, passed around, used

> as models, while these women were, often, artists themselves and much younger). ("Notebooks": 1987: 184–5)

Sherman's comments of course remind us of the disjunction between the Surrealist woman as practicing artist and the Surrealist woman as a figure of representation; a disjunction that instils a crisis of representation. This crisis itself comes to haunt Sherman's parodic revisions of Bellmer's dolls in a way that suggests a dynamic of complicity and resistance in Sherman's own work—and indeed in our own critical reflection on them. This series of images becomes a heuristic model of how feminist and postmodernist accounts of the female body and representation serve to both guide and restrict Sherman's own response to Surrealist images. Although Sherman attempts to counter the misogyny of much Surrealist art, she senses the trap of recuperation:

> ... I had wanted to explore a violent misogynistic direction, á la de Sade and the boys; instead everything seems too "loaded" about sex/violence. I guess that the successful surrealistic ploy here would be to diffuse the ugly-reality of misogyny by bursting the reality-surreal!—voilá! ("Notebooks," 1987: 184–5)

Here Sherman reveals a frustration and an anxiety at the heart of her art practice: a desire to deploy the codes of violence and sex at the heart of Surrealism to undo the very categories that those codes construct, at the same time engaging with the force of their aesthetic and political meaning. Sherman articulates her strategy as an attempt to unfix the "ugly-reality of misogyny" in Surrealist art practice without simply making her work a crude political statement, divested of the very ambiguity that fuels the emotional depth of Bellmer's work. Instead her works offer an interrogation of the violence and eroticism of Bellmer's images without completely forgetting the social and political contexts (including the gendered relations of the Surrealist group) from which they emerge. But the tension for Sherman here is also the desire to remove her work from a more dogmatic feminist polemic, one that might seek to contain the aesthetic function of her images within a static and homogenous political reading, one that loses the ambiguity of the aesthetic function of the image. While Sherman's hybrid sex dolls provide a much more radical rearrangement of the body, one which unsettles a Surrealist avant-garde violation of female form, Sherman nevertheless draws on the political and aesthetic force of Bellmer's work. Confronted with Bellmer's and Sherman's images, we cannot remain passive viewers; our own desires and our own bodies are caught up in the contradictions that abound in these representations. The sense of crisis that these images provoke is exactly our own sense of crisis as to how we are implicated in their social and aesthetic ramifications; questions of violence, gender, sexuality and identity. It is precisely in this sense that Sherman investigates "the darker, savage, unspeakable side of a modernity."

Conclusion

In what sense then does Sherman's engagement with Surrealist iconography constitute an unsettling and disruptive return to the past that echoes Surrealism's own working through of *its* repressed past. Foster defines Surrealism's use of the outmoded as a strategic break with the past, one that nevertheless works through a "dialectic of ruination, recovery and resistance" (166):

> Surrealism is a metaphorical death of the nineteenth century in the sense that it breaks with it—its dominant values concerning art and politics, subjectivity and sexuality. But surrealism breaks with it through comedy, a rhetorical mode of collective reintegration, so it is also a symbolic working-through of the nineteenth century—of its image sphere of broken political promises, suppressed social movements, frustrated utopian desires. (167–8)

In her parodic recreations of Bellmer's dolls, Sherman works through the political and social codes and values underpinning Surrealist art and politics in a way that demonstrates the anxieties and ambiguities of its own "image sphere." Her graphic pornographic tableaux of anatomically correct medical mannequins ciphers the affective resonances of "shock" that emanate from the seductively damaged bodies of Bellmer's dolls in a way that makes apparent the "frustrated utopian desires" of any art practice. While both Bellmer's and Sherman's work stages a certain resistance to authoritarian cultural narratives and traditions, the extent to which they also risk internalizing the very ideologies they set out to critique provides an important heuristic frame in which to examine the relationship between them.

Notes

1 The critical war over Sherman's images exists at two different levels: the level of the more general meaning of the work and at the level of its meaning for feminist politics and aesthetics. Here I have delt with the first level and as I have indicated I will touch on the second level in the final chapter. Of course these different critical approaches overlap but here it has been necessary to look at the first level in order to tease out the implications of the second.

2 Barbara L. Miller writes that "In the early '70s, managers stopped displaying these images in the foyers of their theaters; any existing stills were sent to retail outlets where movie buffs could buy them for pennies. The images became collectors items, fetish objects and camp commodities. It was not the content of these images but, as Sherman confessed in a 1991 interview, the 'cheapness' of these now out-of-date productions that made them so exciting" (5).

3 Rosalind Krauss suggests that Judith Williamson was one of the first feminist critics to fully embrace Sherman's work. In her essay "Images of Woman," Williamson analyses Sherman's work in terms of visual style and performances of femininity. During the 1980s theories of masquerade and performance came to dominate discussions of film theory and gaze theory, culminating in 1990 with the publication of Butler's *Gender*

Trouble which goes back to Riviere's essay on masquerade in order to explore the notion of gender performativity. Krauss contrasts Williamson's essay with attempts by Mulvey and Solomon-Godeau to "recast" Sherman's work within a feminist context by arguing that it goes beyond "mere" feminist polemic (41).

4 In an interview with Noriku Fuku in 1997 Sherman discusses the rejection of this work: "I got a lot of criticism from feminists who said I was promoting negative stereotypes of women as victims … . It bothered me at first when people criticised [the work] … seeing the side I hadn't intended. I finally decided it was something I had to accept" (125).

5 For an important discussion on the ambivalence of reading practices, see Kobena Mercer's two articles on Robert Mapplethorpe's homoerotic photographs: "Skin Head Sex Thing: Racial Difference and the Homoerotic Imaginary" and "Reading Racial Fetishism: The Photographs of Robert Mapplethorpe."

6 Criticism of Sherman's and Mapplethorpe's work, by both the right and the left, reflects the way in which the debate about "political correctness" during the 1980s and early 1990s was itself usurped by the right. As John Guillory argues "The phenomenon of 'political correctness,' recently the object of so much complaint in the right-wing media, can be seen … as the paradoxical triumph in the university of an otherwise defeated liberalism. It is not surprising that a progressive discourse, more or less routed in American culture, should find itself driven to police the borders of its diminished territory. As everyone on the left knows, the concept of political correctness was formulated within left discourse itself to critique the tendency to moralistic posturing provoked by the dire situation of an increasingly reactionary social order" (1993: 342–3).

7 The controversy surrounding Mapplethorpe's exhibition arose when the director of the Cincinnati Contemporary Arts Centre faced obscenity charges for mounting a touring exhibition of Mapplethorpe's work. Mapplethorpe's exhibition "The Perfect Moment" was first mounted in 1988 in Philadelphia before traveling to other cities throughout the states. In the period between its first showing and its arrival in Cincinatti, Mapplethorpe had died of AIDS. When the show had reached Washington, the stop before Cincinnati, Jesse Helms and the religious right mounted a massive campaign against Mapplethorpe's work, which resulted in the gallery caving in and closing the show. When it finally moved to Cincinnati, Helms's campaign continued, resulting in obscenity charges being laid against the director of the Arts Centre.

8 Dubin notes that the art critic Hilton Kramer executed what became a typical ploy for conservative art critics, which was to express outrage at the public funding of art which even a liberated press found too controversial and distasteful to publish (175).

9 In Kobena Mercer's reading of the racial fetishism in Mapplethorpe's portraits of black men, he takes up Raymond Williams's term to explore "the complex structure of feeling" evoked in these images. In a revised reading of an earlier discussion of Mapplethorpe's work, Mercer attempts to "take back the unavoidably moralistic connotation" of the term fetishism, in order to trace his own "ambivalent structure of feeling" in response to Mapplethorpe's images (1995: 179). Mercer's reading is compelling for the way in which he returns to the implications of his earlier reading practice in the context of the political and cultural censure of Mapplethorpe's work.

10 Kobena Mercer explains the way in which Mapplethorpe's images inscribe racial fetishism: "The scopic fixation on black skin thus implies a kind of 'negrophilia,' an

aesthetic idealization and erotic investment in the racial other that inverts and reverses the binary axis of the fears and anxieties invested in or projected onto the other in 'negrophobia'" (1995: 175).

11 In 1947 Bellmer provided illustrations for the second printing of Bataille's *Story of the Eye*. Sue Taylor argues that Bellmer had intuitively grasped many of the ideas around eroticism and transgression that Bataille explores in this novel as well as in his theoretical writings, long before he came to read Bataille's novel (136).

12 Ted Gott suggests that *Document* "is perhaps best remembered for its recognition of photography's potential for sexual totemism" (136).

13 Like *Document*, *Minotaure* was an interdisciplinary magazine, publishing criticism, philosophy, ethnology, anthropology, psychoanalysis as well as articles on music, architecture and art.

14 See Therese Lichtenstein (2001), Sue Taylor (2001), Hal Foster (1993) and Peter Webb (1985).

15 There were a number of episodes in Bellmer's life in which he cross-dressed. The most significant involved a visit with his father to Berlin in 1921. At the conclusion of their journey by train, Bellmer emerged from his cabin fully dressed as a woman, with make-up and wig. He then proceeded, much to his father's outrage and embarrassment, to walk with him through the streets of Berlin. This prank was clearly designed to annoy his father, who had accompanied him on his journey to attend engineering school, what would otherwise be a conventional rite of passage for father and son.

16 Sherman's interest in the abject body and its viscera mirrors a Surrealist fusion of the grotesque and the erotic, in particular in the work of the more dissident Surrealists: Bataille, Leiris and also Bellmer. In an article in *Document*, Michel Leiris examines the painting of a corpse by the artist Antoine Caron. In the painting a soldier shoves his fist into the stomach of the dead man. Discussing this image, Leiris notes that the internal organs have an erotic effect. In a 1930 edition of *Document* Leiris sets the stage for a decade to come, in which Surrealism and those on its edges would become increasingly preoccupied by erotic violence:

> Masochism, sadism and almost all vices are in the end only ways of feeling oneself more human—because one is in a deeper and more direct connection with the body—such that the sight of wrinkles and viscera, terrible for some, take us a step further towards an intensification of our human consciousness … the most atrocious visions, like the cruellest pleasures, are absolutely legitimate if they contribute to such a development of humanity. (Leiris cited in Gott, 1993: 136)s

17 Lichtenstein reveals how Bellmer was influenced by the German neurologist Paul Schilder's ideas on body image. According to Schilder our body image develops through both an individual experience of sensation as well as the perception of our body from the external world. As such our body image is in a constant process of construction and deconstruction (34).

18 The question of complicity and resistance in relation to Bellmer's work unfolds in two recent book length studies of Bellmer's work. In *Behind Closed Doors*, Therese Lichtenstein suggests that although Bellmer's dolls are certainly disturbing and confronting, the dolls' artificiality is always foregrounded so that what we get is a complicated projection of male anxiety directed against an authoritarian masculinist culture. In order to arrive at this reading Lichtenstein leaves out of critical

consideration Bellmer's more explicit pornographic drawings of children as well as his pornographic photographs of his various lovers and partners. On the other hand, Sue Taylor, in *Hans Bellmer: The Anatomy of Anxiety*, seems trapped within a reading of perversion rather than the images themselves. However, she makes some important points which highlight the problematic nature of how to read these images. Taylor concludes that "While Bellmer's doll photographs, with their egregious manipulations of female anatomy, may have been suspect in the sociopolitical context of Nazi Germany, they found immediate acceptance within another patriarchal order, in France—the overwhelmingly male heterosexist Surrealist avant-garde" (98).

19 See discussion in Chapter 7.

Chapter 7

Conclusion: Disturbing the Feminist Subject

> Contemporary feminist debates over the meanings of gender lead time and again to a certain sense of trouble, as if the indeterminacy of gender might eventually culminate in the failure of feminism. Perhaps trouble need not carry such a negative valence.
>
> —Judith Butler, Preface (1990)
>
> *Gender Trouble: Feminism and the Subversion of Identity*

Introduction

In conclusion I want to briefly reflect on feminist theory's ambivalent reception of Cindy Sherman's work; what it tells us about the work itself and what it conveys about the critical climate of feminism in the recent past. Since much of this reaction has centered on Sherman's representation of gender in one form or another, I want to discuss the question of Sherman's representational practice in relation to Judith Butler's work on gender and its often controversial critical reception. My purpose is not simply to use Butler's work as a straightforward illustration of Sherman's art practice, though Butler's work on gender provides important theoretical tools for understanding Sherman's representational practice and vice versa, but rather to examine how their work has become a site of contestation and struggle within feminist theory. While on one level this scene of struggle is itself a sign of the productive diversity of academic feminism, it nevertheless elucidates the fragilities of cohesion that have simultaneously constrained and broadened the political horizon of feminism. As such the very ambivalence of positionality that has shaped the critical discussion of the subjects of this book opens up the broader limitations of any kind of political and intellectual affiliation. While feminism's polarized reaction to Butler's work unravels the problematic nature of the universal female subject within feminist theory and politics, the contention around Sherman's work hinges on whether her work merely reinscribes normative codes of femininity or in fact challenges those codes. What becomes evident then is feminism's practice of inclusion and exclusion; the question of proper and improper feminist acts. I want to argue that the question of an improper feminist act arises in relation to Butler and Sherman in terms of two major concerns. The first is the perceived success of the work that operates to delegitimize its critical power in relation to feminism's traditionally more marginal status as a political and theoretical tool challenging the status quo. In other words how can Butler and Sherman's work be considered as proper feminist acts when the very status of their work is understood to have broad appeal and to be flourishing within and against a traditional feminist politics; that is, how can work seemingly saturated with power be considered feminist? The second concern hinges around their challenge to the ground of the "real" as a transparent field of operations that locate the experience and material conditions of women as the motivating force of feminist politics. Sherman's employment of parodic effects to create highly ambiguous representations of the female body and gendered subjectivity and Butler's emphasis on the radical possibilities of parody and performance in gender subversion shift the political goal of feminism from a paradigm of total transformation (one which is premised on a knowable, objectified set of conditions and their effects) to an illumination of the indeterminacy of gender, a regime that produces identifications, negotiations and refusals, which are never fully transparent to the subject. Central to this debate is a poststructuralist and postmodernist challenge to the privileging of experience and its reliance on certain united claims to truth as the very ground on which social change might be orchestrated. This has opened up what has become a cyclical pattern of divisive contest within feminist politics in the last two decades at least; the tension between a symbolic and material politics, a strategic politics of resignification or a politics of united political action concerned with wide-scale institutional reform. Without attempting to heal this rift or to suggest that either politics need cancel out the other, I want to reflect on the very valency of trouble in order to make some tentative conclusions about why Sherman and Butler's projects—one aesthetic, the other philosophical—are indeed important for feminist cultural theory. The very fact that both Butler and Sherman return to strategic moments within modernity—Sherman to Surrealism and Bellmer, Butler to Lacan and Riviere—discloses the important legacies of Surrealism and psychoanalysis for the present; remembering that for both Surrealism and psychoanalysis, the experience of everyday life was saturated with the residues of fantasy and imagination that thwarted any straightforward understanding of the psychic and material operations that inform aesthetic and political life.

Body Double/Body Trouble

The appearance of Madonna and Cindy Sherman in *Rolling Stone* magazine in 1997 marked a typical postmodern encounter between art and popular culture, one that for many critics might have become the very sign of Sherman's increasing popular appeal and the commodification of her work. The occasion for the meeting between these two blonde icons was Sherman's retrospective exhibition of her *Untitled Film Stills* (1977–80) at the Museum of Modern Art, which was sponsored by Madonna. Madonna's well-known promotion and collection of art—by Robert Mapplethorpe, Frida Kahlo as well as Sherman—reveals a penchant for work that trades on a certain fetish of difference: of women, eroticized black men, and the cultural exotic. Madonna's changing personae as well as her use of camp, itself borrowed from gay subculture, similarly encodes the fetishization of difference as central to the subversion of gendered performance. While Madonna might be rightly accused of a form of subcultural tourism that risks cannabalizing the cultural expressions of marginalized groups, at some level her work obviates the anxieties around authenticity that pertain to any production of difference. While critics castigate Madonna for what they see as a commercially driven cult of difference, one that renders any subversion of gender politically compromised, is there any instance where gender itself is completely located outside of commodity experience. Is this not the lesson of Sherman's film stills; the gap opened up by the performance of femininity as a product of the culture at large and the subversive potential of its ironic or parodic reiteration. As with Sherman, any subversive potential of Madonna's work is only legible if we read the ever-changing performance of femininity in her music and video-clips as ironic reiterations that refuse a seamless or stable identity. What is therefore most striking about the photograph of Madonna and Sherman together is its reproduction of one of Sherman's own Film Stills, *Untitled #13*. In this image a female college student or librarian reaches for a book from a library shelf; but having her attention suddenly distracted, she turns to face the camera and is caught in that moment of knowing that she is being watched. In the photograph of Sherman and Madonna, artist and pop singer pose against the backdrop of what appears to be the MOMA library offices, against shelves of books that resemble the library shelf in the original. The uncanny—or canny—reproduction of this image as well as the doubling of Sherman and Madonna as stand-ins for the blonde woman in the original, evokes precisely the kind of circularity and quotation that challenges the ontological grammar of the original, the authentic, the imaginary elsewhere of feminine being.

According to Abigail Solomon-Godeau, the promotion of Cindy Sherman by both the art world and the media has only been made possible by the erasure of the feminist qualities of her work and that the success of the work "depends on the distortion or repression of the most destabilizing, denaturalizing, and subversive elements in her work" (1991: 115). She argues that with Sherman's transition into major artist status, by 1987 "an apparatus of publicity replaced an apparatus of criticism" (113). Though the photograph of Madonna and Sherman could be read as a perfect example of the apparatus of publicity taking shape around Sherman, is there not the sense in which the photograph itself, in miming Sherman's own work, is not altogether unaware of the publicity/critical dichotomy; indeed that the two need not be mutually exclusive. Since 1987 the academic work on Sherman has continued to flourish, as has the publicity of Sherman and her work, both positive and negative, in the wider media. Moreover, does this kind of reading not risk reducing the critical efficacy of Sherman's work to authorial biography, to Sherman's status as celebrity artist in a way that assumes an instrumental connection between the identity of the author and the meaning of the work. Such a dichotomy also proceeds from the assumption that feminism itself has no investment in the power that circulates in and around images, subjects and institutions, as though feminism can remain outside the sphere of a mediated culture, which produces both celebrity and publicity. Finally, what is achieved by distancing the critical edge of Sherman's work from mediated culture when this is precisely the realm with which Sherman's work provides its most incisive engagement? I therefore want to use this seemingly troubling image of celebrity doubling to frame my reading of the Sherman phenomenon within the context of feminist theory's own troubled relationship with the feminine subject. Since the category of gender remains a constant theme in her work, I want to argue that Sherman's work is important for feminism, but that importance does not overcome either the ambiguity of the work itself nor does it rest on Sherman's own avowal or disavowal of feminism. That feminist critics have been both fascinated and disturbed by Sherman's images attests to the shifting contours of feminism itself.[1] Therefore in order to broadly map the critical reception of Sherman's work within feminist theory it is necessary to return to key moments that constituted the emergence of feminism's ambivalent response to Sherman's work.

Although critics such as Judith Williamson and Rosalind Krauss were quick to praise the critical edge in Sherman's work, others felt that Sherman herself had fallen prey to the very process of fetishization, reproducing stereotypical images of women that reinscribe their denigration within culture. Mira Schor most forcefully put this kind of argument forward in her hostile review of Sherman's work in the late 1980s. In "From Liberation to Lack" Schor lamented the fact that feminism "has little institutional memory" and no "collective absorption of early achievements and ideas" (1989: 15). Inserting herself into the article as "a living bridge across ebb tides of feminist thought" (15), Schor nostalgically defines her role as a feminist art teacher in terms of imparting "the ABCs of feminist art history" to her "unformed art students" in order to remove "the rose-filtered lenses that camouflage patriarchal domination" (15). Implicit in Schor's tone and developed throughout the essay is a binary apparatus of experience and theory, rhetorically elaborated as "good" feminist art based on "personal experiences re-examined in consciousness-raising" (15–16) versus bad feminist art of the kind Sherman produces:

> One has to see a Sherman photograph on a person's wall to understand the nature of its appeal: a wet t-shirt clinging suggestively to breasts is *la même chose*, whether you call it *draperie mouillée* [Kenneth Clarke, *The Nude*] or tits and ass. These negative representations are disturbingly close to the way men have traditionally experienced or fantasized women. Sherman's camera is male. Her images are successful partly because they do not threaten phallocracy, they reiterate and confirm it. (17)

La même chose, a phrase repeated twice in the essay, eschews any sense of a deconstructive practice operating in Sherman's work or indeed an ironic reflection of the cultural material reproduced in her images. According to Schor, Sherman's images are simply "the same as" a traditional western nude, "the same as" a

Playboy centerfold. What the essay reveals, however, is the degree to which Schor's polemical critique of Sherman hinges around an aversion to any kind of reading strategy other than the most literal. For Schor "tits and ass" is simply that no matter what the discursive context or genre. If the operation of parody involves a strategy of encoding *and* decoding through the twin modes of recognition and interpretation, to read Sherman's images simply as the consumption of myth, as "tits and ass," is to recognize but not interpret. Decrying deconstruction's resistance to essentialism—to what she calls the "real" differences experienced by men and women—Schor suggests that feminist representations of female sexuality and the body must strive toward capturing their own experiences in the face of any critical censure that deems such practices as essentialist. That a version of this essay was reprinted in 1994, under the new heading "Appropriation and Backlash" in a volume titled *The Power of Feminist Art: The American Movement of the 1970s, History and Impact*, attests to Schor's ongoing sense that Sherman's work constitutes a backlash to earlier feminist art.

While Schor's review is striking for its overly literal reading of Sherman's work, Rosalind Krauss notes that even when feminists embrace Sherman's work

> they have been disgusted by its consumption as myth. For such consumption, they point out, inverts the terms of Sherman's work, taking the very thing she is holding up for critical inspection and transposing it on the grounds of praise. (1993: 173)

Moreover, Sherman's refusal to speak up as a feminist has perplexed many of her critics. Although Sherman clearly acknowledges the cultural context shaping the production of her images, including feminist theory's important contribution to understanding the cultural construction of female identity and representation, she rejects the idea that the work can be reduced to a straightforward ideological critique. While Mulvey I think rightly argues that Sherman's work is inconceivable "without a prehistory of feminism and its theorization of the body and representation" (1991: 138), this is not the same as suggesting that her work conveys a singular feminist polemic:

> Even though I've never actively thought of my work as a feminist or as a political statement, certainly everything in it was drawn from my observations as a woman in this culture. And a part of that is a love-hate thing—being infatuated with make-up and glamour and detesting it at the same time. (Interview, 1997: 80) [2]

Sherman's ambivalent ("love-hate") relationship to postmodern culture—specifically her identity as a woman within that culture—emerges in the work as a complicated dynamic of complicity and resistance in relation to the authoritarian cultural narratives and traditions with which her work engages, including feminism. The strategies of parody and pastiche that her work utilizes necessarily risk internalizing the very ideologies they set out to critique; but they also disclose the ruses of power latent within the logic of masquerade wherein the citation and reiteration of gender norms is both stabilized and destabilized. In Schor's critique, however, the sense in which parody might work to destabilize traditional subject positions for women is completely negated because the images come too close to the way women have been traditionally subordinated by patriarchal culture. In its parodic reproduction of representational "identities," I would argue that Sherman's work *is* useful for feminism precisely because it exposes the original as itself "a parody of the *idea* of the natural and the original" (Butler, 1990: 31). In other words, as Butler's work has shown, while gender is constructed through the citation of norms and signs which render it legible, this need not imply that gender is *always* socially pre-determined in a way that denies the subject any sense of agency, since in the repetition of those codes, the possibility of negotiation and subversion arise. While Sherman's work, like Butler's, suggests that we cannot entirely escape gender, the images force us to reflect on the naturalized codes of femininity that Schor wants to reinscribe as "real;" it is in the very repetition of those codes that Sherman's images enact a self-reflexiveness around gender stereotypes. We might say that Sherman's images bring into play an agency around identity performance that disrupts the chain of signification that reduces them to reified feminine stereotypes.

More recently Nadine Lemmon has suggested that the ambivalent critical reception of Sherman's work is an indication that "the meaning of the work totters dangerously on the cusp between progressive deconstruction and repressive replication (1993: 101). This leads Lemmon to conclude that Sherman's refusal to speak up about the politics of her work or to name herself as a feminist, to become a model feminist representative, is a successful ploy, "a safe route" in her journey to celebrity artist status. It is as though Lemmon wants to castigate Sherman for not making up her mind, for not being responsible to the work. Such a reading of course rests on an utterly problematic reduction of meaning solely to authorial intention; but even if we allow the usefulness of an artist's comments for a reading of the work, Sherman has suggested time and again that the work is not about her in particular, even if it stems from a "love-hate thing" that defines what is to be a woman in contemporary culture. To acknowledge that love and hate are opposite emotional responses is to underline the enormous power and deception of the images; as Krauss suggests "Sherman as de-myth-ifier is specifically allowing us, encouraging us to look under the hood, even as she is also showing us the tremendous pull to buy into the myth" (1999: 110).

It seems that the very ambiguity of the images produced for the viewer what Kobena Mercer has called "ambivalent structures of feeling" (1994: 171).[3] In Mercer's reading of the racial fetishism in Robert Mapplethorpe's portraits of black men, he takes up Raymond Williams's idea of shared "structures of feeling" that shape particular collective moments in history to explore his own ambivalent subjective and affective response to Mapplethorpe's images. While Mercer had initially found that in framing and objectifying male black bodies Mapplethorpe was complicit in degrading black men, he also suggests that in representing the black male body through traditional codes of classical beauty and formal aesthetics, he also potentially empowers the black male nude by inserting it into traditional Western art where previously it had been absent. In reflecting on his initial response to these images in terms of fascination and disappointment, pleasure and disturbance, Mercer concludes that he was caught in a moment of liminal "textual ambivalence." In his revised reading, however, Mercer attempts to "take back the unavoidably moralistic connotation" of the term fetishism, in order to trace his own "ambivalent structure of feeling" in response to Mapplethorpe's work (1995: 179). By pointing to the way in which emotional ambivalence occurs at the intersection of the psychic and the social, experience and knowledge, Mercer suggests that in his earlier reading he had focused on the negative emotional valences of disappointment, anger and disturbance because of his own location and position as a black male critic. However, reflecting on this position, Mercer argues that this earlier reading could only take place by blocking out one side of his ambivalence, namely pleasure and fascination, which reflect his own fantasies and desires as a viewing subject. What Mercer's reading compellingly divulges is the importance of keeping alive the opposite emotional valences that inform his response to the work as well as the ambivalence conveyed through the images themselves. He therefore concludes that "Mapplethorpe's work is powerful and disturbing precisely because it forces such acknowledgement of the ambivalence of identity and identification we actually inhabit in living with difference (1993: 335).

In Mercer's revised reading there is an important cautionary tale about the wider implications of the politics of representation. In the overly moralistic readings of the sexual fetishization in Sherman's images (by Schor and others) is there not a closing down of the very ambivalence—hate and love—that Sherman suggests structure their production. In reproducing the kind of literal reading that Schor puts forward, one has to position Sherman's, and potentially the viewer's, identification with the subject of her images solely in terms of love and infatuation, when in fact there is also hate and detestation. In other words to privilege such an ideologically structured reading (a particular mode of feminist reading), we have to shut down the very ambivalence around identity and identification that inform actual lived experience. Through his concept of a structure of feeling Williams provided a way of thinking about certain lived social experiences that although felt to be emerging are nevertheless not yet fully codified. In this sense a structure of feeling is often comprised of what is felt strongly but not yet fully articulated, all that which comes through "as disturbance, tension, blockage, emotional trouble" (*Literature and Revolution*: 17). However, one of the ways in which we do get a glimpse of what he calls "a social experience which is still in process" (36), is through works of art, which mange to convey the emergence of new structures of feeling before they become fully coherent. Here Williams attempts to demonstrate how different modes of artistic production may convey a politics of affect that does not necessarily form part of any clear ideological position (35). If Sherman's work, from the *Untitled Film Stills* and the "Centerfolds" through to the "Disasters" series and finally the "Sex Pictures," stage an ongoing crisis of representation for the female body as well as feminine subjectivity, what kind of affective residues of actual lived experience were being mapped in the process? To put it very simply, could it be that the enormous appeal and power of Sherman's work resides precisely in the way that the images tap into the very ambivalence that defines what it feels like to be a woman in contemporary culture; to be fascinated with the myth of femininity as well as to be disturbed by its pervasive power. Indeed as the history of the critical reception of Sherman's work reveals, these works would not slide easily into an existing feminist art paradigm, but bring with them a sense of "disturbance, tension, blockage, emotional trouble"—to use Williams' words.

Gender Trouble

Mulvey's suggestion that the *Untitled Film Stills* arrived on the art scene at a time when the female body was unrepresentable unless framed within the context of feminist theory invites us to read them in part as a critique of feminist representations of the body up until that moment. Similarly, Judith Butler's disarticulation of the traditional link between sex and gender within feminist theory served as a counter move to the proscriptive discourse on gender and sexuality that had dominated feminism up until the 1980s. Central to Butler's project in *Gender Trouble* is her interrogation of the naturalization of the heterosexual matrix; that is how sex/gender and nature/culture dualisms are constructed and naturalized in and through one another (1990: 36). An important part of that argument was to reveal how identity categories within feminism are themselves the site of a violent exclusion, which ultimately constrains the very possibilities that feminism attempts to open up (1999: 197). By drawing attention to the blind spots of feminism's own political enterprise, Butler questioned the presumptive status of the "real" as it came to shape the institutional and political goals of feminism as well as a binary theory of gender. In suggesting that gender identity is both ambivalent and indeterminate, neither fixed nor "real" in the sense of an authentic gendered identity, Butler's theory of performativity allowed for the possibility that gender may become a site of subversion. Ambivalence is important in Butler's work precisely because it opens up a slippage between the regulatory command of gender norms and the indeterminate nature of their articulation. But nevertheless Butler is quick to point out that any act of subversion is also necessarily implicated in the relations of power that it seeks to oppose. As such Butler concludes that there is no "political position purified of power, and perhaps that impurity is what produces agency as the potential interruption and reversal of regulatory regimes" (1999: xxvi).

In the Preface to the tenth anniversary publication of *Gender Trouble*, Butler reflects on her original intention in the writing of the book as well as the subsequent criticism of it:

> As I wrote it, I understood myself to be in an embattled and oppositional relation to certain forms of feminism, even as I understood the text to be part of feminism itself. I was writing in the tradition of immanent critique that seeks to provoke critical examination of the basic vocabulary of the movement of thought to which it belongs. There was and remains warrant for such a mode of criticism and to distinguish between self-criticism that promises a more democratic and inclusive life for the movement and criticism that seeks to undermine it altogether. (1999: vii)

Despite Butler's intention to contribute to "the cultural life of a political struggle" located both inside and outside the academy, the widespread appeal of the book became an indictment of its necessary failure. Nearly a decade after its publication Martha Nussbaum launched a critical and disparaging attack on Butler under the title, "The Professor of Parody—The Hip Defeatism of Judith Butler" (1999). Although the proper names are different and the context has shifted slightly, the terms of the debate in Nussbaum's article uncannily reconstitute Mira Schor's own critique of "good" and "bad" feminism. If "experience" is the defining term of Schor's polemic against Sherman and deconstruction, in Nussbaum's article the category of the "real" is taken up as the sign of an "old style" feminist politics versus the "the new symbolic type" of feminist thinkers—which, according to Nussbaum, Butler personifies. Lined up behind Butler are young feminists brainwashed by French postmodernist thought who produce "fancy words on paper" and think that politics involves "poking fun" at the powers that repress them. In "the new feminism," Nussbaum argues, there is no room for large-scale social change and only the "flimsiest connections with the real situation of real women" (37). Nussbaum suggests that within Butler's politics of "quietism" and "retreat," all one can do is find "spaces within the structures of power in which to parody them, to poke fun at them, to transgress them in speech" (37). This is in contrast to Nussbaum's own feminist politics which are grounded in "the material conditions of real women," in "real bodies" and "real struggles" (37).

While Nussbaum is not the first to draw the conclusion that poststructuralism has infected feminism with its "empty" politics, what is distinctive in her attack on Butler is the sense in which it has become the very sign of feminism's failure:

> … there is a despair at the heart of the cheerful Butlerian enterprise. The big hope, the hope for a world of real justice, where laws and institutions protect the dignity of all citizens, has been banished, even perhaps mocked as sexually tedious. Judith Butler's hip quietism is a comprehensible response to the difficulty of realizing justice in America. But it is a bad response. It collaborates with evil. Feminism demands more and women deserve better. (1999: 37)

Nussbaum restages the traditional feminist debate between theory and practice in terms of narcissistic symbolic theory and productive "real" politics. As Robyn Wiegman cogently argues, Nussbaum attempts to "retrieve a humanist subject animated by 'the suffering of others', a subject who sees the future in a "real" world now disarticulated from the academy's illusory attachment to abstraction"

(1999: 130). For Nussbaum, the category of the "real" becomes a polemical weapon against theory, against interpretation, and most of all against a feminist theory that does not embrace her own political goals. In Nussbaum's article the "real" is tied to an "old-style" feminist politics which is set up in opposition to the symbolic and parodic work of "the new feminism."[4]

While Schor's and Nussbaum's critiques unleash a familiar debate about the competing claims of theory and practice, or theory and experience, their polemical force serves to prescribe the female subject of feminism within a rigidly defined "real," a category which for Nussbaum is the only ground on which political agency may be conceived. Moreover, it is precisely this kind of reification of the "real" that the work of both Butler and Sherman, in their different ways, brings into question; particularly its essentialist figuration within feminist and other representational discourses. Politically aligned to an ontologically stable feminist subject, Nussbaum misreads the political efficacy of parody despite Butler's insistence that it may be a useful political tool precisely because of its paradoxical strategy as authoritarian and transgressive, which within the politics of feminine masquerade unfolds "the slippery distinction between 'appearing' and 'being'" (1990: 47).

For Schor and Nussbaum, however these theoretical and aesthetic interventions reflect a crisis that is perceived within the rubric of "'the idiom of failure' pervasive to academic feminism's perception of itself" (Weigman, 1999). Closely tied to this notion of failure is the sense in which the widespread influence of feminism outside the academy has resulted in its preoccupation with celebrity and self-obsession rather than justice and social reform. Indeed with Sherman's increasing celebrity critics have suggested that there has been a concomitant decline in feminist analyses of her work; whether this can be substantiated or not, underpinning such claims is the sense in which Sherman's supposed celebrity status has tainted her usefulness for feminist theory. Although *Gender Trouble* was never intended as a work of popular theory, its appeal both inside and outside the academy is used by Nussbaum as the very sign of feminism's increasing concern with its career advancement; condemned as "hip" and "cheerful" on the one hand and as "a collaboration with evil" on the other, Nussbaum implies that Butler has sold out for the sake of academic stardom and in the process infected young feminists with the fashionableness of her theories.

In the new Preface Butler responds to the question of the usefulness of her politics of resignification:

> It has been one of the most gratifying experiences for me that the text continues to move outside the academy to this day. At the same time that this book was taken up by Queer Nation … it was among the materials that also helped to prompt members of the American Psychoanalytic Association and the American Psychological Association to reassess some of their current doxa on homosexuality. (1999: xvii)

Butler's text, far from signifying a move towards abstraction, has precipitated a rethinking of gender that has had far reaching effects on the material conditions of men and women. In other words, a symbolic politics does not operate outside the social relations and practices that inform it, but rather works to unmask the discursive investments and the will to power that inform the production of normative social subjects. As such her interrogation of identity categories does not suggest that we can dispense with identity altogether, but aims to reveal the way in which such categories are constructed as "natural" and "universal" across space and time. In this sense, Butler's critique, far from being disconnected from a feminism concerned with the material effects of gender subordination, actually provides important tactical tools for responding to precisely those exclusionary systemic practices that enact subordination.

Underlying the critical attacks on Sherman and Butler, however, is a potent sense of loss over a form of political idealism that we would not want to deny achieved something quite remarkable. For even if we reject the logic of such arguments for the present and the future, the affective charge of the promise underlying such political convictions is something we might not want to lose entirely. As Wendy Brown has suggested, "to identify politically conservative tendencies" in feminism "does not vitiate" its achievement (2005: 110), nor does the strategic loss of ground in one area of feminist politics necessarily herald its total demise: "Certainly it is possible to expand the subject of feminism while narrowing feminism's political vision" (110). Rather than lamenting the past as a way of pointing to the failures of the present, Brown contends, "avowing our loss may enable us to cultivate the memory—and with Benjamin—ignite that memory—of the utopian imaginary of the revolutionary paradigm and so make that imaginary part of our knowledge for working in the present" (115). In this sense perhaps we also need to retrieve the notion of "crisis" from its sole association with failure and narcissistic danger, remembering instead that crisis lies at the very heart of a revolutionary paradigm. In Butler and Sherman's work crisis seems to mark a critical turning point, a productive tension in which the very conditions and possibilities of aesthetic and theoretical work are interrogated. The concept of crisis must therefore assert itself as a moment of renegotiation, one in which the production of dissonant mechanisms and strategies extends our concept of the feminist subject in its theoretical and political contexts. In their different ways, Sherman and Butler have interrogated the very concept of what it means to produce "feminist" theory and art in a way that obviates the productive political dimensions of the notion of "crisis." These kinds of self-reflexive approaches invariably produce work that is by its very nature both "troubled" and "troubling." But, I would argue, it is this very capacity to trouble that sustains vibrant intellectual debate and nurtures a relationship between the past and the present, between theory and experience or theory and politics, which generates new critical positions for the future. While the dream of revolution may appear to be historically outmoded, it may well be that through the utopian imaginary of the revolutionary paradigm, Surrealism and feminism still have a great deal to teach us.

Notes

1 See Barbara L. Miller's article for a discussion of the ambivalent attitude to Sherman's work.

2 In response to Sherman's refusal to speak up as a feminist Rosalind Krauss concludes that: "The idea that the artist has a responsibility to come forward with an explicit reading of her or his work seems just as peculiar as the idea that the only way to produce such a reading … would be through words" (1993: 207).

3 Laura Mulvey (1991), Nadine Lemmon (1993) and Abigail Solomon-Godeau (1995) in various ways reflect a critical ambivalence in relation to Sherman's work.

4 In her reflective piece, "Remembering Women's Studies," Alice Gambrell observes that "In the present … we are witnessing the reemergence of a constant within academic feminist debate, one that reconstitutes itself every few years, each time with a slightly different terminological or methodological tonality" (93).

Bibliography

Adams, Bronte and Trudi Tate, eds. *That Kind of Woman: Stories From the Left Bank and Beyond.* London: Virago, 1991.

Angeles, Paul de. "Interview With Leonora Carrington," in *Leonora Carrington: The Mexican Years, 1943–1985*. San Francisco: Mexican Museum, 1991.

———. "Interview With Leonora Carrington", *El Paseante 17*, ed. Nadine van Hasselt. Trans. Cecilia Martinez. N.d., n.p.

Appignanesi, Lisa and John Forrester. *Freud's Women*. Harmondsworth: Penguin, 2000.

Apter, Emily and William Pietz, eds. *Fetishism and Cultural Discourse*. Ithaca and London: Cornell University Press, 1993.

Assa, Sonia. "Gardens of Delight or What's Cookin'? Leonora Carrington in the Kitchen," *Studies in Twentieth Century Literature*, 15. Summer (1991), 213–27.

Baker, Michael. *Our Three Selves: The Life of Radclyffe Hall*. London: Hamilton, 1985.

Barron, Stephanie, ed. *Degenerate Art: The Fate of Avant-Garde Art in Nazi Germany*, Exhibition Catalogue. Los Angeles, CA: Los Angeles County Museum of Art, 1991.

Barthes, Roland. *Camera Lucida*. London: Vintage, 1993. First published in 1980.

Bataille, Georges. "The Metaphor of the Eye," in George Bataille, *Story of the Eye*. Penguin, 1979. First published in 1963.

———. *Story of the Eye*. Trans. Joachim Neugroschal. Great Britain: Penguin, 1982. First published in 1928 under the pseudonym Lord Auch.

———. *Visions of Excess: Selected Writings*. Ed. Allan Stoekl. Minneapolis: University of Minnesota Press, 1985.

———. *The Absence of Myth: Writings on Surrealism*. Ed. and trans. Michael Richardson. London and New York: Verso, 1994.

———. *Eroticism*. Trans. Mary Dalwood. London and New York: Marion Boyars, 1994. First published in 1957.

Beauvoir, Simone de. *The Prime of Life: The Autobiography of Simone de Beauvoir, 1929–1944*. Trans. Peter Green. Intro. Toril Moi. New York: Paragon House, 1992.

Bell, Michael. *Literature, Modernism and Myth: Belief and Responsibility in the Twentieth Century*. Cambridge: Cambridge University Press, 1997.

Bellmer, Hans. *Hans Bellmer: Photographs*. Exhibition Catalogue, Krannert Art Museum. Illinois: University of Illinois, 1991.

———. "The Father" (1936). Trans. Allen S. White. Reprinted in Therese Lichtenstein, *Behind Closed Doors: The Art of Hans Bellmer*. Berkeley: University of California Press, 2001.

———. "Memories of the Doll Theme" (1934). Trans. Peter Chametzky, Susan Felleman and Jochen Schindler. Reprinted in Therese Lichtenstein, *Behind Closed Doors: The Art of Hans Bellmer*. Berkeley: University of California Press, 2001.

Benjamin, Walter. "The Work of Art in the Age of Mechanical Reproduction", *Illuminations*. Trans. Harry Zohn. Intro. Hannah Arendt. New York: Schocken Books, 1968.

———. "Surrealism: The Last Snapshot of the European Intelligentsia", *Selected Writings*, Vol. 2, 1927–34. Trans. Rodney Livingstone. Cambridge, MA and London, England: Harvard University Press, 1999.

———. *The Arcades Project*. Trans. Howard Eiland and Kevin McLaughlan. Ed. Rolf Tiedemann. Cambridge, MA: Harvard University Press, 2002.

Benstock, Shari. *Women of the Left Bank: Paris, 1900–1940*. Austin: University of Texas Press, 1986.

Bhabha, Homi K. *The Location of Culture*. London and New York: Routledge, 1994.

Boldt-Irons, Leslie Anne (ed). *On Bataille: Critical Essays*. Albany: State University of New York Press, 1995.

Breton, André. *Nadja*. Trans. Richard Howard. New York: Grove Press, 1960. First published 1928.

———. *Manifestoes of Surrealism*. Trans. Richard Seaver and Helen R. Lane. Ann Arbor: University of Michigan Press, 1972.

———. *Conversations: The Autobiography of Surrealism*. With André Parinaud and others. Trans. and intro. Mark Polizzotti. New York: Marlowe and Company, 1993. First published 1952.

———. *Anthology of Black Humour*. Trans. and intro. Mark Polizzotti. San Francisco: City Lights Books, 1997. First published 1941.

Bronfen, Elisabeth. *Over Her Dead Body: Death, Femininity and the Aesthetic*. Manchester: Manchester University Press, 1992.

Brophy, Kevin. *Creativity: Psychoanalysis, Surrealism and Creative Writing*. Melbourne, Victoria: Melbourne University Press, 1998.

Burke, Carolyn. "Lee Miller in Hitler's Bathtub," *Heat*, 12 (1999), 148–157.

Butler, Judith, "Imitation and Gender Insubordination," in Diana Fuss, ed. *Inside/Out: Lesbian Theories, Gay Theories*. New York and London: Routledge, 1991.

———. *Gender Trouble. Feminism and the Subversion of Identity*. New York and London: Routledge, 1990. Reprinted in 1999 with a new Preface.

Byatt, Helen. "Introduction," Leonora Carrington, *The Hearing Trumpet*. Boston: Exact Change, 1996. First published 1991.

Cahoone, Lawrence E., ed. and intro. *From Modernism to Postmodernism: An Anthology*. Oxford: Blackwell, 1996.

Cahun, Claude. "La 'Salomé' d'Oscar Wilde. Le procès Billing et les 47.000 pervertis du Livre noir". *Mercure de France*, No. 481, 1 July, 1918.

———. "Captive Balloon", "Poetry Keeps Its Secret", "The Invisible Adventure," in Penelope Rosemont, ed. *Surrealist Women: An International Anthology*. Austin: University of Texas Press, 1998.

Cahun, Claude. "La 'Salomé d'Oscar Wilde: Les procès Billing et les 47.000 pervertis du Livre Noir," in *Mercure de France*, VII, 1918.

———. *Claude Cahun Photographe, 1894–1954*. Exhibition Catalogue, Musée d'Art Moderne de la Ville de Paris. Paris: Jean-Michel, 1995.

Calinescu, Matei. *The Five Faces of Modernity: Modernism, Avant-Garde, Decadence, Kitsch, Postmodernism*. Durham, NC: Duke University Press, 1987.

Carrington, Leonora. "The Debutante" (1939), *The House of Fear. Notes From Down Below*. Trans. Katherine Talbot and Marina Warner. Intro. Marina Warner. London: Virago Press, 1989.

———. *Down Below*, in *The House of Fear: Notes from Down Below*. Trans. Katherine Talbot and Marina Warner. Intro. Marina Warner. London: Virago Press, 1989. First published 1944.

———. Leonora Carrington. *Paintings, Drawings and Sculptures 1940–1990*. Ed. Andrea Schlieker. Exhibition Catalogue, Serpentine Gallery, London, 1991.

———. *The Hearing Trumpet*. Exact Change: Boston, 1996. First published 1974.

Carrol, Rachel. "Something to See: Spectacle and Savagery in Leonora Carrington's Fiction," *Critique: Studies in Contemporary Fiction*, 9.2 (Winter, 1998), 154–67.

Carroll, Lewis. *Through The Looking Glass*. Harmondsworth: Penguin, 1994. First published 1872.

Carter, Angela. "The Alchemy of the Word" (1978), in *Expletives Deleted: Selected Writings*. London: Vintage, 1992.

——— (ed.) *Wayward Girls and Wicked Women: An Anthology of Stories*. London: Virago, 1986.

Castle, Terry. *Noel Coward and Radclyffe Hall: Kindred Spirits*. New York: Columbia University Press, 1996.

Caws, Mary Ann. *The Surrealist Look: An Erotics of Encounter*. Cambridge, MA: MIT Press, 1997.

Caws, Mary Ann, Rudolf Kuenzli and Gwen Raaberg, eds. *Surrealism and Women*. Cambridge, MA: MIT Press, 1991.

Chadwick, Whitney. *Women Artists and the Surrealist Movement*. London: Thames and Hudson, 1985.

——— and Isabelle de Courtivron, eds. *Significant Others: Creativity and Intimate Partnership*. London: Thames and Hudson, 1993.

Christensen, Peter. G. "The Flight From Passion in Leonora Carrington's Literary Work,"in Mary Ann Caws, Rudolf E. Kuenzli and Gwen Raaberg, eds, *Surrealism and Women*. Cambridge, MA and London: MIT Press, 1991.

Coffman, Christine E. "The Papin Enigma," *GLQ: A Journal of Lesbian and Gay Studies*, 5.3 (1999), 331–59.

Cohen, Margaret. *Profane Illumination. Walter Benjamin and the Paris of Surrealist Revolution*. Berkeley, Los Angeles and London: University of California Press, 1993.

Conley, Katharine. *Automatic Woman: The Representation of Woman in Surrealism*. Lincoln and London: University of Nebraska Press, 1996.

———. "Calude Cahun's Iconic Heads: From 'The Sadistic Judith' to *Human Frontier*," in Papers of Surrealism 2 (Summer 2004): http://www.surrealismcentre.ac.uk/publications/papers/journal2/index.htm.

Copjec, Joan "The Sartorial Superego," *October*, 50 (Fall 1990), 57–95.

Dean, Carolyn J. "Claude Cahun's Double," *Yale French Studies*. 90 June (1996), 71–92.

Derrida, Jaques. *Margins of Philosophy*. Trans. Alan Bass. Brighton: Harvester Press, 1982.

Doan, Laura. "Passing Fashions: Reading Female Masculinities in the 1920s," *Feminist Studies*, 24.3 (Fall 1998), 663–700.

———. *Fashioning Sapphism: The Origins of Modern English Lesbian Culture*. New York: Columbia University Press, 2001.

Dubin, Steven C. *Arresting Images: Impolitic Art and Uncivil Actions*. London and New York: Routledge, 1992.

Ellis, Havelock. "Sexual Inversion" (1897), *Studies in the Psychology of Sex, Volume 1*. New York: Random House, 1936.

Feldstein, Richard and Judith Roof, eds. *Feminism and Psychoanalysis*. Ithaca, NJ and London: Cornell University Press, 1989.

Fine, Reuben. *The History of Psychoanalysis.* New York: Continuum, 1990.

Flanner, Janet. *Paris was Yesterday 1925–39.* Ed. Irving Drutmen. London: Angus and Robertson, 1973.

Flugel, J.C. *Men and their Motives*. London: Kegan Paul, 1934.

———. *The Psychology of Clothes.* London: The Hogarth Press and The Institute of Psychoanalysis, 1950. First published 1930.

Foster, Hal. *Compulsive Beauty.* Cambridge, MA and London: MIT Press, 1993.

Foucault, Michel. *The History of Sexuality, Vol. 1*. Trans. Robert Hurley. Harmondsworth, England: Penguin, 1984. First published 1976.

———. *Foucault Live: Interviews, 1961–1984*. Ed. Sylvere Lotringer. Trans. Lysa Hochroth and John Johnston. New York: Semiotext(e), 1996.

———. "A Preface to Transgression", *Aesthetics: Essential Works of Foucault, 1954–1984*, Vol. 2. Ed. James D. Faubion. Trans. Robert Hurley et al. Harmondsworth: Penguin, 1998.

Freud, Sigmund. "Delusions and Dreams in Jenden's 'Gradiva'" (1907), *The Penguin Freud Library*, Vol. 14: *Art and Literature: Jensen's 'Gradiva', Leonardo Da Vinci and Other Works*. Ed. Albert Dickinson. Trans. Kames Strachey. Harmondsworth: Penguin, 1990.

———. "The 'Uncanny'" (1919), *The Penguin Freud Library*, Vol. 14: *Art and Literature: Jensen's 'Gradiva', Leonardo Da Vinci and Other Works*. Ed. Albert Dickinson. Trans. James Strachey. Harmondsworth: Penguin, 1990.

———. "Fetishism" (1927), *The Penguin Freud Library*, Vol. 7: *On Sexuality.* Harmondsworth, England: Penguin, 1991.

———. *The Interpretation of Dreams*. The Penguin Freud Library, Vol. 4, 1991.

———. "On Narcissism: An Introduction" (1920), *The Penguin Freud Library*, Vol. 2: *On Metapsychology: The Theory of Psychoanalysis*, Harmondsworth, England: Penguin, 1991.

———. "Psychoanalytic Notes on an Autobiographical Account of a Case of Paranoia" (1911), *The Penguin Freud Library*, Vol. 9. Harmondsworth: Penguin, 1991.

———. "Creative Writers and Daydreaming" (1909), *The New Penguin Freud: The Uncanny*. Trans. David McLintock. London: Penguin, 2003.

Fuku, Noriko. "A Woman of Parts: An Interview with Cindy Sherman," *Art in America*, 85.6 June (1997), 74–125.

Gambrell, Alice. *Women Intellectuals, Modernism and Difference: Transatlantic Culture, 1919–1945*. Cambridge: Cambridge University Press, 1997.

———. "Remembering Women's Studies," in Krzysztof Ziarek and Seamus Deane, eds, *Future Crossings: Literature Between Philosophy and Cultural Studies*. Evanston, IL: Northwestern University Press, 2000.

Garelick, Rhonda K. *Rising Star: Dandyism, Gender, and Performance in the Fin de Siècle*. Princeton, NJ: Princeton University Press, 1998.

Gott, Ted. "Lips of Coral: Sex and Violence in Surrealism," *Surrealism: Revolution By Night*. Exhibition Catalogue, National Gallery of Australia, 1993.

Guggenheim, Peggy. *Out of This Century: Confessions of an Art Addict*. Foreward Gore Vidal. New York: Universe Books, 1987.

Guillory, John. *Cultural Capital: The Problem of Literary Canon Formation*. Chicago: University of Chicago Press, 1993.

Guerlac, Suzanne. *Literary Polemics: Bataille, Sartre, Valéry, Breton*. Stanford, CA: Stanford University Press, 1997.

Gunning, Tom. "The Exterior as Intérieur: Benjamin as Optical Detective," *Boundary*, 2, 30. 1 (2003), 105–30.

Heath, Stephen. "Joan Riviere and the Masquerade," in Victor Burgin, James Donald and Cora Kaplan, eds, *Formations of Fantasy*. London and New York: Methuen, 1986.

Hall, Radclyffe. *The Well of Loneliness*. New York: Convici Friede, 1929.

Hedges, Inez. *Languages of Revolt: Dada and Surrealist Literature and Film.* Durham, NC: Duke University Press, 1983.

Hubert, Renée Riese. *Magnifying Mirrors: Women, Surrealism and Partnership.* Lincoln and London: University of Nebraska Press, 1994.

———. *Surrealism and the Book*. Berkeley: University of California Press, 1988.

Hughes, Athol (ed.). *The Inner World of Joan Riviere. Collected Papers: 1920–1958*. London: Karnac Books, 1991.

Huxley, Aldous. *Eyeless in Gaza*. Harmondsworth: Penguin, 1965. First published 1936.

Jacobus, Mary. *First Things: The Maternal Imaginary in Literature, Art and Psychoanalysis*. New York: Routledge, 1995.

James, Edward. *Swans Reflecting Elephants: My Early Years*. Ed. George Melly. London: Weidenfeld and Nicolson, 1982.

Jameson, Fredric. *Marxism and Form: Twentieth Century Dialectical Theories of Literature*. Princeton, NJ: Princeton University Press, 1971.

———. *A Singular Modernity: Essay on the Ontology of the Present*. New York: Verso, 2002.

Jay, Martin. *Downcast Eyes: The Denigration of Vision in Twentieth-Century Thought*. Berkeley, Los Angeles and London: University of California Press, 1994.

Jean, Marcel. *The History of Surrealist Painting*. Trans. Simon Watson Taylor. New York: Grove Press, 1960. First published 1959.

Jocobus, Mary. "Is There a Woman in This Text?," *New Literary History*, Vol. 1 (Autumn, 1982), pp. 117–41.

———. *First Things: The Maternal Imaginary in Literature, Art, and Psychoanalysis*. New York and London: Routledge, 1995.

Jones, Ernest. "The Early Development of Female Sexuality", *The International Journal of Psycho-Analysis*, V.viii, October (1927).

———. *The Life and Works of Sigmund Freud*. Ed. Lionel Trilling. Harmondsworth, Penguin, 1974.

Kamenish, Paula K. "Naming the Crime: Responses to the Papin Murders From Lacan, Beauvoir, and Flanner," *The Comparatist*, 20 (1996), 93–110.

Kaplan, Janet A. *Unexpected Journey: The Art and Life of Remedios Varo*. New York: Abbeville Press, 1988.

Krauss, Rosalind. *The Optical Unconscious*. Cambidge, MA: MIT Press, 1993.

———. *Bachelors*. Cambridge, MA and London: MIT Press, 1999.

——— and Jane Livingstone, eds. *L'Armour Fou: Photography and Surrealism*. New York: Abbeville Press, 1985.

Lacan, Jaques. "Motives of Paranoiac Crime: The Crime of the Papin Sisters," *Critical Texts: A Review of Theory and Criticism*, 5.3 (1988). First published *in Le Minotaure*, 3-4 (December, 1933).

Lambert, Angela. *1939: The Last Season of Peace*. London: Weidenfeld and Nicolson, 1989.

Lane, Christopher. "'The Delerium of Interpretation': Writing the Papin Affair," *Differences: A Journal of Feminist Cultural Studies*, 5.2 (1993), 25–61.

Lauretis, Teresa de. *Technologies of Gender: Essays on Theory, Film, and Fiction*. Bloomington: Indiana Press, 1987.

Lichtenstein, Therese. *Behind Closed Doors: The Art of Hans Bellmer*. Berkeley: University of California Press, 2001.

Love, Heather K. "'Spoiled Identity': Stephen Gordon's Loneliness and the Difficulties of Queer History," *GLQ: A Journal of Lesbian and Gay Studies*, 7.4 (2001), 487–519.

Lusty, Natalya. "Surrealism's Banging Door," *Textual Practice*, 17:2 (2003), 335–56.

Marcus, Laura, ed. *Sigmund Freud's The Interpretation of Dreams: New Interdisciplinary Essays*. Manchester and New York: Manchester University Press, 1999.

Matthews J.H. *Languages of Surrealism*. Columbia: University of Missouri Press, 1986.

———. *Surrealism, Insanity, and Poetry*. New York: Syracuse University Press, 1982.

Merck, Mandy. *Perversions: Deviant Readings*. New York: Routledge, 1993.

Mercer, Kobena. "Reading Racial Fetishism: The Photographs of Robert Mapplethorpe," in *Welcome to the Jungle: New Positions in Black Cultural Studies*, New York and London: Routledge, 1994.

———. "Skin Head Sex Thing: Racial Difference and the Homoerotic Imaginary," in *Welcome to the Jungle: New Positions in Black Cultural Studies*, New York and London: Routledge, 1994.

Miller, Barbara L. "Sherman's Mass Appeal," *Afterimage*, 24.3 November–December (1997), 5.

Mitford, Nancy. *Love in a Cold Climate*. London: Penguin Classics, 1986. First published 1949.

Monahan, Laurie. "Radical Transformations: Claude Cahun and the Masquerade of Womanliness," in M. Catherin de Zegher, ed., *Inside the Visible: An Elliptical Traverse of Twentieth Century Art in, of, and from, the Feminine*. Cambridge MA: The MIT Press, 1996.

Mulvey, Laura. "A Phantasmagoria of the Female Body: The Work of Cindy Sherman," *New Left Review*, 188 (1991), 136–50.

Newton, Esther. "The Mythic Mannish Lesbian: Radclyffe Hall and the New Woman," in M.B. Dubberman, M. Vicinius, and G. Chauncey, eds, *Hidden from History: Reclaiming the Gay and Lesbian Past*. Hardmondsworth: Penguin, 1989.

Nicholls, Peter. *Modernisms: A Literary Guide*. Basingstoke and London: Macmillan, 1995.

Nussbaum, Martha C. "The Professor of Parody: The Hip Defeatism of Judith Butler," *The New Republic*, 22 February (1999), 37–45.

Nye, Robert. "Medical Origins of Fetishism," in Emily Apter and William Pietz, eds, *Fetishism As Cultural Discourse*. New York: Cornell University Press, 1993.

Paglia, Camille. *Sexual Personae: Art and Decadence From Nefertiti to Emily Dickinson*. London and New Haven: Yale University Press, 1990.

Paskauskas, R. Andrew, ed. *The Complete Correspondence of Sigmund Freud and Ernest Jones, 1908–1939*. Cambridge, MA and London: The Belknap Press, 1995.

Pellegrini, Ann. "Femmes Futiles: Womanliness, Whiteness, and the Masquerade," in *Performance Anxieties: Staging Psychoanalysis, Staging Race*. New York and London: Routledge, 1997.

Phillips, Adam. *On Kissing, Tickling and Being Bored: Psychoanalytic Essays on the Unexamined Life*. London: Faber and Faber, 1993.

Pierre, José. Ed. *Investigating Sex: Surrealist Discussions, 1928–1932*. Trans. Malcom Imrie. London and New York: Verso, 1992.

Polizzotti, Mark. *Revolution of the Mind: The Life of André Breton*. New York: Da Capo Press, 1997.

Pringle, Margaret. *Dance Little Ladies: The Days of the Debutante*. London: Orbis Books, 1977.

Probyn, Elspeth. *Sexing the Self: Gendered Positions in Cultural Studies*. London and New York: Routledge, 1994.

Resnik, Salomon. *Personne et Psychose: études sur le langage du corps*. Paris: Payot, 1973.

Rice, Shelley (ed). *Inverted Odysseys: Claude Cahun, Maya Deren, Cindy Sherman*. Cambridge, MA and London: MIT Press, 1999.

Richardson, Michael. "Seductions of the Impossible: Love, the Erotic and Sacrifice in Surrealist Discourse," *Theory, Culture, and Society*. Special Issue on Love and Eroticism, 15.3–4 (1998), 375–92.

Riviere, Joan. "Womanliness as a Masquerade," *The International Journal of Psycho-Analysis*, V.x, April–July (1929).

Rose, Jacqueline. "Femininity and Its Discontents" in *Sexuality in the Field of Vision*. London and New York: Verso, 2005. First published in 1983.

Rrose is a Rrose is a Rrose: Gender Performance in Photography. Exhibition Catalogue, Guggenheim Museum, 1997. Intro. Jennifer Blessing. New York: Guggenheim Museum Publications, 1997.

Rosemont, Penelope, ed. *Surrealist Women. An International Anthology*. Intro. Penelope Rosemont. Austin: University of Texas Press, 1998.

Roudinesco, Elisabeth. *Jacques Lacan and Co.: A History of Psychoanalysis in France, 1925–1985*. Trans. Jeffry Mehlman. Chicago: University of Chicago Press, 1990.

———. *Jacques Lacan*. Trans. Barbara Bray. New York: Columbia University Press, 1997.

Russo, Mary. *The Female Grotesque. Risk. Excess and Modernity*. New York and London, Routledge, 1994.

Sawin, Martica. *Surrealism in Exile and the Beginning of the New York School*. Cambridge, MA and London, England: MIT Press, 1997.

Schor, Naomi. "Fetishism and Its Ironies," in Emily Apter and William Pietz, eds, *Fetishism as Cultural Discourse*. Ithaca, NJ and London: Cornell University Press, 1993.

Sedgwick, Eve Kosofsky. *Between Men: English Literature and Male Homosocial Desire*. New York: Columbia University Press, 1985.
———. *Epistemology of the Closet.* Harmondsworth: Penguin, 1990.
——— and Adam Frank. “Shame in the Cybernetic Fold: Reading Silvan Tomkins,” in *Shame and Its Sisters: A Silvan Tomkins Reader.* Durham, NC: Duke University Press, 1995.
Sherman, Cindy. “Notebooks,” *Cindy Sherman: Retrospective*. Exhibition Catalogue. Essays by Amada Cruz, Elizabeth A.T. Smith and Amelia Jones. New York: Thames and Hudson, 1997.
———. *Cindy Sherman, 1975–1993*. Text by Rosalind Krauss, New York: Rizzoli, 1993.
———. *Cindy Sherman: Photographic Work*, 1975–1995. Exhibition Catalogue. Eds. Zdenek Felix and Martin Schwander. Essay by Elisabeth Bronfen. Munich; London: Schirmer Art Books, 1995.
Solomon-Godeau, Abigail. “The Equivocal ‘I’: Claude Cahun as Lesbian Subject” in Shelley Rice, ed., *Inverted Odysseys: Claude Cahun, Maya Deren, Cindy Sherman*. Cambridge, MA and London: MIT Press, 1999.
———. “Suitable for Framing: The Critical Casting of Cindy Sherman,” *Parkett*, 29 (1991), 112–15.
Simmel, George. *Simmel on Culture: Selected Writings*. Eds David Frisby and Mike Featherstone. London: Sage Publications, 1997.
Sontag, Susan. *On Photography*. Harmondsworth: Penguin, 1977. First published in 1973.
———. “The Pornographic Imagination” in George Bataille, *Story of the Eye*. Penguin, 1979. First published in 1967.
———. “Notes on Camp,” in Fabio Cleto, ed., *Camp: Queer Aesthetics and the Performing Subject: A Reader*. Ann Arbor: University of Michigan Press, 1999.
Stewart, Susan. *Crimes of Writing: Problems in the Containment of Representation.* New York and Oxford: Oxford University Press, 1991.
———. *On Longing: Narratives of the Miniature, the Gigantic, the Souvenir, the Collection*. Durham, NC and London: Duke University Press, 1993.
Stoekl, Allan. “Introduction,” in Georges Bataille. *Visions of Excess. Selected Writings 1927–39*. Minneapolis: University of Minnesota Press, 1993.
Suleiman, Susan Rubin. *Subversive Intent: Gender, Politics and the Avant-Garde*. Cambridge, MA and London, England: Harvard University Press, 1990.
———. *Risking Who One Is: Encounters With Contemporary Art and Literature*. Cambridge, MA and London, England: Harvard University Press, 1994.
———. “Bataille in the Street: The Search for Virility in the 1930s,” in Carolyn Bailey Gill, ed., *Bataille: Writing the Sacred*. London and New York: Routledge, 1995.
———. “Dialogue and Double Allegiance: Some Contemporary Women Artists and the Historical Avant-garde,” in Whitney Chadwick, ed., *Mirror Images:*

Women, Surrealism, and Self-Reproduction. Cambridge, MA: MIT Press, 1998.

Surya, Michel. *Georges Bataille: An Intellectual Biography*. Trans. Krzystof Fijalkowski and Michael Richardson. London and New York: Verso, 2002.

Tagg, John. *The Burden of Representation: Essays on Photographies and Histories*. Basingstoke: Macmillan Education, 1988.

Taylor, Sue. *Hans Bellmer: The Anatomy of Anxiety*. Cambridge, MA and London: MIT Press, 2000.

Theweleit, Klaus. *Male Fantasies*. Trans. Stephen Conway with Erica Carter and Chris Turner. Minneapolis: University of Minnesota Press, 1989.

Warner, Marina. "Leonora Carrington's Spirit Bestiary; or the Art of Playing Make-Belief," *Leonora Carrington: Paintings, Drawings and Sculptures 1940–1990*. Exhibition Catalogue, Serpentine Gallery, 1991.

Webb, Peter, with Robert Short. *Hans Bellmer*. London: Quartet Books, 1985.

Weeks, Jeffrey. "Havelock Ellis and the Politics of Sex Reform," in Shelia Rowbotham and Jeffrey Weeks, *Socialism and the New Left: The Personal and Sexual Politics of Edward Carpenter and Havelock Ellis*. London: Pluto Press, 1977.

Wiegman, Robyn. "Object Lessons: Men. Masculinity, and the Sign Women," *Signs*, 26.2 (Winter 2001), 355–72.

———. "Feminism, Institutionalism, and the Idiom of Failure," *Differences: A Journal of Feminist Cultural Studies,* 11.3 (1999), 107–36.

Williams, Raymond. *Marxism and Literature*. Oxford: Oxford University Press, 1977.

Williamson, Judith. "Images of Woman," *Screen*, 24 November (1983), 102–17.

Wilson, Elizabeth *Adorned in Dreams: Fashion and Modernity*. London: Virago Press, 1985.

Wilson, Sarah. "Max Ernst and England," *Max Ernst: A Retrospective*. Exhibition Catalogue. Ed. Werner Spies. Munich: Presetel-Verlag, 1991.

Wren, Celia. "Geriatric Goddess," *The Village Voice*, September (2000).

Wright, Elizabeth. "The Uncanny and Surrealism," in *Modernism and the European Unconscious*. Cambridge: Polity Press, 1990.

Index

(References to illustrations are in **bold**)